Renée Mill

A Therapist Guide for an Effective
10-session CBT Treatment Program

The Anxiety Management

MANUAL

www.
AUSTRALIANACADEMIC**PRESS**
.com.au

Other titles in this program:
The Anxiety Management Workbook

The Anxiety Management Manual
First published 2017
Australian Academic Press Group Pty. Ltd.
18 Victor Russell Drive
Samford Valley QLD 4520
Australia
www.australianacademicpress.com.au

ISBN 9781922117687

ISBN 9781922117687

Disclaimer
Every effort has been made in preparing this work to provide information based on accepted standards and practice at the time of publication. The publisher, however, makes no warranties of any kind of psychological outcome relating to use of this work and disclaims all responsibility or liability for direct or consequential damages resulting from any use of the material contained in this work.

Publisher: Stephen May

Cover design and typesetting: Luke Harris, Working Type Studio

Printing: Lightning Source

Contents

An Important Note for Therapists

At the end of each session of this program are two important tools that requirethe client to briefly check-in on how their thoughts are going and note them down — the ***Anxiety Management Sheet*** and the ***Daily Monitoring Diary***. To help the success of this program clients should continue to use these tools for a period of time after completing the 10 sessions.

Extra copies of the Anxiety Management Sheet and the Daily Monitoring Diary are available from the author's practice — Anxiety Solutions CBT.

For further information go to

www.anxietysolutionscbt.com

Introduction

Who is Renee Mill?

The Anxiety Management Manual represents a synthesis and consolidation of the clinical work I have carried out with people since 1974.

My career began as an occupational therapist in Johannesburg, South Africa where I worked in hospitals with diverse medical conditions. I discovered that patients recovered well when they understood why we were giving them particular tasks and the benefits they would reap from engaging in the process. Another key to successful treatment was assigning activities that were practical and relevant to their lives.

As occupational therapists, we were responsible for motivating patients, getting them moving and helping them function in everyday life. At that time, when psychodynamic and humanistic psychology was revered, the work we were doing was undervalued and seen as merely 'keeping the patients busy'.

Owing to a back injury, my focus became 'psych OT' which meant I worked full time with psychiatric patients. It is in this milieu that I discovered my passion. I studied for an additional five years to qualify (with distinction) as a clinical psychologist in 1982. At the University of the Witwatersrand, the focus was psychodynamic. My particular interest was in the work of psychoanalyst Melanie Klein and I worked within her model with extensive supervision for nine years. As a Kleinian therapist, I drilled deep into the unconscious without any overt treatment plan or direction. It couldn't have been more different from my work as an occupational therapist.

In addition to working with private patients, I ran various groups in the 1980's. As a young mother of four children, I had many acquaintances who begged me for practical parenting workshops where they obtained solutions to their problems. They just wanted to know how to communicate better without understanding the reason they were getting it wrong. Responding to this need, the occupational therapist in me wrote and ran parenting courses for parents of children and adolescents.

A common problem I noted amongst this normal population of parents was anger, frustration, stress and sadness. I realised that no number of strategies would help if an emotion such as anger got in the way. And so was born my interest in emotion regulation. In 1989 I began a weekly cognitive behavioural therapy (CBT) group for women to teach strategies for emotion regulation. It was highly successful and no one was more surprised than me. Without delving into the past, or developing insight, these women became calmer and happier, simply by learning tools. I was bemused to find that CBT encourages exercise, socialising and keeping busy — precisely the activities which had attracted the corn of psychoanalysts in my earlier years.

In 1995, with the popularisation of emotional intelligence, I synthesised the process I had been teaching for six years into an emotion regulation program and began using it with my individual clients (feeling slightly guilty about it and hoping my Kleinian supervisor would not find out).Again and again, I observed the benefits of this approach with hundreds if not thousands of people from different cultures and of all different ages.

In 1997, I migrated to Sydney Australia with my family. I was excited to discover that the techniques I utilised benefited the multicultural Australian population. I also learned that working analytically with mums and dads was difficult in a culture where there is no home help. I was grateful for my experience as an occupational therapist which verified the usefulness of practical, relevant skills. I was also appreciative that I had experience with CBT as that is the dominant approach in psychology in Australia

What I have discovered after 42 years, is that there is not a one size fits all approach. Working in a psychodynamic way is very useful for many patients but does not yield results for a client suffering from a panic attack in the moment. When it comes to emotion regulation generally, and anxiety and anger in particular, practical, relevant, easy to use tools are the most effective way of managing symptoms.

Since 1972, I have studied and taught. I have worked with clients one-on-one, couples, families and groups. I have delivered workshops in corporate settings, schools and shelters for the disabled and disenfranchised. I have written 3 practical, self-help books for lay people. They all teach emotion regulation although the first two are niched as parenting books. I continue to write a blog and am frequently called on for comment by the media. I work full time in my private practice in Sydney and currently run 3 groups per week teaching emotion regulation.

It is no exaggeration to say that I have devoted most of my life to helping people. I have strived to empower and motivate and to look for the most effective, user friendly way of doing so. I believe that this treatment method achieves that aim.

Is *The Anxiety Management Manual* for me?

If you are a health professional treating clients who suffer from anxiety or stress, then you will find *The Anxiety Management Manual* invaluable. It is an easy to use manualised cognitive behaviour therapy (CBT) treatment program that will deliver results.

No doubt, just like me, you wish to be an excellent clinician able to assist your clients in a meaningful way. This treatment manual has enabled me to achieve this goal.

Over the past 20 years I have developed and employed this method so that 90% of my clients have learned to manage their anxiety in a short space of time.

The Anxiety Management Manual can benefit a wide range of clients, diagnoses and problems. The core of the method is a **4-step** process that can help any person regardless of whether the symptoms of anxiety are mild, moderate or severe. It is effective if the anxiety presents alone or co-exists with other mental health conditions including depression, bipolar disorder and borderline personality disorder.

Even clients who have never received a formal diagnosis, but feel stressed at times, will benefit from this program. *The Anxiety Management Manual* has been used successfully with students struggling with exam stress, sportsmen battling with performance anxiety and managers in business dealing with high levels of work stress. In addition, the tools and 4-step procedure are great for resilience building in the normal population.

What makes this anxiety treatment successful?

1. This treatment method teaches practical tools which are effective in lowering and managing anxiety. The key word here is practical. The tools are not merely concepts but can be incorporated into daily living in a useful manner.

2   The tools are easy to understand and are taught in a way that the regular lay person can grasp quickly, easily and with success.

3. All your clients will find the tools, and the process, simple to learn and easy to apply. Intellectual and conceptual abilities are not necessary for progress to be made.

4. This treatment process has been formalised into this manual and accompanying client workbook which is included as the Appendix to this manual — ***The Anxiety Management Workbook***. Therefore the treatment you offer will be no different from the one I have successfully offered to hundreds of clients since 1995.

5. *The Anxiety Management Workbook* is not a text book about anxiety. It is simple, practical and applicable to everyday life which your clients will appreciate. In my experience, anxiety sufferers frequently become overwhelmed with the amount of information offered on many sites. They also do not see the relevance of the information to their unique problems. All they want is relief from their symptoms as quickly as possible and this process offers that.

6. While there are many CBT tools out there, I have chosen those tools that have proven to be the most helpful to my clients and synthesised them in a unique way.

7. This treatment package is based on the premise that just learning about tools, or practising them once or twice, will have no positive effect on symptoms. Practising the tools over 90 days is what leads to real and lasting change. Neuro-psychotherapy has proven that it is rewiring the brain by developing new neural circuits that leads to change. This program provides the wherewithal for your clients to rewire their brains.

8. I attest that this methodology has a track record of success over many years, with hundreds of diverse individuals. I am not a researcher in an ivory tower. I am on the ground like you, working with real people every day and totally familiar with the complexities of psychotherapy. I would like you to benefit from my experience.

What are the advantages for me?

1. You can jump right in and begin immediately to work with your client. No preparation is required. All you need to do is read this introduction then follow the weekly session content provided to clients in *The Anxiety Management Workbook* and repeated in this manual at the end of this Introduction.

2. The tools are provided in a ten session format. This aligns perfectly with the ten sessions which attract a Medicare rebate in Australia.

3. The therapy is structured. I have found that clients today love structure and predictability. In particular, the anxious-perfectionistic client thrives on the format.

4. Your clients will feel part of their therapeutic process which increases your success rate. When clients feel empowered with knowledge, they are more likely to take ownership for getting better.

5. You will have an increased retention rate with your clients. This is because clients know what they are in for and it is a doable commitment — ten sessions. Often clients baulk at the thought that their therapy could go on for months and even years and this leads to them dropping out and feeling helpless.

6. Your clients will be more willing to commit to the fees because there is a known cost which they can budget for. Endless sessions mean an open ended expense which often results in dropouts.

7. You will experience less resistance from families because *The Anxiety Management Workbook* enables them to understand the process. Clients can come home with their manual and discuss the tools that they learned that day. Parents and spouses no longer feel excluded from, or threatened by, the therapy process.

8. General Practitioners (GP) and specialist doctors respect the notion that this is a prescribed process with tangible goals and results. They too can discuss the therapy with your knowledgeable client.

9. You will come across as an expert to your clients and their doctors. You have a plan and a proven process that brings results. This will increase the referrals you will receive.

10. Clients are more likely to complete the ten sessions because they understand the need to do so. You will find that there will be an excellent retention rate of clients.

11. You can utilise the identical process with a group. Therefore you can utilise the group session Medicare rebate too and lower costs for clients.

12. You can market your anxiety treatment groups to many different markets including GP's, schools and businesses.

What do I bring to the process?

In the domain of emotion regulation, research has revealed that symptom management, and self-regulation of emotions, can successfully be managed without face-to-face therapy.

Today there are many universities offering evidence-based online e-therapy courses. Apps on smart phones have been found to be effective in keeping individuals focused, and consistent, in practicing tools such as mindfulness. Statistics indicate that practicing tools, as opposed to talking to a therapist, yields the best results for anxiety management in today's world.

Therefore, clients who are self-motivated, can move through the process prescribed in this workbook on their own and be successful in lowering their anxiety and managing their symptoms with a minimum of therapist direction.

There is also a large population of clients that require more directive face-to-face therapy.

- Clients who are not self-motivated need a therapist to work with them through the process.
- Many people do not enjoy online learning and prefer to learn with a human teacher.
- Also, clients who are not that literate or intelligent may be unable to understand the tools on their own but have no problem once a therapist has explained them.
- Clients with poor insight need a therapist to help them gain clarity about their symptoms and required treatment.
- Clients who are looking for more than just tools. They may be looking for a support person as well and/or they want to explore their issues in a deeper manner.
- Clients with more complicated mental health issues require more than symptom management. Symptom management may make up a small proportion of the work that needs to be done.

How do I use this treatment within my normal practice?

Following are some examples of how I have utilised this treatment method with various clients.

Thomas

Thomas was referred to me by his doctor because he was unable to sleep, eat or concentrate. He gave me some background information but was unable to think about anything else except his symptoms. Therefore, we immediately launched into the ten session process enumerated on in this manual. By session eight, Thomas was feeling calmer. He could now begin to analyse his primary relationship and admit that it was a major source of discontent. He could also begin to think about what he wanted from the relationship long term. We completed the ten sessions but continued working together in therapy aiming to get clarity about the relationship.

Allison

Allison hated her job but felt unable to make a change. Every time an acquaintance told her to stop whinging and start doing something constructive, Allison would shut down and be unable to think straight. We plunged into the ten week treatment process without exploring the external issues. By session six, Allison was able to face her fears. By session ten, Allison was free of anxiety symptoms, and she was able to move forward in her career.

Lisa

Lisa is a client that presented with parenting issues. We spent several months evaluating her parenting style, the personality profiles of herself and her children and trying different ways of gaining cooperation. Lisa's progress was slow. One day she broke down saying that she was so worried that something terrible would happen to her children that she tended to overprotect them. Lisa's admission alerted me to her anxiety and how it was interfering with her functioning as a parent. I changed direction and I began to teach Lisa anxiety management tools. After seven sessions of this CBT treatment, Lisa was able to implement parenting strategies effectively.

I have found the following clients are not good candidates for the CBT process at the beginning of their treatment:

- Clients who are grieving a death need space to feel their emotions and proceed through the mourning process. Teaching tools to manage emotions at this stage is not appropriate.
- Clients who are "anti CBT". I have had several people over the years tell me that they do not believe in CBT for a multitude of reasons. I do not try and convince them otherwise.
- Clients who have tried CBT before and it did not help them.
- Clients who do not want a structure.
- Clients looking for a place to unload/vent/explore/discover.
- Clients who are oppositional and who will not comply with the requirements such as filling in the daily monitoring diary.
- Clients who wish to explore the roots of their anxiety and are not interested in simply managing their symptoms.
- Individuals who are not ready to commit to a process or to ten sessions.

- Individuals who are ambivalent about therapy in general and who need time to come to terms with it.

My approach is to build trust first. I do this by creating a safe space for the client where they feel that they are being heard and that their needs are being met. As I was originally trained psycho-dynamically, this comes naturally to me. However, I have supervised many psychologists who are only familiar with CBT and who find this difficult. If you are one of these, I recommend that you refer your client on to a more suitable psychologist. Alternatively, you could attend supervision with an experienced clinician with a different orientation such as psycho-analysis, narrative therapy or humanistic psychotherapy.

Some of my clients with anxiety symptoms, who were originally resistant to CBT, do come round to doing the CBT treatment process later on, when they feel ready and/or when they have built up trust in my opinion and abilities.

Beginning Treatment

How the treatment process works

The Anxiety Management Workbook is divided into ten sessions which comprise the actual treatment program. However, you will require at least one additional session, the introductory session, before you can start the process. The initial session is where you meet your potential new client, assess his/her mental health and decide if you are the appropriate therapist to meet their needs.

Introductory Session

Take a full client history in the initial session. In particular focus on what symptoms are present, lifestyle factors, longevity of symptoms and previous treatments. Sometimes you might be able to decide right away that *The Anxiety Management Workbook* is suitable, although I find that often up to 3 sessions are required to make a thorough assessment of the client's needs and suitability.

Besides taking a history, the assessment session is also the time to explain the treatment package that you offer. Your client must know exactly what is on offer to "buy into" the program. Begin by giving some facts about neurobiology, but keep it simple. Most clients react most favourably to this introduction because it illuminates their problem for them.

Using the two diagrams shown as Figure 1 and Figure 2 over the page , explain:

There is a primitive part of the brain that fires when you are anxious. When it fires, a neural circuit is formed. The more the primitive brain fires, the thicker the neural circuit becomes.

It looks like this. (Show Figure 1)

The aim of this CBT treatment program is to stop your primitive brain firing. The way we do this is by utilising your smart brain and teaching you new ways of thinking and behaving. By consistently practicing new thoughts and behaviours over 90 days, you will develop a thick neural circuit in the smart brain while the neural circuit in your primitive brain will reduce in size.

What this means, is that you will automatically think and behave in a rational manner as you will have rewired your brain to a new default position.

At the end of ten sessions, your brain will look like this. (Show Figure 2)

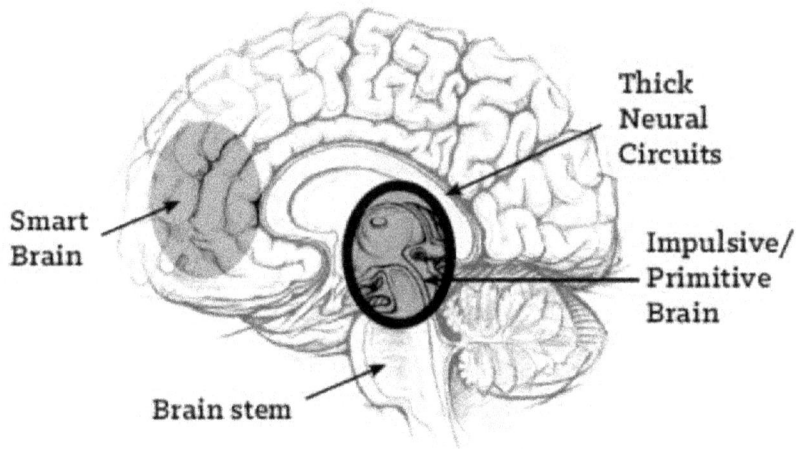

Figure 1 — Sketch of the brain showing thick neural circuits when the primitive brain fires repeatedly.

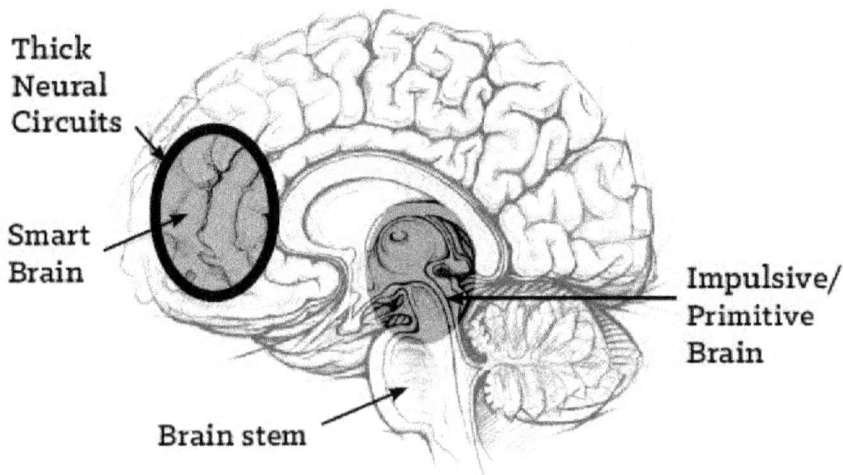

Figure 2 — Sketch of the brain showing thick neural circuits when the smart brain fires repeatedly.

By showing your client these diagrams, you are demonstrating the importance of learning new thought patterns and practicing them religiously for 90 days. You are also making the focus of your assessment and treatment the actual process of neuronal activity not the cause of that activity.

Sometimes it is useful to examine the causes of the anxiety but in regards to efficacy of the treatment, the cause is irrelevant. Many clients prefer this because they do not want to 'blame' anyone for their condition. Other clients prefer it because no time is wasted on trying to hypothesise a cause when it is not readily obvious.

It is also helpful to stress to a new client that:

- Even if you have a genetic tendency for anxiety, or you have been anxious for a long time, it is still possible to make changes. We now know that a brain is neuro-plastic which means it can develop new neuronal pathways, at any age, with practice and repetition.

- Anxiety has nothing to do with your personality or your star sign. It is the result of activity of the neurons in your primitive brain. When you learn to stop your primitive brain from working so much, and train your smart brain to use helpful neuronal circuits instead, your anxiety will reduce.

- Since medication targets neurotransmitters, which is the connecting substance between neurons, it does not promote the development of new neural circuits. This means that medication may be useful in calming you down in the present moment but it does not make structural changes.

- The optimum method for treatment should aim at stimulating helpful neurons to develop new, adaptive neural circuits.

In order that a new client understands the requirements of the treatment, you should show them *The Anxiety Management Workbook* including the worksheets. Explain that these worksheets and a daily monitoring diary will need to be completed for effective treatment . Reassure them that as their therapist you are there to 'hold their hand' for the entire process and that there is nothing to fear. It is a treatment that is based on well established principles and has been used successfully since 1995.

You should also explain the fees which apply to therapy, including ten sessions plus any extra costs such as the workbook.

Clients generally leave the initial session feeling optimistic and hopeful for a good outcome.

Guidelines for Conducting Sessions

The First Session

In session 1, give the client their copy of *The Anxiety Management Workbook* and begin by letting them know that the way the session will run is that they will work through the initial section of the workbook with you by reading aloud the contents and undertaking the exercises. Tell them that during reading they can stop to clarify something they don't understand and that you also may ask them to pause to allow you to talk a little bit more about some aspects of the treatment.

Although the workbook is self-explanatory, it is helpful to add your own comments to make the sessions interesting and to maintain concentration. It is good practice to add information that relates to the client. For example, when the client is reading about behaviours that maintain anxiety and comes to rumination, you could say:

> *You told me last time we met that your thoughts go round and round. That is exactly what rumination is.*

Interjecting at relevant moments is where a therapist's expertise is invaluable. You may want to re-explain to a client who seems not to understand an important point. You may want to draw a parallel between what the client is reading and something they have told you about themselves. Or you may want to embroider a point with current events, or with an analogy, making it more likely your client will remember.

Daily Monitoring Diary

Following the session content is a daily monitoring diary. This 7-day diary is repeated at the end of each successive session. Explain to the client that it will make a huge difference to their improvement if they fill it out every day. Research has shown that self-monitoring improves outcomes. My own clinical observation has been that when a client measures a before and after score, they quickly learn that tools (such as exercise) make a difference and that motivates them to keep going at it.

You should also point out that this is not school and there is no 'punishment' for not completing homework. I say this because I have had clients drop out because they feared punishment and felt like a failure for not completing the diary. You should stress that all homework is for the client's own benefit and that you will continue to motivate the client to comply. Usually, by session 4, most clients are seeing the benefits and filling out the diary weekly.

Anxiety Management Worksheet

The Anxiety Management Worksheet is the core of the treatment program. It is the process that enables rewiring of thought patterns. Seven copies of the 2-page back-to-back worksheet are provided at the end of every session following the Daily Monitoring Diary to allow for daily completion by the client. Here the client briefly records an event during the previous day where they felt anxious and then completes the worksheet. Every tool that is learned in the weekly sessions is on the worksheet.

The worksheet is made up of four steps. It is the practical application of the EBB FLOW model. If you look at the margins of the worksheet you will see the letters of EBB FLOW indicating the process.

There is no need to 'teach' the worksheet as it is self-explanatory. (I have found that attempting to explain it creates confusion. Therefore, I simply ask my client to read aloud and fill in as they go.)

Practical Tips on Using the Anxiety Management Worksheet

Step 1 — The Event

Watch out that your client does not get lost in detail when recording the event. There are only a few lines for the 'story' which in truth is not central. The focus is on learning what it was about an event that triggered stress. The underpinning of CBT is that it is our beliefs that lead to anxiety, not an external situation. Therefore, what is vital is for your client to acknowledge that they stressed themselves in a particular situation.

An example of too much event detail would be:

I started a new job. I introduced myself to the team leader and she was rude. I guessed it was because I am going to a second rate university. My peers went to New York. You have no idea how easy it is there. They are let off work by 12 o'clock. I wanted a meaningful experience. Also I may want to work in this hospital one day…

A better description of an event would be:

I started a new job. I introduced myself to the team leader and she was rude. That is when I began to work myself up.

Step 2

Keep an eye out during this step for what the client's beliefs are and what they might relate to. Many clients suffer a debilitating anxiety attack and then judge themselves harshly for it.

For example, a client might describe an event in step 1 as:

A young driver dented my car. That is when I began to work myself up to 100%. I really lost it and could not control myself.

The client then lists in step 2 that they lost *control* and *respect*, judged themselves as *untogether*, and worried that they would suffer *mental collapse* when what they wanted was *tranquility*.

In this illustration, the client is focusing on their reaction to the collision. This is incorrect. The purpose of the worksheet is to help them to learn what beliefs about the collision caused them to work themselves up into an anxious state. A more useful step 2 listing would be that they lost *validation* in themselves as a driver, judged themselves as *incompetent* (as a driver), and worried that they would suffer *financial hardship* (because of the repairs), when what they wanted was *for life to go smoothly*.

Step 3

The first time that a client fills in a worksheet, step 3 can be overwhelming. Therefore, you should encourage your client to read through all the tools and then choose those that feel helpful to them in relation to the event described.

If your client gets flustered, reassure them that they need to 'just do it' — just keep re-reading and filling in the worksheets and after a few days it will make sense.

Step 4

This step is always difficult for Session One because the wording is 'in the past I would have…but this time I…'. With Session One of course there is no previous time. Therefore it is best to make suggestions to role model what it could sound like such as 'In the past I would have felt helpless but this time I have a worksheet and tools that I can learn and be empowered by.' After Session One this first worksheet becomes the benchmark for the before and after scenario in later worksheets.

After all four steps have been completed make sure you encourage your client by endorsing them for the progress they have made. Make sure such encouragement is appropriate and avoid statements such as: 'You are amazing', or 'I am so proud of you'. Instead you should be specific about gains made, for example: 'You can endorse yourself for filling out that worksheet even though you felt panicked. That shows determination.'

What to Expect Across the Sessions

Frequently the second session is a bit overwhelming for a client. There is a lot of information and a new process that needs to be taken in. I always reassure my client that by the fourth session they will be adept at the process and it will make sense. All they need to do is to keep going and filling in the worksheets and daily monitoring diary and soon they will 'get the hang of it'.

By session 5, most clients will have reduced their anxiety markedly. That is the time you can consider reducing sessions to fortnightly, especially if your client is diligently filling out the worksheets. If I have a client who does not practice the worksheets, encourage them to keep coming weekly because at least that way you can ensure that they practice the process once a week in my rooms.

The challenge by session 6 is to keep clients coming to therapy. By this time they begin to feel well, their symptoms have often disappeared, and they question the necessity of continuing. Remind them of the importance of practice and repetition to make real and lasting change at the level of their brain's neural circuits. With some clients, once they are feeling better, it is still effective to meet monthly — as long as worksheets are filled out regularly.

When the ten sessions are over, make sure the client fills in the evaluation form. By doing so, they make a commitment to continuing to utilise the process they have learnt through therapy.

General Pointers

1. No matter what else you do in a session, be sure to have your client fill out and read to you at least one anxiety management worksheet. The worksheet is the main tool and key to improvement.

2. At the beginning of every session, go through the daily monitoring diary. It is invaluable to see the anxiety scores, when they escalate during a week and what may be triggering the escalation. It is also important to monitor the general progression as the weeks go by. Clients feel motivated when they see their scores drop and can see patterns which can be rectified.

3. If your client has not filled out the daily monitoring diary, explain that they are not at school and therefore not in 'trouble'. However, because it is in their interest to complete the diary you will need to keep encouraging them to do so. You should clearly explain this to the client so that they understand why you keep asking about the diary and reinforcing its importance to them. (In all my years of practice I have had only one client who never filled out anything. He attended all sessions and reassured me that he had greatly improved. He simply did not enjoy doing paperwork of any kind.)

4. It is best if the **first four sessions** are done weekly. It may even be necessary to have the first two sessions in the same week if the client is extremely distressed and anxious to get started.

5. On the rare occasion that you may find it is necessary to not follow the scheduled session in a week because of other issues that have arisen with the client since last seeing them, make sure that you gain the agreement of the client. This is important because you have formed a contract with the client for ten sessions.

6. Always be aware that some clients will intentionally try and avoid completing worksheets. For instance, borderline personality disordered people often have lots of drama in their life which they want to unload. However, what will benefit them the most is to learn to regulate their emotions. Be firm about sticking to

the program until your client's anxiety is well managed. Then you can have less structured sessions but remember to have your client fill out at least one anxiety management worksheet per week. Clients without a formal diagnosis but who are dramatic, very emotive or attention-seeking can also be problematic . Stick to the program and reassure them that it is only for a few weeks. Other clients may avoid the worksheets due to a lack of self-discipline, procrastination, or an aversion to taking responsibility for their own wellbeing. Utilise your expertise to motivate your client to participate in the process. You may even reflect that what is happening in the session (e.g. procrastination) is what they do outside the session to their disadvantage.

7. Finish the final session on a positive note and an open door policy. Reassure your client that if ever they need some help you are there. Finishing the manual does not mean the end of the relationship. It means they have mastered a technique to manage their symptoms.

In Conclusion

In order to motivate your clients, you need to believe in the process. Like them, it will take a few sessions to get a feel of how this anxiety treatment program works. It will usually take the success of about three clients to become passionate about this successful and helpful treatment.

I am asking you to do what you will be asking your clients to do — follow the process and you will see the benefits. When you do, you will be able to empathise with your client's uncertainty at the beginning. When you have seen results after a few individuals you will be able to identify with my passion for the process and conviction of its efficacy.

I wish you every success in your role as a therapist. May you have the same feelings of satisfaction and meaning that I derive, even after 20 years, from using *The Anxiety Management Manual.*

Good luck and all the best.

Renee.

Appendix

The Anxiety Management Workbook

Session 1

TOOLS FOR TACKLING ANXIETY

This course is based on the principles of Cognitive Behavioural Therapy (CBT) which is:

- An effective, evidence-based intervention in treating anxiety.

- An approach based on the relationship that exists between cognition (thoughts), emotion and behaviour (including physiological responses).

Aim: To modify the behavioural, cognitive and mood difficulties that bring a person to seek treatment.

How: By learning and practising tools/strategies for the cognitions, behaviours and moods associated with anxiety.

Group Process Outline

(only read if there is a group of 2 or more, otherwise, skip to the next section — The Nature of Anxiety.)

During each of the 10 sessions in this program, we will look at a different cognitive or behavioural tool for reducing anxiety. At the end of every session, one person will read out a worksheet that they filled out. This enables individuals to practice the tools within the group and to receive positive support from the group. It also provides a forum for others to learn from the presenter and be inspired to make better choices too.

Only everyday events should be presented to the group. This is not a deep psychological group where loss and grief are shared. Nonetheless, the group needs to be a safe space and therefore the following guidelines should be adhered to.

Group Guidelines

- Confidentiality: anything discussed within the group stays within the group.

- Be sensitive and appropriate to others in the group.

- Use 'I' statements rather than telling others what to do e.g. 'I feel it is important to be active' rather than 'you should exercise otherwise you won't feel better'.

- Endorse the presenter for their growth.

- Do not give advice, reassurance or personal accolades.

The Nature of Anxiety

It is important to understand that anxiety is an in-built human function and can be useful at times. This can be illustrated by the following example:

A man is having his morning swim at the beach and suddenly, some distance away he spots a fin moving above the water. The man identifies it as a shark, realises the danger and responds with fear. This is appropriate and functional.

This fear response is also called the *fight or flight response*. It occurs when a person is in danger or believes they are in danger. It is adaptive in circumstances such as the one above because it helps the man to swim away quickly or to fight the danger, thereby saving his life.

We often activate the fight or flight response when there is no real danger and so we become anxious. By realising that the perceived danger is not a real threat, your response will be reduced. You can ultimately stop yourself setting off a fight or flight response.

So what happens when your fight or flight response is activated?

Three major types of responses occur:

1. Thoughts (also called Cognitions).

2. Actions (also called Behaviours).

3. Bodily reactions (also called Physiological responses).

What causes anxiety?

Research has shown that it is your **thoughts**, and principally your thoughts, that cause your anxiety. Simply put, it is what you tell yourself in a particular situation that sets off your emotions, behaviours and bodily reactions.

Like most of us, you may not be aware of what you are thinking when you become stressed. The majority of your thoughts occur automatically and at a subliminal level. This prevents you from being able to link your thoughts to your stress.

As you proceed through this program, however, you will learn to identify your personal thinking style, and particular thoughts, that precipitate your anxiety.

Session 1

Which thoughts precipitate anxiety?

Thoughts can be neutral, positive or negative.

For example, let's say that you notice your bicycle leaning on the fence.

- You could have a **neutral thought** like 'I will ride my bike later today'.

- You could have a **positive thought** like 'I can ride a bicycle very well'.

- You could have a **negative thought** like 'have not ridden my bike for a few days so I will probably fall if I ride today'.

It is your **negative automatic thoughts that cause distress** and can make it difficult for you to function effectively in your daily life.

By working through the program content and participating in the exercises, you will soon learn what your specific negative, unconscious thoughts are. You will also learn more helpful ways of thinking and how to supplant your negative thoughts with positive ones.

Changing thoughts is an easy process which you will learn in a step by step manner. Practice and repetition over 90 days will ensure that your new way of thinking endures.

The EBB FLOW model of CBT

CBT is an approach that focuses on the relationship that exists between thoughts (cognitions), behaviours, and bodily reactions. The **EBB FLOW model** adapts the standard A-B-C model of CBT and indicates optimism and fluidity. Just as the sea ebbs and flows with ease, so too you will learn how to move easily from a state of stress and anxiety to a state of calm.

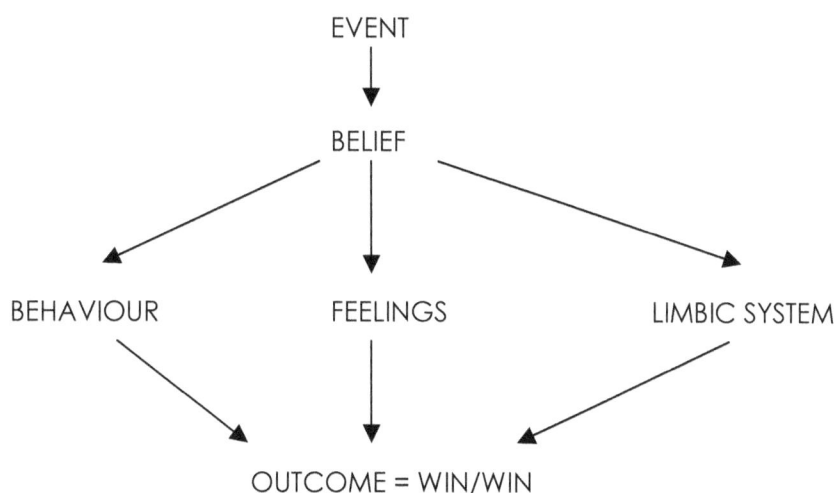

EVENT
↓
BELIEF
↙   ↓   ↘
BEHAVIOUR   FEELINGS   LIMBIC SYSTEM
↘   ↓   ↙
OUTCOME = WIN/WIN

The components in the model spell out its name:

E = Event

B = Belief about the event

B = Behaviour

F = Feelings

L = Limbic system

O = Outcome

W = Win/win

E=Event: Any occurrence, no matter how small, that takes place in your day to day activities.

B=Belief: When an event occurs, you will automatically have a thought about it. You may not be aware of the thought since it races through your mind automatically, unconsciously and very, very quickly. Your thought can be positive or negative. For instance, if you are thinking that it is exciting to find a giant python, the thought is positive. Alternatively, if you are thinking that you might be killed, the thought is negative.

Thought Examples:

- Neutral — 'There is a huge python snake in my guest bedroom. I suspected for many years that it was living in my ceiling'.

- Positive — 'Wow, what an interesting creature! Let me catch it on camera and send it to ABC news'.

- Negative — 'That snake is about to lunge at me and kill me'.

In this example I have used a snake in order to make a strong case for the assertion that most of life's events are neutral. Many people have argued 'Come on. Snakes cannot be neutral. Everybody finds them scary.' However, these people are not correct.

On 22nd June 2016, a giant python was discovered by home owner Trina Hibberd in far North Queensland, Australia. The python was 5m long and stretched across 2 rooms. When interviewed on TV, Trina was neutral. She told the ABC that the scrub python had been living in the walls and ceiling of the home for more than a decade and she first saw it 15 years ago. 'We knew the snake was there but I had never seen it inside, not that I know of,' she said. 'I've never seen it in its full length.'

She demonstrates that she was not bothered by having a huge snake in her ceiling and was matter of fact when she found it indoors. The snake catcher on the other hand was excited at finding such a large python saying it was the second biggest he had ever seen and calling it 'a good monster'.

These Queenslanders confirm that it is not the snake itself that causes fear but the thought that goes with seeing the snake.

B=Behaviour: Your behaviour during an event will be determined by your thoughts. Therefore, if you have the positive thought that you are privileged to view a giant python in real life, you will act in a curious and accepting manner toward it. However, if you have a negative thought, namely, that it is dangerous and you'll be eaten, you will act in a threatened and fearful manner.

F=Feelings: Your automatic thought will influence the way you feel as well. The positive thought will result in you feeling excited, or interested, while the negative thought will result in you feeling anxious and terrified.

L=Limbic System: When you think a negative thought, it activates the limbic system which is responsible for setting off the 'fight or flight' reaction in your body. The limbic system is part of your primitive brain and prepares your breathing, heart rate, muscles and digestion for danger (or perceived danger). These bodily reactions can be very distressing for an anxious person. Some individuals have been known to rush to the emergency room of the nearest hospital fearing that they are suffering a heart attack when in fact they are experiencing a panic attack.

O=Outcome: The outcome of an event is totally connected to your initial thought about it. A positive thought may help to create a positive outcome as you may act calmly near the snake and observe its slow, non threatening movement. A negative thought may result in a negative outcome e.g. screaming and stamping could cause the snake to move more quickly and thus startle you even more.

W=Win/Win: The purpose of this course is to teach you to achieve a winning solution. Your ability to reduce and manage your fight/flight response system will enhance your ability to find helpful solutions.

The basic philosophy of the EBB FLOW model is that everyday life events are neutral in and of themselves. What makes us react in a positive or negative manner to an event is the belief that we ascribe to an event.

Catastrophic life events, such as an airplane crash, cannot be said to be neutral. How one deals with cataclysmic life events is not dealt with in this course. The tools of this course assist people living everyday lives, with everyday problems, and who suffer from anxiety and stress.

An Illustration of the EBB FLOW model

The following illustration will reveal just how fluid thoughts are and how quickly we can move from one emotional state to another. Anger, or the 'fight' response, demonstrates it well.

Mr. Jones catches a ferry every Sunday morning. He regards it as his special time to relax and enjoy Sydney harbour at its best. One Sunday, as he leaves the city, some children begin to behave badly. They yell, and jump up and down. Mr. Jones is infuriated and is about to yell at them to shut up when a man comes up to him. 'I am so sorry my children are being disruptive' he says', 'but we have just come from the hospital. Their mum has just died.'

In a flash, Mr. Jones transforms from fury to compassion. Suddenly he wants to help the children and their unruly behaviour does not bother him.

When the ferry arrives in Manly, the captain of the ferry sees Mr. Jones. 'I hope Mr. X did not tell you his fabricated story about his wife dying? He tells it to everybody so that he does not have to discipline his kids.'

In an instant, Mr. Jones is furious again.

See how quickly that happened? Mr. Jones moved from fury, to compassion and back to fury easily and quickly.

Once you learn to identify your thoughts and challenge them, you too can move from anxiety to calm quickly and easily. When you master the 4-step process on the worksheet following each session in this program, you will be able to move from a negative thought to a neutral or positive thought with ease, thereby lifting your mood and feeling calmer.

Behaviours

Certain behaviours will keep your anxiety at a high level once it has been activated. Before we head into the first exercise tick the behaviours in the list below that are relevant to you:

- You avoid anxiety provoking situations. Such as when you isolate yourself because you fear meeting new people. Avoidance maintains fear and may even increase it. Facing your fear and socialising would help you to reduce your anxiety.

- You do not stay in your feared situation long enough. For example, when you flee as soon as a crowd starts to build around you. Fleeing maintains the fear and may also intensify it. Staying in the crowd and breathing through it would assist you to lower your panic over time.

- You do not do things you would really like to do nor do you achieve certain goals.

- You over-plan to prevent your highly feared predicted event from occurring. For example, you research to every last detail the background to a speech you will be making for fear you will otherwise look incompetent.

- You over-prepare as a safety behaviour because you believe it will stop the feared event from happening. Over-preparing may mean practicing your speech hundreds of times before you deliver it.

- You ruminate. This is unproductive worry where you constantly chew on your thoughts without a result or purpose.

- You are hyper-vigilant. You keep your eyes peeled for a potential threat and/or you pay greater attention to your body sensations.

- You do not practice skills you have been taught like relaxation, meditation, mindfulness.

- You do not challenge your thoughts.
- You maintain behaviours that promote anxiety. This includes continuing to consume stimulants or staying in a stressful job.

EXERCISE ONE

Did you know that certain substances may be contributing to your anxiety? Please tick if you consume any of the following and assign a weekly amount.

- Alcohol   _____pw
- Marijuana   _____pw
- Nicotine   _____pw
- Coffee   _____pw
- Medications that are stimulants   _____pw
- Cortisone /steroids   _____pw
- Speed   _____pw
- Appetite suppressants   _____pw

Certain lifestyle behaviours may be contributing to your anxiety. Please tick those that apply to you and elaborate below.

- insufficient sleep
- broken sleep
- eating irregularly
- poor nutrition

_____

_____

_____

_____

_____

Have you identified any substances, or lifestyle behaviours, that may be contributing to your anxiety? YES/NO

If yes, commit to make changes below. Make small changes that you will be able to sustain.

Example: My medications increase my heart rate. I will speak to my doctor about other options. OR From today I will reduce my coffee intake by 1 cup per day.

_____

_____

_____

_____

EXERCISE TWO

Bodily Reactions

Your body reacts when you are fearful or anxious. Tick the symptoms in the list below that you experience when you are anxious:

- Breathing rate and depth increases to make more oxygen available to the muscles for fight or flight. You can experience yawning, breathlessness, smothering feelings, tightness in the chest. This may reduce blood supply to the head (not dangerous) which can lead to dizziness, light-headedness, blurred vision, confusion, hot flushes and feelings of unreality.

- Heart rate and blood pressure increase enabling blood and oxygen to be pumped around the body quicker. You may experience this as a 'pounding heart'.

- Sweating increases. This cools the body preventing it from overheating when strenuous physical activity begins.

- Muscle tension increases preparing your body to respond quickly. You may experience this as aches, pains, trembling, shaking, and feelings of exhaustion.

- Digestive system activity slows allowing more energy to be diverted to the fight/flight systems. You would experience a dry mouth, nausea, heavy stomach.

- Blood redistribution to muscles occurs often resulting in tingling of fingers or toes and/or numbness.

- Immune system slows down. This allows your body to put all its efforts into escaping. You may have noticed that you frequently suffer from coughs, colds and sore throats.

Remember, these responses are vital to your survival when you are facing real danger. However, when you are not in danger, ongoing bodily reactions are distressing.

Do you have any other symptoms that are not mentioned here? Please list them.

_____

_____

_____

_____

Did you learn about symptoms that you have but were not aware that they are a consequence of anxiety?

If yes, please elaborate.

_____

_____

_____

Now that you have learned the theory behind this process, you can immediately learn the tools.

Calming Tool One: Relaxation

'Breathing and deep relaxation lowers anxiety'.

It is a valuable exercise to take the time to breathe deeply every day. It is also beneficial to practice a relaxation method at least twice a day. First thing in the morning and last thing at night is easy to work into your schedule. You cannot overdose on relaxation so feel free to do it as many times as you need. Any method of relaxation that you enjoy can be utilised.

If you do not have a deep breathing method, it is recommended that you utilise the method below and make it a daily practice. You can download more on this technique from http://anxietysolutionscbt.com/about/our-tools/.

Five breaths to calm.

The 'five breaths to calm,' approach follows these core steps:

1. Focus on your breath.

2. When you inhale, fill your lungs to maximum capacity.

3. When you exhale, push out as much air as possible.

4. The word 'relax' must be said aloud, as an instruction.

5. In short, breathe deeply and as you exhale, say the word 'relax' out loud.

Repeat these steps five times. For maximum benefit, breathing this way should be done at least twice a day.

This type of breathing can be used as a tool when you are feeling anxious. Over time, it will train your body to be in an ongoing relaxed state.

Calming Tool Two: Exercise

'Exercise lifts my mood'

There is no health discipline today that does not encourage regular exercise. Twenty minutes a day of brisk walking is all you need to get your metabolism going.

Whatever exercise you choose, it will enhance your feeling of well-being owing to the endorphins which are released. Furthermore, an agile body is better able to cope with stress and illness, and generally has a better immune system.

EXERCISE THREE

What types of exercise do you enjoy?

_____

_____

_____

What exercise do you actually do?

_____

_____

_____

If you have not been exercising, make a commitment, now, on paper as follows:

I commit to (type of exercise)

_____

_____ times a week, starting _____

Daily Monitoring Diary

As part of this course you are requested to fill out a quick-diary each day to help you monitor your progress. Each day you will need to fill out the following information:

- If you exercised and for how long — Anxiety level before and after

- If and for how long you engaged in relaxation — Anxiety level before and after

- How often you had a catastrophic/negative thought — Your belief in that thought (rating) before and after challenging it

- Overall anxiety rating for the day on a scale from 0–10 (0 being not at all; 10 being extremely high anxiety)

The first weekly diary is on page 13.

You will get the most out of this course if you do this. You will learn to identify what's going on for you at any given time (in terms of beliefs/thoughts, feelings and behaviours/responses).

You can then utilise one or more appropriate tools you have learned through the course to help with the difficult moment. By taking notice of the changes you experience, you will feel motivated to keep using the tools.

The Anxiety Management Worksheet

The Anxiety Management Worksheet is the major tool of this program. More than anything else, filling out one worksheet every day is what will most effect change in your life.

Do this for 90 days consecutively. After 90 days, you may reduce to one worksheet every second day for the next three months. After that, filling out one anxiety management worksheet per week will be sufficient to keep your new helpful thoughts wired.

Warning: If you stop filling out worksheets altogether, you could relapse and become anxious again over time.

How it works

This worksheet is the practical application of the EBB FLOW paradigm. It is a four step process that is easy to do. In fact, the worksheet is self-explanatory. I recommend that you fill one in now to get the gist of it.

The first worksheet is on page 15. There are 7 worksheets at the end of each session for you to fill out every week.

At the end of every session is a page for you to make notes. The first one can be found on page 30.

DAILY MONITORING DIARY

WEEK ENDING _____

Day	M	T	W	T	F	S	S
Overall Anxiety Rating for the day (0-10)							

1. EXERCISE

	M	T	W	T	F	S	S
How long?							
Anxiety level before (0-10)							
Anxiety level after (0-10)							

2. BREATHING & RELAXATION

	M	T	W	T	F	S	S
How long?							
Anxiety level before (0-10)							
Anxiety level after (0-10)							

Session 1

Anxiety Management Worksheet

The purpose of this worksheet is to help you to see every stressful event as an opportunity for
1. greater understanding of yourself, your anxiety and the people around you, and
2. practicing tools to manage your anxiety.

Step One: An Event

Briefly describe an event when you became anxious. Give such details as time, place and people involved, and end with "That's when I began to work myself up..."

_____

_____ E

_____

_____ Rate your anxiety on a scale of 0 to 100%: [   ] %

Step Two: The Working-Up Process

Learn about your working up process by identifying your thoughts, feelings, behaviours and bodily reactions during the event. Tick the ones that most resonate with you.

Undermining Beliefs

I fear that I have lost...
- ☐ approval
- ☐ control
- ☐ co-operation
- ☐ face
- ☐ respect
- ☐ success
- ☐ trust
- ☐ validation
- ☐ love

This event proves that I am...
- ☐ stupid
- ☐ abnormal
- ☐ incompetent
- ☐ lazy
- ☐ irresponsible
- ☐ a total failure
- ☐ undisciplined
- ☐ untogether
- ☐ useless

B

I worry that I will suffer...
- ☐ mental collapse
- ☐ illness
- ☐ financial hardship

What I want is...
- ☐ total control
- ☐ respect
- ☐ success
- ☐ perfection
- ☐ comfort
- ☐ fairness
- ☐ tranquility
- ☐ all the answers
- ☐ for life to go smoothly
- ☐ to be all things to all people

Self-destructive Behaviour

Active
- ☐ get violent
- ☐ swear
- ☐ slam doors
- ☐ run away
- ☐ overeat
- ☐ harm myself
- ☐ criticise

Passive
- ☐ take it too seriously
- ☐ give up
- ☐ wallow in self pity
- ☐ sulk
- ☐ space out
- ☐ procrastinate
- ☐ give in
- ☐ be controlled

Intense Feelings

Angry feelings
- ☐ hateful
- ☐ aggravated
- ☐ annoyed
- ☐ hostile
- ☐ outraged
- ☐ punitive
- ☐ resentful
- ☐ vengeful

Fearful feelings
- ☐ helpless
- ☐ hopeless
- ☐ disappointed
- ☐ sad
- ☐ attacked
- ☐ worn out
- ☐ rejected
- ☐ jealous
- ☐ afraid
- ☐ exploited
- ☐ lonely
- ☐ abandoned
- ☐ guilty
- ☐ insulted
- ☐ confused
- ☐ disillusioned
- ☐ misunderstood
- ☐ trapped

Bodily Reactions (Limbic System)

I am uncomfortable because I am experiencing...
- ☐ tremors
- ☐ nausea
- ☐ sweaty palms
- ☐ stomach-ache
- ☐ pounding heart
- ☐ general tension
- ☐ fatigue
- ☐ imagination on fire
- ☐ headache
- ☐ dry mouth
- ☐ jaw clenching
- ☐ shortness of breath

Continued over

B   F   L

Step Three: The Working-Down Process

Begin with, "Suddenly I realised that I was anxious and that I had choices..." This is the step of self-leadership and trust in one's ability to handle the situation.

Choose helpful thoughts:

I choose to depersonalise
There is no intention to hurt me. He is doing the best he can with the tools he has at the moment.

I choose realism over romanticism
Life presents many obstacles. I lower or raise standards as needed.

There is no right or wrong
Unless it is a moral issue, I will see it simply as a difference of opinion and/or taste.

I choose the total view of positivity
Even though this event is negative, the total view of his behaviour is positive.

I surrender control
Since I cannot change this situation, I choose to let go of it

I choose to put this event in perspective
This event is not a catastrophe because it is not life threatening. It can be viewed as a trivial life event, a normal life problem that needs to be solved not dramatised.

I choose to view this event as average, falling within the normal range
This event is not exceptional; many people have gone through this.

It's temporary - "this too shall pass"
Life is constantly changing and moving through phases and this situation will also change.

Fears or facts?
Why fear? It may not happen!

I choose to focus on this as a learning experience
Every problem that comes my way is an opportunity for me to learn about my strengths and weaknesses, others and life.

Feel soothing emotions:

I choose to feel warm, loving emotions. I do this by focusing on my heart and letting love, trust forgiveness, compassion, hope or gratitude fill my heart space.

Behave constructively:

I choose to work in part acts:
I will break the overwhelming job into manageable parts.

Do the difficult:
I will face what I fear and act with self-discipline

I choose to solutionise:
I will find a solution by taking advice or doing research.

Prioritise myself:
I will keep my life balanced by meeting friends, doing exercise or laughing.

Compartmentalise:
I will not let this event cloud my whole day; I will focus on something else now.

Utilise calming strategies:

When I:
- relax,
- breathe deeply,
- go for a run,
- shower,
- lie down,
- read,
- watch TV,
- climb into a mental helicopter
- practice mindfulness, meditation, my mind and body calm down.

Step Four: The Self Motivation Process

Endorse yourself for any growth no matter how small.

In the past I would have...

_____

_____

But this time I...

_____

_____

Tick off the traits that you strengthened when you worked down your anxiety:

- ☐ generosity
- ☐ kindness
- ☐ compassion
- ☐ consideration
- ☐ helpfulness
- ☐ respectfulness
- ☐ honesty
- ☐ fairness
- ☐ patience
- ☐ peacefulness
- ☐ self-discipline
- ☐ forgiveness
- ☐ courage
- ☐ responsibility
- ☐ reliability
- ☐ loyalty
- ☐ love
- ☐ humility

Rate your anxiety on a scale of 0 to 100%:

☐ %

O   W

Anxiety Management Worksheet

The purpose of this worksheet is to help you to see every stressful event as an opportunity for
1. greater understanding of yourself, your anxiety and the people around you, and
2. practicing tools to manage your anxiety.

Step One: An Event

Briefly describe an event when you became anxious. Give such details as time, place and people involved, and end with "That's when I began to work myself up..."

_____

_____ E

_____

_____ Rate your anxiety on a scale of 0 to 100%: [   ] %

Step Two: The Working-Up Process

Learn about your working up process by identifying your thoughts, feelings, behaviours and bodily reactions during the event. Tick the ones that most resonate with you.

Undermining Beliefs

I fear that I have lost...

- ☐ approval
- ☐ control
- ☐ co-operation
- ☐ face
- ☐ respect
- ☐ success
- ☐ trust
- ☐ validation
- ☐ love

This event proves that I am...

- ☐ stupid
- ☐ abnormal
- ☐ incompetent
- ☐ lazy
- ☐ irresponsible
- ☐ a total failure
- ☐ undisciplined
- ☐ untogether
- ☐ useless

B

I worry that I will suffer...

- ☐ mental collapse
- ☐ illness
- ☐ financial hardship

What I want is...

- ☐ total control
- ☐ respect
- ☐ success
- ☐ perfection
- ☐ comfort
- ☐ fairness
- ☐ tranquility
- ☐ all the answers
- ☐ for life to go smoothly
- ☐ to be all things to all people

Self-destructive Behaviour

Active

- ☐ get violent
- ☐ swear
- ☐ slam doors
- ☐ run away
- ☐ overeat
- ☐ harm myself
- ☐ criticise

Passive

- ☐ take it too seriously
- ☐ give up
- ☐ wallow in self pity
- ☐ sulk
- ☐ space out
- ☐ procrastinate
- ☐ give in
- ☐ be controlled

Intense Feelings

Angry feelings

- ☐ hateful
- ☐ aggravated
- ☐ annoyed
- ☐ hostile
- ☐ outraged
- ☐ punitive
- ☐ resentful
- ☐ vengeful

Fearful feelings

- ☐ helpless
- ☐ hopeless
- ☐ disappointed
- ☐ sad
- ☐ attacked
- ☐ worn out
- ☐ rejected
- ☐ jealous
- ☐ afraid
- ☐ exploited
- ☐ lonely
- ☐ abandoned
- ☐ guilty
- ☐ insulted
- ☐ confused
- ☐ disillusioned
- ☐ misunderstood
- ☐ trapped

Bodily Reactions (Limbic System)

I am uncomfortable because I am experiencing...

- ☐ tremors
- ☐ nausea
- ☐ sweaty palms
- ☐ stomach-ache
- ☐ pounding heart
- ☐ general tension
- ☐ fatigue
- ☐ imagination on fire
- ☐ headache
- ☐ dry mouth
- ☐ jaw clenching
- ☐ shortness of breath

Continued over

B   F   L

www.anxietysolutionscbt.com

Step Three: The Working-Down Process

Begin with, "Suddenly I realised that I was anxious and that I had choices..." This is the step of self-leadership and trust in one's ability to handle the situation.

Choose helpful thoughts:

I choose to depersonalise
There is no intention to hurt me. He is doing the best he can with the tools he has at the moment.

I choose realism over romanticism
Life presents many obstacles. I lower or raise standards as needed.

There is no right or wrong
Unless it is a moral issue, I will see it simply as a difference of opinion and/or taste.

I choose the total view of positivity
Even though this event is negative, the total view of his behaviour is positive.

I surrender control
Since I cannot change this situation, I choose to let go of it

I choose to put this event in perspective
This event is not a catastrophe because it is not life threatening. It can be viewed as a trivial life event, a normal life problem that needs to be solved not dramatised.

I choose to view this event as average, falling within the normal range
This event is not exceptional; many people have gone through this.

It's temporary - "this too shall pass"
Life is constantly changing and moving through phases and this situation will also change.

Fears or facts?
Why fear? It may not happen!

I choose to focus on this as a learning experience
Every problem that comes my way is an opportunity for me to learn about my strengths and weaknesses, others and life.

Feel soothing emotions:

I choose to feel warm, loving emotions. I do this by focusing on my heart and letting love, trust forgiveness, compassion, hope or gratitude fill my heart space.

Behave constructively:

I choose to work in part acts:
I will break the overwhelming job into manageable parts.

Do the difficult:
I will face what I fear and act with self-discipline

I choose to solutionise:
I will find a solution by taking advice or doing research.

Prioritise myself:
I will keep my life balanced by meeting friends, doing exercise or laughing.

Compartmentalise:
I will not let this event cloud my whole day; I will focus on something else now.

Utilise calming strategies:

When I:
- relax,
- breathe deeply,
- go for a run,
- shower,
- lie down,
- read,
- watch TV,
- climb into a mental helicopter
- practice mindfulness, meditation, my mind and body calm down.

Step Four: The Self Motivation Process

Endorse yourself for any growth no matter how small.

In the past I would have...

_____

_____

But this time I...

_____

_____

Tick off the traits that you strengthened when you worked down your anxiety:

☐ generosity   ☐ peacefulness
☐ kindness   ☐ self-discipline
☐ compassion   ☐ forgiveness
☐ consideration   ☐ courage
☐ helpfulness   ☐ responsibility
☐ respectfulness   ☐ reliability
☐ honesty   ☐ loyalty
☐ fairnesy   ☐ love
☐ patience   ☐ humility

Rate your anxiety on a scale of 0 to 100%:

[____]%

O

W

Anxiety Management Worksheet

The purpose of this worksheet is to help you to see every stressful event as an opportunity for
1. greater understanding of yourself, your anxiety and the people around you, and
2. practicing tools to manage your anxiety.

Step One: An Event

Briefly describe an event when you became anxious. Give such details as time, place and people involved, and end with "That's when I began to work myself up..."

E

Rate your anxiety on a scale of 0 to 100%: ____ %

Step Two: The Working-Up Process

Learn about your working up process by identifying your thoughts, feelings, behaviours and bodily reactions during the event. Tick the ones that most resonate with you.

Undermining Beliefs

I fear that I have lost...
- approval
- control
- co-operation
- face
- respect
- success
- trust
- validation
- love

This event proves that I am...
- stupid
- abnormal
- incompetent
- lazy
- irresponsible
- a total failure
- undisciplined
- untogether
- useless

B

I worry that I will suffer...
- mental collapse
- illness
- financial hardship

What I want is...
- total control
- respect
- success
- perfection
- comfort
- fairness
- tranquility
- all the answers
- for life to go smoothly
- to be all things to all people

Self-destructive Behaviour

Active
- get violent
- swear
- slam doors
- run away
- overeat
- harm myself
- criticise

Passive
- take it too seriously
- give up
- wallow in self pity
- sulk
- space out
- procrastinate
- give in
- be controlled

Intense Feelings

Angry feelings
- hateful
- aggravated
- annoyed
- hostile
- outraged
- punitive
- resentful
- vengeful

Fearful feelings
- helpless
- hopeless
- disappointed
- sad
- attacked
- worn out
- rejected
- jealous
- afraid
- exploited
- lonely
- abandoned
- guilty
- insulted
- confused
- disillusioned
- misunderstood
- trapped

Bodily Reactions (Limbic System)

I am uncomfortable because I am experiencing...
- tremors
- nausea
- sweaty palms
- stomach-ache
- pounding heart
- general tension
- fatigue
- imagination on fire
- headache
- dry mouth
- jaw clenching
- shortness of breath

Continued over

B   F   L

                   www.anxietysolutionscbt.com

Step Three: The Working-Down Process

Begin with, "Suddenly I realised that I was anxious and that I had choices..." This is the step of self-leadership and trust in one's ability to handle the situation.

Choose helpful thoughts:

I choose to depersonalise
There is no intention to hurt me. He is doing the best he can with the tools he has at the moment.

I choose realism over romanticism
Life presents many obstacles. I lower or raise standards as needed.

There is no right or wrong
Unless it is a moral issue, I will see it simply as a difference of opinion and/or taste.

I choose the total view of positivity
Even though this event is negative, the total view of his behaviour is positive.

I surrender control
Since I cannot change this situation, I choose to let go of it

I choose to put this event in perspective
This event is not a catastrophe because it is not life threatening. It can be viewed as a trivial life event, a normal life problem that needs to be solved not dramatised.

I choose to view this event as average, falling within the normal range
This event is not exceptional; many people have gone through this.

It's temporary - "this too shall pass"
Life is constantly changing and moving through phases and this situation will also change.

Fears or facts?
Why fear? It may not happen!

I choose to focus on this as a learning experience
Every problem that comes my way is an opportunity for me to learn about my strengths and weaknesses, others and life.

Feel soothing emotions:

I choose to feel warm, loving emotions. I do this by focusing on my heart and letting love, trust forgiveness, compassion, hope or gratitude fill my heart space.

Behave constructively:

I choose to work in part acts:
I will break the overwhelming job into manageable parts.

Do the difficult:
I will face what I fear and act with self-discipline

I choose to solutionise:
I will find a solution by taking advice or doing research.

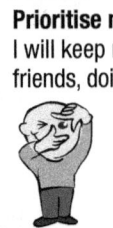

Prioritise myself:
I will keep my life balanced by meeting friends, doing exercise or laughing.

Compartmentalise:
I will not let this event cloud my whole day; I will focus on something else now.

Utilise calming strategies:

When I:
• relax,
• breathe deeply,
• go for a run,
• shower,
• lie down,
• read,
• watch TV,
• climb into a mental helicopter
• practice mindfulness, meditation, my mind and body calm down.

Step Four: The Self Motivation Process

Endorse yourself for any growth no matter how small.

In the past I would have...

_____

_____

But this time I...

_____

_____

Tick off the traits that you strengthened when you worked down your anxiety:

☐ generosity	☐ peacefulness		
☐ kindness	☐ self-discipline		
☐ compassion	☐ forgiveness		
☐ consideration	☐ courage		
☐ helpfulness	☐ responsibility		
☐ respectfulness	☐ reliability		
☐ honesty	☐ loyalty		
☐ fairness	☐ love		
☐ patience	☐ humility		

Rate your anxiety on a scale of 0 to 100%:

_____ %

O

W

Session 1

Anxiety Management Worksheet

The purpose of this worksheet is to help you to see every stressful event as an opportunity for
1. greater understanding of yourself, your anxiety and the people around you, and
2. practicing tools to manage your anxiety.

Step One: An Event

Briefly describe an event when you became anxious. Give such details as time, place and people involved, and end with "That's when I began to work myself up..."

E

Rate your anxiety on a scale of 0 to 100%: ____ %

Step Two: The Working-Up Process

Learn about your working up process by identifying your thoughts, feelings, behaviours and bodily reactions during the event. Tick the ones that most resonate with you.

Undermining Beliefs

I fear that I have lost...
- approval
- control
- co-operation
- face
- respect
- success
- trust
- validation
- love

This event proves that I am...
- stupid
- abnormal
- incompetent
- lazy
- irresponsible
- a total failure
- undisciplined
- untogether
- useless

B

I worry that I will suffer...
- mental collapse
- illness
- financial hardship

What I want is...
- total control
- respect
- success
- perfection
- comfort
- fairness
- tranquility
- all the answers
- for life to go smoothly
- to be all things to all people

Self-destructive Behaviour

Active
- get violent
- swear
- slam doors
- run away
- overeat
- harm myself
- criticise

Passive
- take it too seriously
- give up
- wallow in self pity
- sulk
- space out
- procrastinate
- give in
- be controlled

Intense Feelings

Angry feelings
- hateful
- aggravated
- annoyed
- hostile
- outraged
- punitive
- resentful
- vengeful

Fearful feelings
- helpless
- hopeless
- disappointed
- sad
- attacked
- worn out
- rejected
- jealous
- afraid
- exploited
- lonely
- abandoned
- guilty
- insulted
- confused
- disillusioned
- misunderstood
- trapped

Bodily Reactions (Limbic System)

I am uncomfortable because I am experiencing...
- tremors
- nausea
- sweaty palms
- stomach-ache
- pounding heart
- general tension
- fatigue
- imagination on fire
- headache
- dry mouth
- jaw clenching
- shortness of breath

Continued over

B   F   L

Copyright Renee Mill 2014   www.anxietysolutionscbt.com

Page 21

Step Three: The Working-Down Process

Begin with, "Suddenly I realised that I was anxious and that I had choices..." This is the step of self-leadership and trust in one's ability to handle the situation.

Choose helpful thoughts:

I choose to depersonalise
There is no intention to hurt me. He is doing the best he can with the tools he has at the moment.

I choose realism over romanticism
Life presents many obstacles. I lower or raise standards as needed.

There is no right or wrong
Unless it is a moral issue, I will see it simply as a difference of opinion and/or taste.

I choose the total view of positivity
Even though this event is negative, the total view of his behaviour is positive.

I surrender control
Since I cannot change this situation, I choose to let go of it

I choose to put this event in perspective
This event is not a catastrophe because it is not life threatening. It can be viewed as a trivial life event, a normal life problem that needs to be solved not dramatised.

I choose to view this event as average, falling within the normal range
This event is not exceptional; many people have gone through this.

It's temporary - "this too shall pass"
Life is constantly changing and moving through phases and this situation will also change.

Fears or facts?
Why fear? It may not happen!

I choose to focus on this as a learning experience
Every problem that comes my way is an opportunity for me to learn about my strengths and weaknesses, others and life.

Feel soothing emotions:

I choose to feel warm, loving emotions. I do this by focusing on my heart and letting love, trust forgiveness, compassion, hope or gratitude fill my heart space.

Behave constructively:

I choose to work in part acts:
I will break the overwhelming job into manageable parts.

Do the difficult:
I will face what I fear and act with self-discipline

I choose to solutionise:
I will find a solution by taking advice or doing research.

Prioritise myself:
I will keep my life balanced by meeting friends, doing exercise or laughing.

Compartmentalise:
I will not let this event cloud my whole day; I will focus on something else now.

Utilise calming strategies:

When I:
• relax,
• breathe deeply,
• go for a run,
• shower,
• lie down,
• read,
• watch TV,
• climb into a mental helicopter
• practice mindfulness, meditation, my mind and body calm down.

Step Four: The Self Motivation Process

Endorse yourself for any growth no matter how small.

In the past I would have...

_____

_____

But this time I...

_____

_____

Tick off the traits that you strengthened when you worked down your anxiety:

☐ generosity   ☐ peacefulness
☐ kindness   ☐ self-discipline
☐ compassion   ☐ forgiveness
☐ consideration ☐ courage
☐ helpfulness   ☐ responsibility
☐ respectfulness ☐ reliability
☐ honesty   ☐ loyalty
☐ fairness   ☐ love
☐ patience   ☐ humility

Rate your anxiety on a scale of 0 to 100%:

[____]%

O   W

Anxiety Management Worksheet

The purpose of this worksheet is to help you to see every stressful event as an opportunity for
1. greater understanding of yourself, your anxiety and the people around you, and
2. practicing tools to manage your anxiety.

Step One: An Event

Briefly describe an event when you became anxious. Give such details as time, place and people involved, and end with "That's when I began to work myself up…"

_____

_____ E

_____

_____ Rate your anxiety on a scale of 0 to 100%: [   ] %

Step Two: The Working-Up Process

Learn about your working up process by identifying your thoughts, feelings, behaviours and bodily reactions during the event. Tick the ones that most resonate with you.

Undermining Beliefs

I fear that I have lost...

- ☐ approval
- ☐ control
- ☐ co-operation
- ☐ face
- ☐ respect
- ☐ success
- ☐ trust
- ☐ validation
- ☐ love

This event proves that I am...

- ☐ stupid
- ☐ abnormal
- ☐ incompetent
- ☐ lazy
- ☐ irresponsible
- ☐ a total failure
- ☐ undisciplined
- ☐ untogether
- ☐ useless

B

I worry that I will suffer...

- ☐ mental collapse
- ☐ illness
- ☐ financial hardship

What I want is...

- ☐ total control
- ☐ respect
- ☐ success
- ☐ perfection
- ☐ comfort
- ☐ fairness
- ☐ tranquility
- ☐ all the answers
- ☐ for life to go smoothly
- ☐ to be all things to all people

Self-destructive Behaviour

Active
- ☐ get violent
- ☐ swear
- ☐ slam doors
- ☐ run away
- ☐ overeat
- ☐ harm myself
- ☐ criticise

Passive
- ☐ take it too seriously
- ☐ give up
- ☐ wallow in self pity
- ☐ sulk
- ☐ space out
- ☐ procrastinate
- ☐ give in
- ☐ be controlled

Intense Feelings

Angry feelings
- ☐ hateful
- ☐ aggravated
- ☐ annoyed
- ☐ hostile
- ☐ outraged
- ☐ punitive
- ☐ resentful
- ☐ vengeful

Fearful feelings
- ☐ helpless
- ☐ hopeless
- ☐ disappointed
- ☐ sad

- ☐ attacked
- ☐ worn out
- ☐ rejected
- ☐ jealous
- ☐ afraid
- ☐ exploited
- ☐ lonely
- ☐ abandoned
- ☐ guilty
- ☐ insulted
- ☐ confused
- ☐ disillusioned
- ☐ misunderstood
- ☐ trapped

Bodily Reactions (Limbic System)

I am uncomfortable because I am experiencing...

- ☐ tremors
- ☐ nausea
- ☐ sweaty palms
- ☐ stomach-ache
- ☐ pounding heart
- ☐ general tension
- ☐ fatigue
- ☐ imagination on fire
- ☐ headache
- ☐ dry mouth
- ☐ jaw clenching
- ☐ shortness of breath

Continued over

B   F   L

www.anxietysolutionscbt.com

Step Three: The Working-Down Process

Begin with, "Suddenly I realised that I was anxious and that I had choices..." This is the step of self-leadership and trust in one's ability to handle the situation.

Choose helpful thoughts:

I choose to depersonalise
There is no intention to hurt me. He is doing the best he can with the tools he has at the moment.

I choose realism over romanticism
Life presents many obstacles. I lower or raise standards as needed.

There is no right or wrong
Unless it is a moral issue, I will see it simply as a difference of opinion and/or taste.

I choose the total view of positivity
Even though this event is negative, the total view of his behaviour is positive.

I surrender control
Since I cannot change this situation, I choose to let go of it

I choose to put this event in perspective
This event is not a catastrophe because it is not life threatening. It can be viewed as a trivial life event, a normal life problem that needs to be solved not dramatised.

I choose to view this event as average, falling within the normal range
This event is not exceptional; many people have gone through this.

It's temporary - "this too shall pass"
Life is constantly changing and moving through phases and this situation will also change.

Fears or facts?
Why fear? It may not happen!

I choose to focus on this as a learning experience
Every problem that comes my way is an opportunity for me to learn about my strengths and weaknesses, others and life.

Feel soothing emotions:

I choose to feel warm, loving emotions. I do this by focusing on my heart and letting love, trust forgiveness, compassion, hope or gratitude fill my heart space.

Behave constructively:

I choose to work in part acts:
I will break the overwhelming job into manageable parts.

Do the difficult:
I will face what I fear and act with self-discipline

I choose to solutionise:
I will find a solution by taking advice or doing research.

Prioritise myself:
I will keep my life balanced by meeting friends, doing exercise or laughing.

Compartmentalise:
I will not let this event cloud my whole day; I will focus on something else now.

Utilise calming strategies:

When I:
• relax,
• breathe deeply,
• go for a run,
• shower,
• lie down,
• read,
• watch TV,
• climb into a mental helicopter
• practice mindfulness, meditation, my mind and body calm down.

Step Four: The Self Motivation Process

Endorse yourself for any growth no matter how small.

In the past I would have...

_____

_____

But this time I...

_____

_____

Tick off the traits that you strengthened when you worked down your anxiety:

☐ generosity	☐ peacefulness
☐ kindness	☐ self-discipline
☐ compassion	☐ forgiveness
☐ consideration	☐ courage
☐ helpfulness	☐ responsibility
☐ respectfulness	☐ reliability
☐ honesty	☐ loyalty
☐ fairness	☐ love
☐ patience	☐ humility

Rate your anxiety on a scale of 0 to 100%:

☐ %

O

W

Session 1

Anxiety Management Worksheet

The purpose of this worksheet is to help you to see every stressful event as an opportunity for
1. greater understanding of yourself, your anxiety and the people around you, and
2. practicing tools to manage your anxiety.

Step One: An Event

Briefly describe an event when you became anxious. Give such details as time, place and people involved, and end with "That's when I began to work myself up..."

_____

_____ E

_____

Rate your anxiety on a scale of 0 to 100%: [   ] %

Step Two: The Working-Up Process

Learn about your working up process by identifying your thoughts, feelings, behaviours and bodily reactions during the event. Tick the ones that most resonate with you.

Undermining Beliefs

I fear that I have lost...
- [ ] approval
- [ ] control
- [ ] co-operation
- [ ] face
- [ ] respect
- [ ] success
- [ ] trust
- [ ] validation
- [ ] love

This event proves that I am...
- [ ] stupid
- [ ] abnormal
- [ ] incompetent
- [ ] lazy
- [ ] irresponsible
- [ ] a total failure
- [ ] undisciplined
- [ ] untogether
- [ ] useless

B

I worry that I will suffer...
- [ ] mental collapse
- [ ] illness
- [ ] financial hardship

What I want is...
- [ ] total control
- [ ] respect
- [ ] success
- [ ] perfection
- [ ] comfort
- [ ] fairness
- [ ] tranquility
- [ ] all the answers
- [ ] for life to go smoothly
- [ ] to be all things to all people

Self-destructive Behaviour

Active
- [ ] get violent
- [ ] swear
- [ ] slam doors
- [ ] run away
- [ ] overeat
- [ ] harm myself
- [ ] criticise

Passive
- [ ] take it too seriously
- [ ] give up
- [ ] wallow in self pity
- [ ] sulk
- [ ] space out
- [ ] procrastinate
- [ ] give in
- [ ] be controlled

Intense Feelings

Angry feelings
- [ ] hateful
- [ ] aggravated
- [ ] annoyed
- [ ] hostile
- [ ] outraged
- [ ] punitive
- [ ] resentful
- [ ] vengeful

Fearful feelings
- [ ] helpless
- [ ] hopeless
- [ ] disappointed
- [ ] sad
- [ ] attacked
- [ ] worn out
- [ ] rejected
- [ ] jealous
- [ ] afraid
- [ ] exploited
- [ ] lonely
- [ ] abandoned
- [ ] guilty
- [ ] insulted
- [ ] confused
- [ ] disillusioned
- [ ] misunderstood
- [ ] trapped

Bodily Reactions (Limbic System)

I am uncomfortable because I am experiencing...
- [ ] tremors
- [ ] nausea
- [ ] sweaty palms
- [ ] stomach-ache
- [ ] pounding heart
- [ ] general tension
- [ ] fatigue
- [ ] imagination on fire
- [ ] headache
- [ ] dry mouth
- [ ] jaw clenching
- [ ] shortness of breath

Continued over

B   F   L

Copyright Renee Mill 2014 · www.anxietysolutionscbt.com

Page 25

Step Three: The Working-Down Process

Begin with, "Suddenly I realised that I was anxious and that I had choices..." This is the step of self-leadership and trust in one's ability to handle the situation.

Choose helpful thoughts:

I choose to depersonalise
There is no intention to hurt me. He is doing the best he can with the tools he has at the moment.

I choose realism over romanticism
Life presents many obstacles. I lower or raise standards as needed.

There is no right or wrong
Unless it is a moral issue, I will see it simply as a difference of opinion and/or taste.

I choose the total view of positivity
Even though this event is negative, the total view of his behaviour is positive.

I surrender control
Since I cannot change this situation, I choose to let go of it

I choose to put this event in perspective
This event is not a catastrophe because it is not life threatening. It can be viewed as a trivial life event, a normal life problem that needs to be solved not dramatised.

I choose to view this event as average, falling within the normal range
This event is not exceptional; many people have gone through this.

It's temporary - "this too shall pass"
Life is constantly changing and moving through phases and this situation will also change.

Fears or facts?
Why fear? It may not happen!

I choose to focus on this as a learning experience
Every problem that comes my way is an opportunity for me to learn about my strengths and weaknesses, others and life.

Feel soothing emotions:

I choose to feel warm, loving emotions. I do this by focusing on my heart and letting love, trust forgiveness, compassion, hope or gratitude fill my heart space.

Behave constructively:

I choose to work in part acts:
I will break the overwhelming job into manageable parts.

Do the difficult:
I will face what I fear and act with self-discipline

I choose to solutionise:
I will find a solution by taking advice or doing research.

Prioritise myself:
I will keep my life balanced by meeting friends, doing exercise or laughing.

Compartmentalise:
I will not let this event cloud my whole day; I will focus on something else now.

Utilise calming strategies:

When I:
• relax,
• breathe deeply,
• go for a run,
• shower,
• lie down,
• read,
• watch TV,
• climb into a mental helicopter
• practice mindfulness, meditation, my mind and body calm down.

Step Four: The Self Motivation Process

Endorse yourself for any growth no matter how small.

In the past I would have...

But this time I...

Tick off the traits that you strengthened when you worked down your anxiety:

☐ generosity ☐ peacefulness
☐ kindness ☐ self-discipline
☐ compassion ☐ forgiveness
☐ consideration ☐ courage
☐ helpfulness ☐ responsibility
☐ respectfulness ☐ reliability
☐ honesty ☐ loyalty
☐ fairness ☐ love
☐ patience ☐ humility

Rate your anxiety on a scale of 0 to 100%:

☐ %

O   W

Session 1

Anxiety Management Worksheet

The purpose of this worksheet is to help you to see every stressful event as an opportunity for
1. greater understanding of yourself, your anxiety and the people around you, and
2. practicing tools to manage your anxiety.

Step One: An Event

Briefly describe an event when you became anxious. Give such details as time, place and people involved, and end with "That's when I began to work myself up..."

_____

_____

_____

_____ Rate your anxiety on a scale of 0 to 100%: [   ] %

E

Step Two: The Working-Up Process

Learn about your working up process by identifying your thoughts, feelings, behaviours and bodily reactions during the event. Tick the ones that most resonate with you.

Undermining Beliefs

I fear that I have lost...
- ☐ approval
- ☐ control
- ☐ co-operation
- ☐ face
- ☐ respect
- ☐ success
- ☐ trust
- ☐ validation
- ☐ love

This event proves that I am...
- ☐ stupid
- ☐ abnormal
- ☐ incompetent
- ☐ lazy
- ☐ irresponsible
- ☐ a total failure
- ☐ undisciplined
- ☐ untogether
- ☐ useless

B

I worry that I will suffer...
- ☐ mental collapse
- ☐ illness
- ☐ financial hardship

What I want is...
- ☐ total control
- ☐ respect
- ☐ success
- ☐ perfection
- ☐ comfort
- ☐ fairness
- ☐ tranquility
- ☐ all the answers
- ☐ for life to go smoothly
- ☐ to be all things to all people

Self-destructive Behaviour

Active
- ☐ get violent
- ☐ swear
- ☐ slam doors
- ☐ run away
- ☐ overeat
- ☐ harm myself
- ☐ criticise

Passive
- ☐ take it too seriously
- ☐ give up
- ☐ wallow in self pity
- ☐ sulk
- ☐ space out
- ☐ procrastinate
- ☐ give in
- ☐ be controlled

Intense Feelings

Angry feelings
- ☐ hateful
- ☐ aggravated
- ☐ annoyed
- ☐ hostile
- ☐ outraged
- ☐ punitive
- ☐ resentful
- ☐ vengeful

Fearful feelings
- ☐ helpless
- ☐ hopeless
- ☐ disappointed
- ☐ sad
- ☐ attacked
- ☐ worn out
- ☐ rejected
- ☐ jealous
- ☐ afraid
- ☐ exploited
- ☐ lonely
- ☐ abandoned
- ☐ guilty
- ☐ insulted
- ☐ confused
- ☐ disillusioned
- ☐ misunderstood
- ☐ trapped

Bodily Reactions (Limbic System)

I am uncomfortable because I am experiencing...
- ☐ tremors
- ☐ nausea
- ☐ sweaty palms
- ☐ stomach-ache
- ☐ pounding heart
- ☐ general tension
- ☐ fatigue
- ☐ imagination on fire
- ☐ headache
- ☐ dry mouth
- ☐ jaw clenching
- ☐ shortness of breath

Continued over

B   F   L

Step Three: The Working-Down Process

Begin with, "Suddenly I realised that I was anxious and that I had choices..." This is the step of self-leadership and trust in one's ability to handle the situation.

Choose helpful thoughts:

I choose to depersonalise
There is no intention to hurt me. He is doing the best he can with the tools he has at the moment.

I choose realism over romanticism
Life presents many obstacles. I lower or raise standards as needed.

There is no right or wrong
Unless it is a moral issue, I will see it simply as a difference of opinion and/or taste.

I choose the total view of positivity
Even though this event is negative, the total view of his behaviour is positive.

I surrender control
Since I cannot change this situation, I choose to let go of it

I choose to put this event in perspective
This event is not a catastrophe because it is not life threatening. It can be viewed as a trivial life event, a normal life problem that needs to be solved not dramatised.

I choose to view this event as average, falling within the normal range
This event is not exceptional; many people have gone through this.

It's temporary - "this too shall pass"
Life is constantly changing and moving through phases and this situation will also change.

Fears or facts?
Why fear? It may not happen!

I choose to focus on this as a learning experience
Every problem that comes my way is an opportunity for me to learn about my strengths and weaknesses, others and life.

Feel soothing emotions:

I choose to feel warm, loving emotions. I do this by focusing on my heart and letting love, trust forgiveness, compassion, hope or gratitude fill my heart space.

Behave constructively:

I choose to work in part acts:
I will break the overwhelming job into manageable parts.

Do the difficult:
I will face what I fear and act with self-discipline

I choose to solutionise:
I will find a solution by taking advice or doing research.

Prioritise myself:
I will keep my life balanced by meeting friends, doing exercise or laughing.

Compartmentalise:
I will not let this event cloud my whole day; I will focus on something else now.

Utilise calming strategies:

When I:
• relax,
• breathe deeply,
• go for a run,
• shower,
• lie down,
• read,
• watch TV,
• climb into a mental helicopter
• practice mindfulness, meditation, my mind and body calm down.

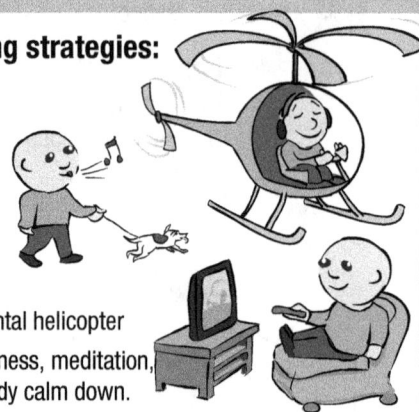

Step Four: The Self Motivation Process

Endorse yourself for any growth no matter how small.

In the past I would have...

_____

_____

But this time I...

_____

_____

Tick off the traits that you strengthened when you worked down your anxiety:

☐ generosity   ☐ peacefulness
☐ kindness   ☐ self-discipline
☐ compassion   ☐ forgiveness
☐ consideration   ☐ courage
☐ helpfulness   ☐ responsibility
☐ respectfulness   ☐ reliability
☐ honesty   ☐ loyalty
☐ fairness   ☐ love
☐ patience   ☐ humility

Rate your anxiety on a scale of 0 to 100%:

_____ %

O   W

NOTES

NOTES

NOTES

Session 2

COGNITIVE TOOL: PERSPECTIVE

'I choose to put this incident in perspective. This event is not a catastrophe because it is not life-threatening. It can be viewed as a trivial life problem that needs to be solved not dramatised.'

The word catastrophise refers to the process of taking an everyday event and turning it into a major catastrophe in your mind or with your words. This process may be conscious and deliberate, or unconscious. Either way, catastrophising will get your fight/flight responses going unnecessarily. Our brains are programmed to understand what a catastrophe is and the need to respond to it with life saving energy. But what exactly is a catastrophe?

The Webster dictionary defines a catastrophe as follows:

1. an event causing great and usually sudden damage or suffering; a disaster.

2. a momentous tragic event ranging from extreme misfortune to utter overthrow or ruin.

3. a violent and sudden change in a feature of the earth.

4. a violent usually destructive natural event (as a supernova).

As you can see from this definition, a catastrophe is something major that causes real damage. Yet hundreds of people refer to everyday events as if they were real catastrophes.

Watch your language

Do you use catastrophic language to describe every day events? Here are some common examples:

*   The dinner turned out to be a disaster!

*   I did not get the job that I want, this will be my ruination!

*   She spilled milk on the floor. What a calamity!

*   My hair is too short, this is a crisis!

*   This traffic jam is horrendous!

*   I've got a killer headache! I probably have a tumour.

Other commonly used catastrophic words used in day to day life include *tragedy, blow, shock, horror, abuse* and *trauma.*

When you use catastrophic terms to describe everyday hassles, your brain believes there is danger and sets off a fight/flight reaction. Therefore, it is important that you watch what you say. Use your words carefully and describe what you see in real terms such as:

- Some of the food was burnt at dinner but we snacked on crackers and got through it okay.

- I am so disappointed that I did not get the job I applied for. Luckily I have savings that will see me through.

- No use crying over spilt milk. Better to clean it up so nobody slips.

- My hair is too short, I hate it. I can't wait for it to grow out in 3 weeks.

- This traffic jam is an inconvenience that will dissipate in the next few hours.

- My headache is from bad posture. All I need to do is stretch to get relief.

Notice that you are not pretending that things are perfect. Nor are you trying to see a silver lining. Rather, you are describing realistically what happened instead of exaggerating negatively. Realistic assessments will activate coping mechanisms whereas catastrophic assessments will activate the 'fight or flight ' reaction.

The Reality Check Ruler

A very effective way to help you to see situations realistically is to utilise this ruler.

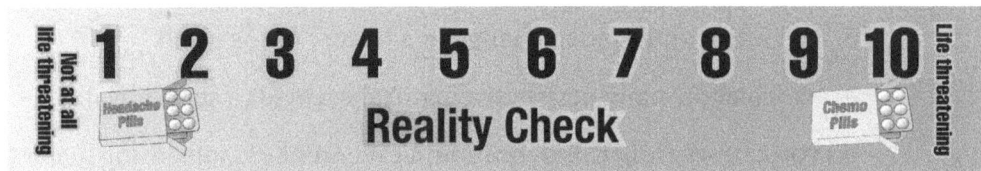

On one end of the ruler is number 1, which is the number depicting a situation that is not at all life-threatening. At the other end of the ruler is number 10, depicting situations which are life-threatening.

And by life-threatening I mean here an objective measure — life-threatening situations include falling off a cliff, being caught in a rip in the ocean, being inside your house while it is on fire, someone holding a knife to your throat.

There are many events which may be major and incur a loss but they are still not life-threatening. When you are watching your house burn down, it is devastating but not life-threatening. When you fall on a road, it may be painful but your life is not at risk. When a large wave knocks you over, it may be uncomfortable and, you may need some assistance, but your life is not on the line.

Whenever a situation arises and you feel that you are becoming panicky, *as if you are in mortal danger*, use this tool. Ask yourself: 'On a scale from 1 to 10, how life-threatening is this incident? ' What you will find is that very few situations, in fact, are life-threatening. As you 'score ' your event lower down on the scale, you will immediately feel your stress levels drop.

The ruler enables you to 'test out' whether or not, in fact, your body is responding realistically. Are you looking at the facts?

Events that are not life-threatening are called 'trivialities '. This does not mean that they are not important or that your worried feelings are not valid. It is just a way of forcing you to view the event in terms of a more realistic perspective and help you become aware that, in the broader scheme of things, most issues that worry you are relatively trivial.

Illustration

Let us say that you are irritated by the fact that a new neighbour talks loudly on the phone near your front door. You get worked up about it and, believing it will disturb your peaceful existence, even curse the man behind his back. Then you discover that a member of your family is dying. Suddenly the irritation is of no significance as your thoughts are totally consumed by the tragic news. The tragic news brought home to you that in the broader scheme of things (life and death situations), the irritation (loud speaking) is a triviality.

This does not mean you have to put up with the new neighbour's loud talking and deny your irritation. *It just means that you do not need to react as if you are about to die.* Rather, you handle it as a problem that needs to be dealt with rationally, without all the emotionality.

EXERCISE FOUR

Fill out the columns below. Column 1 refers to past events in your life that have evoked catastrophic conclusions and major stress reactions. Column 2 refers to the point on the scale where you placed the events at the time. In column 3, write down how you would rate those same events at present. In column 4, write down the wording of this tool. (Writing things down helps you to develop a memory bank of how to rate events realistically).

Life Events	Previous Score	Current Score	Calming Thought
Demonstration: When I had my hair done for my engagement party, it looked awful and I had no time to correct it.	10 I sobbed like a baby at first and then sulked all night ruining my party for myself.	1	This event was not life threatening. A bad hair do is uncomfortable but not dangerous.

Please note: When you are in the midst of catastrophising, you may not be able to utilise the ruler. However, once you have calmed down somewhat, it is still beneficial to use this tool as it will place the situation into perspective for you. Doing this after the fact will have a preventative effect in the future.

Remember: This tool is only effective if the event is not really life-threatening. If an event is truly life-threatening, or catastrophic, do not try and minimise it. Instead, look for a more appropriate tool to help you.

COGNITIVE TOOL: FEARS OR FACTS

'Why fear? It may not happen!'

An important premise of CBT is that irrational thoughts lead to fear and anxiety. A primary tool of CBT is to gather facts to prove that these thoughts are not rational. The aim is to replace the irrational thoughts with rational thoughts which are based on facts. This is what lessens your fear.

A common question utilised in CBT is 'What is the evidence?' What facts do you have to confirm your fear? For instance, where is the proof that you will definitely make a fool of yourself when you deliver your speech?

The idea that is emphasised with this tool is that fears are not always facts. Fears may feel real but until they are confirmed by reality, they are simply that — fears. Humans tend to ruminate about possible negative outcomes, and women seem to do it more than men. We tend to forget the old but true cliché that 90% of the things we worry about never actually materialise.

Compare this to a child who is afraid of the dark. She imagines that there are things that are waiting in the cupboard to pounce when in fact, nothing of the sort exists.

As adults we do this, too. Let us say, for example, that your manager asks you to swap desks with a newcomer; you then start to imagine that after the desk, you will be asked to relinquish your senior position in the company to the newcomer and ultimately, you will be answering to the newcomer. The starting off point was being asked to swap desks; your fears push you to take it to an end-point where you would have to answer to the newcomer.

Many other 'end-points' exist in possibility but you have chosen the one that reflects your fears. Until the boss actually tells you that you are demoted in relation to the newcomer, it is only your fear that leads you to believe that you will be demoted.

The following exercise is here to assist you to hold on calmly through scary moments. Before you succumb to worry and despair, this tool will assist you to wait until you have the facts before jumping to conclusions.

EXERCISE FIVE

For the scenarios presented below, write out possible fearful thoughts and then calm yourself by repeating the wording of this tool.

Example: Your manager asks you to swap desks.

Fearful thought: I will soon be answering to the newcomer.

Calming thought: 'Why waste energy on worry and fear? Until the boss tells me otherwise, I will continue in my job as before, albeit at a new desk.'

1. You find a lump on your hand:

    a) Fearful thought: _____

    b) Calming thought: _____

2. Your boss calls you to his office unexpectedly:

    a) Fearful thought: _____

    b) Calming thought: _____

3. A police car is just behind you and initiates the siren:

    a) Fearful thought: _____

    b) Calming thought: _____

4. Your partner does not eat the soup you especially prepared:

    a) Fearful thought: _____

    b) Calming thought: _____

5. Your best friend's car has gone in for repairs for a month:

    a) Fearful thought: _____

    b) Calming thought: _____

6. Your company has merged with another, larger company:

    a) Fearful thought: _____

    b) Calming thought: _____

7. A fellow passenger on the bus moves from the seat next to you to the back of the bus:

    a) Fearful thought: _____

    b) Calming thought: _____

8. Your partner is late and is not answering his/her phone.

    a) Fearful thought: _____

    b) Calming thought: _____

EXERCISE SIX

Have you ever predicted a negative outcome that proved to be incorrect?

YES/NO

If yes, what was it and how did it turn out in reality?

_____

_____

_____

_____

This tool is particularly helpful when it is difficult to move from a negative thought to a positive one. Sometimes we are so convinced that there will be a negative outcome that our brain cannot process a positive possibility. When you try to think more positively, your brain responds as if it is a 'trick' question and may become even more skeptical.

This tool moves you from a negative thought to a neutral thought. You are not trying to disprove your fears. You are simply putting possible conclusions on hold or in the 'too hard basket'. You are also reassuring yourself that you will be free to start worrying when you have evidence that your fear is a fact.

For example, when you discover a lump on your hand, it is nearly impossible to try and convince yourself that it is nothing. After all, a lump is a lump and should not be there. However, it is possible to move into a neutral position. You say 'Why fear the worst, it may not be the truth. Until the doctor gives me a reliable diagnosis, I will think about other things and not focus on it.'

DAILY MONITORING DIARY

WEEK ENDING _____

Day	M	T	W	T	F	S	S
Overall Anxiety Rating for the day (0-10)							

1. EXERCISE

	M	T	W	T	F	S	S
How long?							
Anxiety level before (0-10)							
Anxiety level after (0-10)							

2. BREATHING & RELAXATION

	M	T	W	T	F	S	S
How long?							
Anxiety level before (0-10)							
Anxiety level after (0-10)							

3. CATASTROPHIC THINKING

	M	T	W	T	F	S	S
How often this type of thought occurred							
Belief in thoughts before challenging (0-10)							
Belief in thoughts after challenging (0-10)							

4. FEARS NOT FACTS

	M	T	W	T	F	S	S
How often this type of thought occurred							
Belief in thoughts before challenging (0-10)							
Belief in thoughts after challenging (0-10)							

Anxiety Management Worksheet

The purpose of this worksheet is to help you to see every stressful event as an opportunity for
1. greater understanding of yourself, your anxiety and the people around you, and
2. practicing tools to manage your anxiety.

Step One: An Event

Briefly describe an event when you became anxious. Give such details as time, place and people involved, and end with "That's when I began to work myself up…"

_____

_____ E

_____

_____ Rate your anxiety on a scale of 0 to 100%: [   ] %

Step Two: The Working-Up Process

Learn about your working up process by identifying your thoughts, feelings, behaviours and bodily reactions during the event. Tick the ones that most resonate with you.

Undermining Beliefs

I fear that I have lost...
- ☐ approval
- ☐ control
- ☐ co-operation
- ☐ face
- ☐ respect
- ☐ success
- ☐ trust
- ☐ validation
- ☐ love

This event proves that I am...
- ☐ stupid
- ☐ abnormal
- ☐ incompetent
- ☐ lazy
- ☐ irresponsible
- ☐ a total failure
- ☐ undisciplined
- ☐ untogether
- ☐ useless

B

I worry that I will suffer...
- ☐ mental collapse
- ☐ illness
- ☐ financial hardship

What I want is...
- ☐ total control
- ☐ respect
- ☐ success
- ☐ perfection
- ☐ comfort
- ☐ fairness
- ☐ tranquility
- ☐ all the answers
- ☐ for life to go smoothly
- ☐ to be all things to all people

Self-destructive Behaviour

Active
- ☐ get violent
- ☐ swear
- ☐ slam doors
- ☐ run away
- ☐ overeat
- ☐ harm myself
- ☐ criticise

Passive
- ☐ take it too seriously
- ☐ give up
- ☐ wallow in self pity
- ☐ sulk
- ☐ space out
- ☐ procrastinate
- ☐ give in
- ☐ be controlled

Intense Feelings

Angry feelings
- ☐ hateful
- ☐ aggravated
- ☐ annoyed
- ☐ hostile
- ☐ outraged
- ☐ punitive
- ☐ resentful
- ☐ vengeful

Fearful feelings
- ☐ helpless
- ☐ hopeless
- ☐ disappointed
- ☐ sad

- ☐ attacked
- ☐ worn out
- ☐ rejected
- ☐ jealous
- ☐ afraid
- ☐ exploited
- ☐ lonely
- ☐ abandoned
- ☐ guilty
- ☐ insulted
- ☐ confused
- ☐ disillusioned
- ☐ misunderstood
- ☐ trapped

Bodily Reactions (Limbic System)

I am uncomfortable because I am experiencing...
- ☐ tremors
- ☐ nausea
- ☐ sweaty palms
- ☐ stomach-ache
- ☐ pounding heart
- ☐ general tension
- ☐ fatigue
- ☐ imagination on fire
- ☐ headache
- ☐ dry mouth
- ☐ jaw clenching
- ☐ shortness of breath

Continued over

B   F   L

Step Three: The Working-Down Process

Begin with, "Suddenly I realised that I was anxious and that I had choices..." This is the step of self-leadership and trust in one's ability to handle the situation.

Choose helpful thoughts:

I choose to depersonalise
There is no intention to hurt me. He is doing the best he can with the tools he has at the moment.

I choose realism over romanticism
Life presents many obstacles. I lower or raise standards as needed.

There is no right or wrong
Unless it is a moral issue, I will see it simply as a difference of opinion and/or taste.

I choose the total view of positivity
Even though this event is negative, the total view of his behaviour is positive.

I surrender control
Since I cannot change this situation, I choose to let go of it

I choose to put this event in perspective
This event is not a catastrophe because it is not life threatening. It can be viewed as a trivial life event, a normal life problem that needs to be solved not dramatised.

I choose to view this event as average, falling within the normal range
This event is not exceptional; many people have gone through this.

It's temporary - "this too shall pass"
Life is constantly changing and moving through phases and this situation will also change.

Fears or facts?
Why fear? It may not happen!

I choose to focus on this as a learning experience
Every problem that comes my way is an opportunity for me to learn about my strengths and weaknesses, others and life.

Feel soothing emotions:

I choose to feel warm, loving emotions. I do this by focusing on my heart and letting love, trust forgiveness, compassion, hope or gratitude fill my heart space.

Behave constructively:

I choose to work in part acts:
I will break the overwhelming job into manageable parts.

Do the difficult:
I will face what I fear and act with self-discipline

I choose to solutionise:
I will find a solution by taking advice or doing research.

Prioritise myself:
I will keep my life balanced by meeting friends, doing exercise or laughing.

Compartmentalise:
I will not let this event cloud my whole day; I will focus on something else now.

Utilise calming strategies:

When I:
- relax,
- breathe deeply,
- go for a run,
- shower,
- lie down,
- read,
- watch TV,
- climb into a mental helicopter
- practice mindfulness, meditation, my mind and body calm down.

Step Four: The Self Motivation Process

Endorse yourself for any growth no matter how small.

In the past I would have...

_____

_____

But this time I...

_____

_____

Tick off the traits that you strengthened when you worked down your anxiety:

☐ generosity	☐ peacefulness
☐ kindness	☐ self-discipline
☐ compassion	☐ forgiveness
☐ consideration	☐ courage
☐ helpfulness	☐ responsibility
☐ respectfulness	☐ reliability
☐ honesty	☐ loyalty
☐ fairness	☐ love
☐ patience	☐ humility

Rate your anxiety on a scale of 0 to 100%:

[____] %

O

W

Anxiety Management Worksheet

The purpose of this worksheet is to help you to see every stressful event as an opportunity for
1. greater understanding of yourself, your anxiety and the people around you, and
2. practicing tools to manage your anxiety.

Step One: An Event

Briefly describe an event when you became anxious. Give such details as time, place and people involved, and end with "That's when I began to work myself up..."

E

Rate your anxiety on a scale of 0 to 100%: ____ %

Step Two: The Working-Up Process

Learn about your working up process by identifying your thoughts, feelings, behaviours and bodily reactions during the event. Tick the ones that most resonate with you.

Undermining Beliefs

I fear that I have lost...
- ☐ approval
- ☐ success
- ☐ control
- ☐ trust
- ☐ co-operation
- ☐ validation
- ☐ face
- ☐ love
- ☐ respect

This event proves that I am...
- ☐ stupid
- ☐ a total failure
- ☐ abnormal
- ☐ undisciplined
- ☐ incompetent
- ☐ untogether
- ☐ lazy
- ☐ useless
- ☐ irresponsible

B

I worry that I will suffer...
- ☐ mental collapse
- ☐ illness
- ☐ financial hardship

What I want is...
- ☐ total control
- ☐ tranquility
- ☐ respect
- ☐ all the answers
- ☐ success
- ☐ for life to go smoothly
- ☐ perfection
- ☐ comfort
- ☐ to be all things to all people
- ☐ fairness

Self-destructive Behaviour

Active
- ☐ get violent
- ☐ swear
- ☐ slam doors
- ☐ run away
- ☐ overeat
- ☐ harm myself
- ☐ criticise

Passive
- ☐ take it too seriously
- ☐ give up
- ☐ wallow in self pity
- ☐ sulk
- ☐ space out
- ☐ procrastinate
- ☐ give in
- ☐ be controlled

Intense Feelings

Angry feelings
- ☐ hateful
- ☐ attacked
- ☐ aggravated
- ☐ worn out
- ☐ annoyed
- ☐ rejected
- ☐ hostile
- ☐ jealous
- ☐ outraged
- ☐ afraid
- ☐ punitive
- ☐ exploited
- ☐ resentful
- ☐ lonely
- ☐ vengeful
- ☐ abandoned

Fearful feelings
- ☐ guilty
- ☐ helpless
- ☐ insulted
- ☐ hopeless
- ☐ confused
- ☐ disappointed
- ☐ disillusioned
- ☐ sad
- ☐ misunderstood
- ☐ trapped

Bodily Reactions (Limbic System)

I am uncomfortable because I am experiencing...
- ☐ tremors
- ☐ nausea
- ☐ sweaty palms
- ☐ stomach-ache
- ☐ pounding heart
- ☐ general tension
- ☐ fatigue
- ☐ imagination on fire
- ☐ headache
- ☐ dry mouth
- ☐ jaw clenching
- ☐ shortness of breath

Continued over

B   F   L

Step Three: The Working-Down Process

Begin with, "Suddenly I realised that I was anxious and that I had choices..." This is the step of self-leadership and trust in one's ability to handle the situation.

Choose helpful thoughts:

I choose to depersonalise
There is no intention to hurt me. He is doing the best he can with the tools he has at the moment.

I choose realism over romanticism
Life presents many obstacles. I lower or raise standards as needed.

There is no right or wrong
Unless it is a moral issue, I will see it simply as a difference of opinion and/or taste.

I choose the total view of positivity
Even though this event is negative, the total view of his behaviour is positive.

I surrender control
Since I cannot change this situation, I choose to let go of it

I choose to put this event in perspective
This event is not a catastrophe because it is not life threatening. It can be viewed as a trivial life event, a normal life problem that needs to be solved not dramatised.

I choose to view this event as average, falling within the normal range
This event is not exceptional; many people have gone through this.

It's temporary - "this too shall pass"
Life is constantly changing and moving through phases and this situation will also change.

Fears or facts?
Why fear? It may not happen!

I choose to focus on this as a learning experience
Every problem that comes my way is an opportunity for me to learn about my strengths and weaknesses, others and life.

Feel soothing emotions:

I choose to feel warm, loving emotions. I do this by focusing on my heart and letting love, trust, forgiveness, compassion, hope or gratitude fill my heart space.

Behave constructively:

I choose to work in part acts:
I will break the overwhelming job into manageable parts.

Do the difficult:
I will face what I fear and act with self-discipline

I choose to solutionise:
I will find a solution by taking advice or doing research.

Prioritise myself:
I will keep my life balanced by meeting friends, doing exercise or laughing.

Compartmentalise:
I will not let this event cloud my whole day; I will focus on something else now.

Utilise calming strategies:

When I:
- relax,
- breathe deeply,
- go for a run,
- shower,
- lie down,
- read,
- watch TV,
- climb into a mental helicopter
- practice mindfulness, meditation, my mind and body calm down.

Step Four: The Self Motivation Process

Endorse yourself for any growth no matter how small.

In the past I would have...

But this time I...

Tick off the traits that you strengthened when you worked down your anxiety:

- generosity
- kindness
- compassion
- consideration
- helpfulness
- respectfulness
- honesty
- fairness
- patience
- peacefulness
- self-discipline
- forgiveness
- courage
- responsibility
- reliability
- loyalty
- love
- humility

Rate your anxiety on a scale of 0 to 100%:

_____%

O   W

Session 2

Anxiety Management Worksheet

The purpose of this worksheet is to help you to see every stressful event as an opportunity for
1. greater understanding of yourself, your anxiety and the people around you, and
2. practicing tools to manage your anxiety.

Step One: An Event

Briefly describe an event when you became anxious. Give such details as time, place and people involved, and end with "That's when I began to work myself up..."

_____

_____ E

_____ Rate your anxiety on a scale of 0 to 100%: [   ] %

Step Two: The Working-Up Process

Learn about your working up process by identifying your thoughts, feelings, behaviours and bodily reactions during the event. Tick the ones that most resonate with you.

Undermining Beliefs

I fear that I have lost...
- ☐ approval
- ☐ control
- ☐ co-operation
- ☐ face
- ☐ respect
- ☐ success
- ☐ trust
- ☐ validation
- ☐ love

This event proves that I am...
- ☐ stupid
- ☐ abnormal
- ☐ incompetent
- ☐ lazy
- ☐ irresponsible
- ☐ a total failure
- ☐ undisciplined
- ☐ untogether
- ☐ useless

B

I worry that I will suffer...
- ☐ mental collapse
- ☐ illness
- ☐ financial hardship

What I want is...
- ☐ total control
- ☐ respect
- ☐ success
- ☐ perfection
- ☐ comfort
- ☐ fairness
- ☐ tranquility
- ☐ all the answers
- ☐ for life to go smoothly
- ☐ to be all things to all people

Self-destructive Behaviour

Active
- ☐ get violent
- ☐ swear
- ☐ slam doors
- ☐ run away
- ☐ overeat
- ☐ harm myself
- ☐ criticise

Passive
- ☐ take it too seriously
- ☐ give up
- ☐ wallow in self pity
- ☐ sulk
- ☐ space out
- ☐ procrastinate
- ☐ give in
- ☐ be controlled

Intense Feelings

Angry feelings
- ☐ hateful
- ☐ aggravated
- ☐ annoyed
- ☐ hostile
- ☐ outraged
- ☐ punitive
- ☐ resentful
- ☐ vengeful

Fearful feelings
- ☐ helpless
- ☐ hopeless
- ☐ disappointed
- ☐ sad
- ☐ attacked
- ☐ worn out
- ☐ rejected
- ☐ jealous
- ☐ afraid
- ☐ exploited
- ☐ lonely
- ☐ abandoned
- ☐ guilty
- ☐ insulted
- ☐ confused
- ☐ disillusioned
- ☐ misunderstood
- ☐ trapped

Bodily Reactions (Limbic System)

I am uncomfortable because I am experiencing...
- ☐ tremors
- ☐ nausea
- ☐ sweaty palms
- ☐ stomach-ache
- ☐ pounding heart
- ☐ general tension
- ☐ fatigue
- ☐ imagination on fire
- ☐ headache
- ☐ dry mouth
- ☐ jaw clenching
- ☐ shortness of breath

Continued over

B   F   L

Step Three: The Working-Down Process

Begin with, "Suddenly I realised that I was anxious and that I had choices..." This is the step of self-leadership and trust in one's ability to handle the situation.

Choose helpful thoughts:

I choose to depersonalise
There is no intention to hurt me. He is doing the best he can with the tools he has at the moment.

I choose realism over romanticism
Life presents many obstacles. I lower or raise standards as needed.

There is no right or wrong
Unless it is a moral issue, I will see it simply as a difference of opinion and/or taste.

I choose the total view of positivity
Even though this event is negative, the total view of his behaviour is positive.

I surrender control
Since I cannot change this situation, I choose to let go of it

I choose to put this event in perspective
This event is not a catastrophe because it is not life threatening. It can be viewed as a trivial life event, a normal life problem that needs to be solved not dramatised.

I choose to view this event as average, falling within the normal range
This event is not exceptional; many people have gone through this.

It's temporary - "this too shall pass"
Life is constantly changing and moving through phases and this situation will also change.

Fears or facts?
Why fear? It may not happen!

I choose to focus on this as a learning experience
Every problem that comes my way is an opportunity for me to learn about my strengths and weaknesses, others and life.

Feel soothing emotions:

I choose to feel warm, loving emotions. I do this by focusing on my heart and letting love, trust forgiveness, compassion, hope or gratitude fill my heart space.

Behave constructively:

I choose to work in part acts:
I will break the overwhelming job into manageable parts.

Do the difficult:
I will face what I fear and act with self-discipline

I choose to solutionise:
I will find a solution by taking advice or doing research.

Prioritise myself:
I will keep my life balanced by meeting friends, doing exercise or laughing.

Compartmentalise:
I will not let this event cloud my whole day; I will focus on something else now.

Utilise calming strategies:

When I:
- relax,
- breathe deeply,
- go for a run,
- shower,
- lie down,
- read,
- watch TV,
- climb into a mental helicopter
- practice mindfulness, meditation, my mind and body calm down.

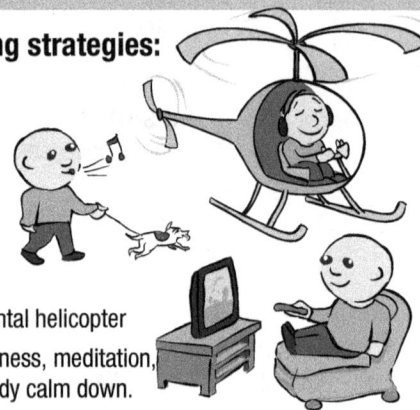

Step Four: The Self Motivation Process

Endorse yourself for any growth no matter how small.

In the past I would have...

_____

_____

But this time I...

_____

_____

Tick off the traits that you strengthened when you worked down your anxiety:

☐ generosity   ☐ peacefulness
☐ kindness   ☐ self-discipline
☐ compassion   ☐ forgiveness
☐ consideration   ☐ courage
☐ helpfulness   ☐ responsibility
☐ respectfulness   ☐ reliability
☐ honesty   ☐ loyalty
☐ fairness   ☐ love
☐ patience   ☐ humility

Rate your anxiety on a scale of 0 to 100%:

_____ %

O

W

Anxiety Management Worksheet

The purpose of this worksheet is to help you to see every stressful event as an opportunity for
1. greater understanding of yourself, your anxiety and the people around you, and
2. practicing tools to manage your anxiety.

Step One: An Event

Briefly describe an event when you became anxious. Give such details as time, place and people involved, and end with "That's when I began to work myself up..."

_____

_____ E

_____

_____ Rate your anxiety on a scale of 0 to 100%: [   ] %

Step Two: The Working-Up Process

Learn about your working up process by identifying your thoughts, feelings, behaviours and bodily reactions during the event. Tick the ones that most resonate with you.

Undermining Beliefs

I fear that I have lost...

- ☐ approval
- ☐ success
- ☐ control
- ☐ trust
- ☐ co-operation
- ☐ validation
- ☐ face
- ☐ love
- ☐ respect

This event proves that I am...

- ☐ stupid
- ☐ a total failure
- ☐ abnormal
- ☐ undisciplined
- ☐ incompetent
- ☐ untogether
- ☐ lazy
- ☐ useless
- ☐ irresponsible

B

I worry that I will suffer...

- ☐ mental collapse
- ☐ illness
- ☐ financial hardship

What I want is...

- ☐ total control
- ☐ tranquility
- ☐ respect
- ☐ all the answers
- ☐ success
- ☐ for life to go smoothly
- ☐ perfection
- ☐ comfort
- ☐ to be all things to all people
- ☐ fairness

Self-destructive Behaviour

Active

- ☐ get violent
- ☐ swear
- ☐ slam doors
- ☐ run away
- ☐ overeat
- ☐ harm myself
- ☐ criticise

Passive

- ☐ take it too seriously
- ☐ give up
- ☐ wallow in self pity
- ☐ sulk
- ☐ space out
- ☐ procrastinate
- ☐ give in
- ☐ be controlled

Intense Feelings

Angry feelings

- ☐ hateful
- ☐ attacked
- ☐ aggravated
- ☐ worn out
- ☐ annoyed
- ☐ rejected
- ☐ hostile
- ☐ jealous
- ☐ outraged
- ☐ afraid
- ☐ punitive
- ☐ exploited
- ☐ resentful
- ☐ lonely
- ☐ vengeful
- ☐ abandoned

Fearful feelings

- ☐ guilty
- ☐ helpless
- ☐ insulted
- ☐ hopeless
- ☐ confused
- ☐ disappointed
- ☐ disillusioned
- ☐ sad
- ☐ misunderstood
- ☐ trapped

Bodily Reactions (Limbic System)

I am uncomfortable because I am experiencing...

- ☐ tremors
- ☐ nausea
- ☐ sweaty palms
- ☐ stomach-ache
- ☐ pounding heart
- ☐ general tension
- ☐ fatigue
- ☐ imagination on fire
- ☐ headache
- ☐ dry mouth
- ☐ jaw clenching
- ☐ shortness of breath

Continued over

B   F   L

Step Three: The Working-Down Process

Begin with, "Suddenly I realised that I was anxious and that I had choices..." This is the step of self-leadership and trust in one's ability to handle the situation.

Choose helpful thoughts:

I choose to depersonalise
There is no intention to hurt me. He is doing the best he can with the tools he has at the moment.

I choose realism over romanticism
Life presents many obstacles. I lower or raise standards as needed.

There is no right or wrong
Unless it is a moral issue, I will see it simply as a difference of opinion and/or taste.

I choose the total view of positivity
Even though this event is negative, the total view of his behaviour is positive.

I surrender control
Since I cannot change this situation, I choose to let go of it

I choose to put this event in perspective
This event is not a catastrophe because it is not life threatening. It can be viewed as a trivial life event, a normal life problem that needs to be solved not dramatised.

I choose to view this event as average, falling within the normal range
This event is not exceptional; many people have gone through this.

It's temporary - "this too shall pass"
Life is constantly changing and moving through phases and this situation will also change.

Fears or facts?
Why fear? It may not happen!

I choose to focus on this as a learning experience
Every problem that comes my way is an opportunity for me to learn about my strengths and weaknesses, others and life.

Feel soothing emotions:

I choose to feel warm, loving emotions. I do this by focusing on my heart and letting love, trust forgiveness, compassion, hope or gratitude fill my heart space.

Behave constructively:

I choose to work in part acts:
I will break the overwhelming job into manageable parts.

Do the difficult:
I will face what I fear and act with self-discipline

I choose to solutionise:
I will find a solution by taking advice or doing research.

Prioritise myself:
I will keep my life balanced by meeting friends, doing exercise or laughing.

Compartmentalise:
I will not let this event cloud my whole day; I will focus on something else now.

Utilise calming strategies:

When I:
- relax,
- breathe deeply,
- go for a run,
- shower,
- lie down,
- read,
- watch TV,
- climb into a mental helicopter
- practice mindfulness, meditation, my mind and body calm down.

Step Four: The Self Motivation Process

Endorse yourself for any growth no matter how small.

In the past I would have...

_____

_____

But this time I...

_____

_____

Tick off the traits that you strengthened when you worked down your anxiety:

☐ generosity	☐ peacefulness
☐ kindness	☐ self-discipline
☐ compassion	☐ forgiveness
☐ consideration	☐ courage
☐ helpfulness	☐ responsibility
☐ respectfulness	☐ reliability
☐ honesty	☐ loyalty
☐ fairness	☐ love
☐ patience	☐ humility

Rate your anxiety on a scale of 0 to 100%:

[____]%

O   W

Anxiety Management Worksheet

The purpose of this worksheet is to help you to see every stressful event as an opportunity for
1. greater understanding of yourself, your anxiety and the people around you, and
2. practicing tools to manage your anxiety.

Step One: An Event

Briefly describe an event when you became anxious. Give such details as time, place and people involved, and end with "That's when I began to work myself up…"

_____

_____ E

_____

_____ Rate your anxiety on a scale of 0 to 100%: [   ] %

Step Two: The Working-Up Process

Learn about your working up process by identifying your thoughts, feelings, behaviours and bodily reactions during the event. Tick the ones that most resonate with you.

Undermining Beliefs

I fear that I have lost...
- ☐ approval
- ☐ control
- ☐ co-operation
- ☐ face
- ☐ respect
- ☐ success
- ☐ trust
- ☐ validation
- ☐ love

This event proves that I am...
- ☐ stupid
- ☐ abnormal
- ☐ incompetent
- ☐ lazy
- ☐ irresponsible
- ☐ a total failure
- ☐ undisciplined
- ☐ untogether
- ☐ useless

B

I worry that I will suffer...
- ☐ mental collapse
- ☐ illness
- ☐ financial hardship

What I want is...
- ☐ total control
- ☐ respect
- ☐ success
- ☐ perfection
- ☐ comfort
- ☐ fairness
- ☐ tranquility
- ☐ all the answers
- ☐ for life to go smoothly
- ☐ to be all things to all people

Self-destructive Behaviour

Active
- ☐ get violent
- ☐ swear
- ☐ slam doors
- ☐ run away
- ☐ overeat
- ☐ harm myself
- ☐ criticise

Passive
- ☐ take it too seriously
- ☐ give up
- ☐ wallow in self pity
- ☐ sulk
- ☐ space out
- ☐ procrastinate
- ☐ give in
- ☐ be controlled

Intense Feelings

Angry feelings
- ☐ hateful
- ☐ aggravated
- ☐ annoyed
- ☐ hostile
- ☐ outraged
- ☐ punitive
- ☐ resentful
- ☐ vengeful

Fearful feelings
- ☐ helpless
- ☐ hopeless
- ☐ disappointed
- ☐ sad
- ☐ attacked
- ☐ worn out
- ☐ rejected
- ☐ jealous
- ☐ afraid
- ☐ exploited
- ☐ lonely
- ☐ abandoned
- ☐ guilty
- ☐ insulted
- ☐ confused
- ☐ disillusioned
- ☐ misunderstood
- ☐ trapped

Bodily Reactions (Limbic System)

I am uncomfortable because I am experiencing...
- ☐ tremors
- ☐ nausea
- ☐ sweaty palms
- ☐ stomach-ache
- ☐ pounding heart
- ☐ general tension
- ☐ fatigue
- ☐ imagination on fire
- ☐ headache
- ☐ dry mouth
- ☐ jaw clenching
- ☐ shortness of breath

Continued over

B   F   L

Step Three: The Working-Down Process

Begin with, "Suddenly I realised that I was anxious and that I had choices..." This is the step of self-leadership and trust in one's ability to handle the situation.

Choose helpful thoughts:

I choose to depersonalise
There is no intention to hurt me. He is doing the best he can with the tools he has at the moment.

I choose realism over romanticism
Life presents many obstacles. I lower or raise standards as needed.

There is no right or wrong
Unless it is a moral issue, I will see it simply as a difference of opinion and/or taste.

I choose the total view of positivity
Even though this event is negative, the total view of his behaviour is positive.

I surrender control
Since I cannot change this situation, I choose to let go of it

I choose to put this event in perspective
This event is not a catastrophe because it is not life threatening. It can be viewed as a trivial life event, a normal life problem that needs to be solved not dramatised.

I choose to view this event as average, falling within the normal range
This event is not exceptional; many people have gone through this.

It's temporary - "this too shall pass"
Life is constantly changing and moving through phases and this situation will also change.

Fears or facts?
Why fear? It may not happen!

I choose to focus on this as a learning experience
Every problem that comes my way is an opportunity for me to learn about my strengths and weaknesses, others and life.

Feel soothing emotions:

I choose to feel warm, loving emotions. I do this by focusing on my heart and letting love, trust forgiveness, compassion, hope or gratitude fill my heart space.

Behave constructively:

I choose to work in part acts:
I will break the overwhelming job into manageable parts.

Do the difficult:
I will face what I fear and act with self-discipline

I choose to solutionise:
I will find a solution by taking advice or doing research.

Prioritise myself:
I will keep my life balanced by meeting friends, doing exercise or laughing.

Compartmentalise:
I will not let this event cloud my whole day; I will focus on something else now.

Utilise calming strategies:

When I:
- relax,
- breathe deeply,
- go for a run,
- shower,
- lie down,
- read,
- watch TV,
- climb into a mental helicopter
- practice mindfulness, meditation, my mind and body calm down.

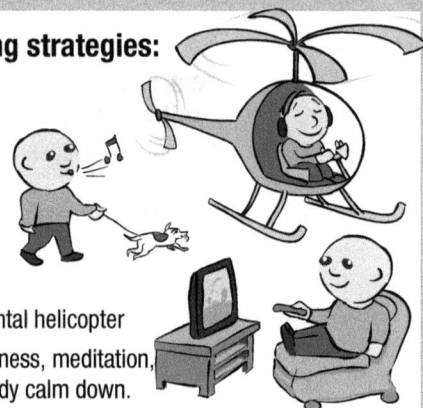

Step Four: The Self Motivation Process

Endorse yourself for any growth no matter how small.

In the past I would have...

_____

_____

But this time I...

_____

_____

Tick off the traits that you strengthened when you worked down your anxiety:

☐ generosity
☐ kindness
☐ compassion
☐ consideration
☐ helpfulness
☐ respectfulness
☐ honesty
☐ fairness
☐ patience
☐ peacefulness
☐ self-discipline
☐ forgiveness
☐ courage
☐ responsibility
☐ reliability
☐ loyalty
☐ love
☐ humility

Rate your anxiety on a scale of 0 to 100%:

_____ %

O

W

Anxiety Management Worksheet

The purpose of this worksheet is to help you to see every stressful event as an opportunity for
1. greater understanding of yourself, your anxiety and the people around you, and
2. practicing tools to manage your anxiety.

Step One: An Event

Briefly describe an event when you became anxious. Give such details as time, place and people involved, and end with "That's when I began to work myself up…"

_____

_____ E

_____

Rate your anxiety on a scale of 0 to 100%: [   ] %

Step Two: The Working-Up Process

Learn about your working up process by identifying your thoughts, feelings, behaviours and bodily reactions during the event. Tick the ones that most resonate with you.

Undermining Beliefs

I fear that I have lost...
- ☐ approval
- ☐ control
- ☐ co-operation
- ☐ face
- ☐ respect
- ☐ success
- ☐ trust
- ☐ validation
- ☐ love

This event proves that I am...
- ☐ stupid
- ☐ abnormal
- ☐ incompetent
- ☐ lazy
- ☐ irresponsible
- ☐ a total failure
- ☐ undisciplined
- ☐ untogether
- ☐ useless

B

I worry that I will suffer...
- ☐ mental collapse
- ☐ illness
- ☐ financial hardship

What I want is...
- ☐ total control
- ☐ respect
- ☐ success
- ☐ perfection
- ☐ comfort
- ☐ fairness
- ☐ tranquility
- ☐ all the answers
- ☐ for life to go smoothly
- ☐ to be all things to all people

Self-destructive Behaviour

Active
- ☐ get violent
- ☐ swear
- ☐ slam doors
- ☐ run away
- ☐ overeat
- ☐ harm myself
- ☐ criticise

Passive
- ☐ take it too seriously
- ☐ give up
- ☐ wallow in self pity
- ☐ sulk
- ☐ space out
- ☐ procrastinate
- ☐ give in
- ☐ be controlled

Intense Feelings

Angry feelings
- ☐ hateful
- ☐ aggravated
- ☐ annoyed
- ☐ hostile
- ☐ outraged
- ☐ punitive
- ☐ resentful
- ☐ vengeful

Fearful feelings
- ☐ helpless
- ☐ hopeless
- ☐ disappointed
- ☐ sad
- ☐ attacked
- ☐ worn out
- ☐ rejected
- ☐ jealous
- ☐ afraid
- ☐ exploited
- ☐ lonely
- ☐ abandoned
- ☐ guilty
- ☐ insulted
- ☐ confused
- ☐ disillusioned
- ☐ misunderstood
- ☐ trapped

Bodily Reactions (Limbic System)

I am uncomfortable because I am experiencing...
- ☐ tremors
- ☐ nausea
- ☐ sweaty palms
- ☐ stomach-ache
- ☐ pounding heart
- ☐ general tension
- ☐ fatigue
- ☐ imagination on fire
- ☐ headache
- ☐ dry mouth
- ☐ jaw clenching
- ☐ shortness of breath

Continued over

B   F   L

Step Three: The Working-Down Process

Begin with, "Suddenly I realised that I was anxious and that I had choices..." This is the step of self-leadership and trust in one's ability to handle the situation.

Choose helpful thoughts:

I choose to depersonalise
There is no intention to hurt me. He is doing the best he can with the tools he has at the moment.

I choose realism over romanticism
Life presents many obstacles. I lower or raise standards as needed.

There is no right or wrong
Unless it is a moral issue, I will see it simply as a difference of opinion and/or taste.

I choose the total view of positivity
Even though this event is negative, the total view of his behaviour is positive.

I surrender control
Since I cannot change this situation, I choose to let go of it

I choose to put this event in perspective
This event is not a catastrophe because it is not life threatening. It can be viewed as a trivial life event, a normal life problem that needs to be solved not dramatised.

I choose to view this event as average, falling within the normal range
This event is not exceptional; many people have gone through this.

It's temporary - "this too shall pass"
Life is constantly changing and moving through phases and this situation will also change.

Fears or facts?
Why fear? It may not happen!

I choose to focus on this as a learning experience
Every problem that comes my way is an opportunity for me to learn about my strengths and weaknesses, others and life.

Feel soothing emotions:

I choose to feel warm, loving emotions. I do this by focusing on my heart and letting love, trust forgiveness, compassion, hope or gratitude fill my heart space.

Behave constructively:

I choose to work in part acts:
I will break the overwhelming job into manageable parts.

Do the difficult:
I will face what I fear and act with self-discipline

I choose to solutionise:
I will find a solution by taking advice or doing research.

Prioritise myself:
I will keep my life balanced by meeting friends, doing exercise or laughing.

Compartmentalise:
I will not let this event cloud my whole day; I will focus on something else now.

Utilise calming strategies:

When I:
• relax,
• breathe deeply,
• go for a run,
• shower,
• lie down,
• read,
• watch TV,
• climb into a mental helicopter
• practice mindfulness, meditation, my mind and body calm down.

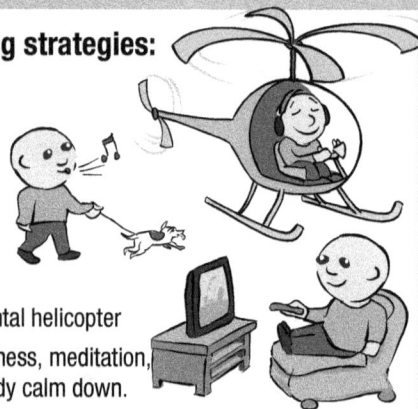

Step Four: The Self Motivation Process

Endorse yourself for any growth no matter how small.

In the past I would have...

_____

_____

But this time I...

_____

_____

Tick off the traits that you strengthened when you worked down your anxiety:

☐ generosity	☐ peacefulness
☐ kindness	☐ self-discipline
☐ compassion	☐ forgiveness
☐ consideration	☐ courage
☐ helpfulness	☐ responsibility
☐ respectfulness	☐ reliability
☐ honesty	☐ loyalty
☐ fairness	☐ love
☐ patience	☐ humility

Rate your anxiety on a scale of 0 to 100%:

☐ %

O

W

Anxiety Management Worksheet

The purpose of this worksheet is to help you to see every stressful event as an opportunity for
1. greater understanding of yourself, your anxiety and the people around you, and
2. practicing tools to manage your anxiety.

Step One: An Event

Briefly describe an event when you became anxious. Give such details as time, place and people involved, and end with "That's when I began to work myself up..."

_____

_____ **E**

_____

_____ Rate your anxiety on a scale of 0 to 100%: [   ] **%**

Step Two: The Working-Up Process

Learn about your working up process by identifying your thoughts, feelings, behaviours and bodily reactions during the event. Tick the ones that most resonate with you.

Undermining Beliefs

I fear that I have lost...

☐ approval   ☐ success
☐ control   ☐ trust
☐ co-operation   ☐ validation
☐ face   ☐ love
☐ respect

This event proves that I am...

☐ stupid   ☐ a total failure
☐ abnormal   ☐ undisciplined
☐ incompetent   ☐ untogether
☐ lazy   ☐ useless
☐ irresponsible

B

I worry that I will suffer...

☐ mental collapse
☐ illness
☐ financial hardship

What I want is...

☐ total control   ☐ tranquility
☐ respect   ☐ all the answers
☐ success   ☐ for life to go
☐ perfection   smoothly
☐ comfort   ☐ to be all things
☐ fairness   to all people

Self-destructive Behaviour

Active

☐ get violent
☐ swear
☐ slam doors
☐ run away
☐ overeat
☐ harm myself
☐ criticise

Passive

☐ take it too seriously
☐ give up
☐ wallow in self pity
☐ sulk
☐ space out
☐ procrastinate
☐ give in
☐ be controlled

Intense Feelings

Angry feelings

☐ hateful   ☐ attacked
☐ aggravated   ☐ worn out
☐ annoyed   ☐ rejected
☐ hostile   ☐ jealous
☐ outraged   ☐ afraid
☐ punitive   ☐ exploited
☐ resentful   ☐ lonely
☐ vengeful   ☐ abandoned

Fearful feelings   ☐ guilty
☐ helpless   ☐ insulted
☐ hopeless   ☐ confused
☐ disappointed   ☐ disillusioned
☐ sad   ☐ misunderstood
                    ☐ trapped

Bodily Reactions (Limbic System)

I am uncomfortable because I am experiencing...

☐ tremors
☐ nausea
☐ sweaty palms
☐ stomach-ache
☐ pounding heart
☐ general tension
☐ fatigue
☐ imagination on fire
☐ headache
☐ dry mouth
☐ jaw clenching
☐ shortness of breath

Continued over

B   **F**   **L**

Step Three: The Working-Down Process

Begin with, "Suddenly I realised that I was anxious and that I had choices…" This is the step of self-leadership and trust in one's ability to handle the situation.

Choose helpful thoughts:

I choose to depersonalise
There is no intention to hurt me. He is doing the best he can with the tools he has at the moment.

I choose realism over romanticism
Life presents many obstacles. I lower or raise standards as needed.

There is no right or wrong
Unless it is a moral issue, I will see it simply as a difference of opinion and/or taste.

I choose the total view of positivity
Even though this event is negative, the total view of his behaviour is positive.

I surrender control
Since I cannot change this situation, I choose to let go of it

I choose to put this event in perspective
This event is not a catastrophe because it is not life threatening. It can be viewed as a trivial life event, a normal life problem that needs to be solved not dramatised.

I choose to view this event as average, falling within the normal range
This event is not exceptional; many people have gone through this.

It's temporary - "this too shall pass"
Life is constantly changing and moving through phases and this situation will also change.

Fears or facts?
Why fear? It may not happen!

I choose to focus on this as a learning experience
Every problem that comes my way is an opportunity for me to learn about my strengths and weaknesses, others and life.

Feel soothing emotions:

I choose to feel warm, loving emotions. I do this by focusing on my heart and letting love, trust forgiveness, compassion, hope or gratitude fill my heart space.

Behave constructively:

I choose to work in part acts:
I will break the overwhelming job into manageable parts.

Do the difficult:
I will face what I fear and act with self-discipline

I choose to solutionise:
I will find a solution by taking advice or doing research.

Prioritise myself:
I will keep my life balanced by meeting friends, doing exercise or laughing.

Compartmentalise:
I will not let this event cloud my whole day; I will focus on something else now.

Utilise calming strategies:

When I:
• relax,
• breathe deeply,
• go for a run,
• shower,
• lie down,
• read,
• watch TV,
• climb into a mental helicopter
• practice mindfulness, meditation, my mind and body calm down.

Step Four: The Self Motivation Process

Endorse yourself for any growth no matter how small.

In the past I would have…

_____

_____

But this time I…

_____

_____

Tick off the traits that you strengthened when you worked down your anxiety:

☐ generosity	☐ peacefulness
☐ kindness	☐ self-discipline
☐ compassion	☐ forgiveness
☐ consideration	☐ courage
☐ helpfulness	☐ responsibility
☐ respectfulness	☐ reliability
☐ honesty	☐ loyalty
☐ fairness	☐ love
☐ patience	☐ humility

Rate your anxiety on a scale of 0 to 100%:

[____]%

0

W

NOTES

NOTES

NOTES

Session 3

COGNITIVE TOOL: TOTAL VIEW

'I choose the total view of positivity. Even though this incident is negative, the total view of my situation/his behaviour is positive'.

When we go through a **specific** negative situation, it often feels to us as though the **whole** situation is negative. For instance, let us say one friend has let you down, you might feel that you cannot trust any of your other friends.

This manner of pessimistic thinking has been described as **pervasive pessimistic thinking** by Martin Seligman It is what happens when you take one negative detail and allow it to contaminate (pervade) the whole picture. This tool helps you to see the total view as positive with only one negative aspect.

EXERCISE SEVEN

This picture of the world is similar to a world map that one sees when watching a weather report on TV. The weather reporter may say something like: 'Clear skies and calm seas overall but a storm gathering at Aceh.'

Take a pen and draw a small circle anywhere on the picture of the world. The small circle you have drawn is representative of a storm that may be occurring at one place in our vast world. Drawing a circle is symbolic of you making a note of an area in your life that hurts, or needs attention. When you stand back and look at the picture of the world in front of you, it all looks clear except for the one spot where you have made a mark.

Similarly, when you have an issue in your life it will be beneficial for you to stand back and look at your life as a whole. Most times you will find that the whole picture is good. However, there is that one issue needs to be addressed.

When you utilise this tool, you are not being hyper-positive and denying that there is pain or stress in your situation. You acknowledge your pain while being realistic about its size in comparison to all the positives in your life.

Viewing the problem in relation to a bigger picture reduces anxiety because the problem becomes small and manageable.

Here are some examples of how to utilise the **Total View** tool:

- You are studying various subjects at school. Your score in maths is below average. You tell yourself 'I am stupid' which is a pervasive pessimistic way of thinking because, overall, you are not stupid.

    Using this tool, you would say 'Even though I am struggling with maths, I am not stupid in every respect. My scores for other subjects are above average. Therefore, the total view of my scholastic ability is positive'.

- You have prepared a 4 course dinner. The soufflé which you made for dessert flopped. Instead of berating yourself and thinking 'I am not a good cook', say 'Even though the soufflé failed to rise, the total view of my cooking ability is good.'

- Your boss yells at you. You feel humiliated and want to leave your job in a fit of anger. Take a minute and ask yourself how many things are bad at your place of employment. If you find that you are satisfied with the income, the hours, your colleagues and the tasks, then calm yourself by saying 'Even though my boss yells at me on occasion and I do not like it, the total view of my job is positive'.

Of course, there will be times when a situation is negative as a whole and this tool would not be applicable. In such a case, you must take action! For instance, if your boss yells at you and underpays you plus the team is unfriendly, then you probably should leave the job.

This tool is appropriate when it feels as though a whole situation is negative when, in fact, it isn't and you need assistance to gain perspective. Gaining that perspective will motivate you and lift your mood.

EXERCISE EIGHT

Circle one response for each of the scenarios below:

1. When you miss an important meeting at work, do you think?

    a) My memory is poor .

    b) I sometimes forget to check my appointment book.

2. When you have prepared an outing with your family and they do not agree with any of your ideas, do you think?

    a) I don't know how to plan outings.

    b) I planned it without asking if they were interested or had free time.

3. When your shares drop to an all-time low, do you think?

    a) I don't know much about the business climate.

    b) I made a poor choice of shares.

4. Do you tend to think?

    a) All people are untrustworthy.

    b) Peter Smith is untrustworthy.

5. Do you ever feel?

    a) I am repulsive.

    b) I am repulsive to Peter Jones.

6. Do you believe?

    a) No courses will ever be able to benefit me.

    b) That course on 'swimming therapy' was not helpful to me.

7. If you are penalised for not returning your income tax forms on time, do you think?

    a) I am disorganised and irresponsible.

    b) I was lazy about getting my taxes done this year.

8. Should a store refuse to honour your credit card, would you think?

    a) I am useless at budgeting.

    b) I sometimes forget to check my balance before I shop.

How many a)'s did you score?

How many b)'s did you score?

In the examples laid out in the above exercise, a) responses are indicative of pervasive pessimistic thinking, while b) responses indicate a negative assessment of a specific area.

Put another way, when you think, 'My memory is poor', you are basically saying that the 'total view of my memory ability is poor'. However, when you say, 'I sometimes forget to check my appointment book', you are saying, 'When I look at the total picture of my memory ability, I can see that it is adequate. However, there are times when I sometimes forget to check my appointment book.'

When you think, 'I am not very good at planning things', you are undermining your organisational abilities in an overall way. However, when you think, 'I planned it without asking if they were interested or had free time', you acknowledge that your organisational abilities as a whole are fine, but in this instance they did not shine through due to a lack of consultation with the people involved.

Similarly, when your shares drop to an all-time low and you attribute it to your lack of knowledge of the entire business climate, it is a pervasive pessimistic belief. On the other hand, when you think that you have a generally thorough understanding of the business climate but in this particular case you erred in your choice, you are looking at the total view of your business abilities in a positive light.

A pervasive pessimistic outlook is de-motivating and de-energising. Seeing the total view as positive will give you a good feeling about yourself, and/or the situation. You will not feel anxious and you will be motivated to persevere and solve the problem.

COGNITIVE TOOL: TEMPORARY

'It's temporary. This too shall pass. Life is constantly changing and moving through phases and this situation will also change.'

Much of the stress we experience in a situation derives from a feeling that the stressful situation will last forever. This is another manner of pessimistic thinking described by Martin Seligman who calls it **permanent pessimistic thinking.**

When you believe that something negative is not going to change and will stay that way forever, you will feel demotivated and maybe even depressed.

Managing physical pain illustrates this perfectly. It has been found that if a patient is told that his surgery would result in excruciating pain for three days, the patient coped well with the pain. However, when a patient with moderate pain was told that his pain could go on indefinitely, the patient struggled much more even though the degree of pain was less. Not knowing when the pain would end, increased stress and maintained focus on the pain.

Put simply, if a person knows that his pain will be short-lived, he will grit his teeth (figuratively and maybe literally) and get through it. However, when there is no end in sight, the suffering becomes difficult to endure.

Watch your language.

When you use words like 'always' and 'never', they indicate a permanent situation. Therefore, when you say, 'It will never get better', or 'it will always be uncomfortable', your stress levels will rise. You may even feel hopeless and give up on things.

This is why it is important to be very specific about situations and speak in temporary terms rather than permanent terms.

Here are some common situations where your language would lower your stress:

- You yell at your husband 'You never take out the garbage!' Is that true? Has he never, ever taken out the garbage? If the reality is that he forgot to take out the garbage two weeks in a row, then say that. 'You have not taken out the garbage for two weeks in a row.' When you do, experience your stress levels reduce.

- Your friend does not invite you out for drinks. You think to yourself 'She never invites me out for a drink.' Is that true? Or does she invite you occasionally but not every time? If it is the latter, describe it factually and you will feel less hurt.

- Your child has not made his bed. You become furious saying 'You always leave your bed unmade. Are you expecting me to make it? When will you do it yourself?' Is this factual? Does the child always leave the bed unmade, or is it only on school days? Or when he is late for school? State the facts and watch your anger subside.

Words and phrases that indicate you might be over-generalising and applying a permanent pessimistic thinking style:

- '(this is) how things always are'

- 'she's always like that'

- 'things never turn out well for me'

EXERCISE NINE

Write down three occasions in your life when you thought things would never get better but they did. This will build up a memory bank that you can draw on in the future. There will come a time when you will feel hopeless again. When this happens, dip into this memory bank to reassure yourself that just like in these examples, the situation will prove to be temporary, and will not stay the same.

Example: I felt hopeless when I lost my job in 1995. After 8 weeks of looking, I believed that I would never find another job. Luckily it did not stay the same. After 6 months, I found another job and it proved to be better paid than the last one.

1.

_____

_____

_____

_____

2.

_____

_____

_____

_____

3.

_____

_____

_____

_____

EXERCISE TEN

Circle one response for each of the scenarios below.

1. Your friend forgets your birthday. You think:

    a) He always forgets my birthday.

    b) He forgot my birthday this year.

2. You are penalised for not returning your income-tax forms on time. You think:

    a) I never get things right.

    b) I was lazy about getting my taxes done this year.

3. You perform particularly badly in a job interview. You think:

    a) I never perform well in job interviews.

    b) I was nervous for this job interview.

4. You lose your temper with a friend. You think:

    a) I am always out of control.

    b) I am in a hostile mood right now.

5. You've been feeling run down lately. You think:

    a) I never get a chance to relax.

    b) I was exceptionally busy this week.

6. Your partner says something that hurts your feelings. You think:

    a) She/he always blurts things out without thinking of others.

    b) She/he was in a bad mood today and momentarily lost control.

7. You gained weight over the holidays and now you are struggling to lose it. You think:

    a) Diets do not work.

    b) The diet I tried did not work.

8. You struggle to get through your first exercise routine. You think:

    a) Exercising is difficult.

    b) My body needs to get used to this.

How many a)'s did you score?

How many b)'s did you score?

In the scenarios of the above exercise: a) responses are indicative of permanent, pessimistic thinking, while b) responses indicate time limited, realistic descriptions of situations.

Put another way, when you think, 'I always put off doing my taxes', you are basically saying that you permanently and at all times put off doing your taxes. However, when you say, 'I was lazy about getting my taxes done this year', you are saying that perhaps on this occasion you did not get your taxes done on time but it is not necessarily a permanent condition. The condition (laziness) is temporary, and next time round you could perform differently.

In sum, when you believe that things will stay the same indefinitely, you will feel hopeless and therefore demotivated. However, when you believe that the situation is a momentary lapse or a temporary hiccup, you will feel able to overcome it and persevere.

Here are some example situations where this tool can be very useful.

- You are sitting on a plane next to a noisy child. Tell yourself: 'This discomfort is not forever. In five hours it will be over. I will walk off the plane into a large airport with plenty of space'.

- It is the end of the day — 'happy hour'. Your kids are acting up and you are becoming infuriated. Tell yourself: 'This will come to an end soon. Only thirty minutes to go until bed time. Soon the kids will be in bed and I will be able to relax'.

- You are extremely busy at work needing to complete a project before a deadline. Tell yourself: 'The deadline is in 3 weeks by which time the project has to be completed. In 3 weeks, I will be able to slow down and resume my normal work pace.'

DAILY MONITORING DIARY

WEEK ENDING _____

Day	M	T	W	T	F	S	S
Overall Anxiety Rating for the day (0-10)							

1. EXERCISE

	M	T	W	T	F	S	S
How long?							
Anxiety level before (0-10)							
Anxiety level after (0-10)							

2. BREATHING & RELAXATION

	M	T	W	T	F	S	S
How long?							
Anxiety level before (0-10)							
Anxiety level after (0-10)							

3. CATASTROPHIC THINKING

	M	T	W	T	F	S	S
How often this type of thought occurred							
Belief in thoughts before challenging (0-10)							
Belief in thoughts after challenging (0-10)							

4. FEARS NOT FACTS

	M	T	W	T	F	S	S
How often this type of thought occurred							
Belief in thoughts before challenging (0-10)							
Belief in thoughts after challenging (0-10)							

5. PERVASIVE PESSIMISTIC THINKING

	M	T	W	T	F	S	S
How often this type of thought occurred							
Belief in thoughts before challenging (0-10)							
Belief in thoughts after challenging (0-10)							

6. PERMANENT PESSIMISTIC THINKING

	M	T	W	T	F	S	S
How often this type of thought occurred							
Belief in thoughts before challenging (0-10)							
Belief in thoughts after challenging (0-10)							

Anxiety Management Worksheet

The purpose of this worksheet is to help you to see every stressful event as an opportunity for
1. greater understanding of yourself, your anxiety and the people around you, and
2. practicing tools to manage your anxiety.

Step One: An Event

Briefly describe an event when you became anxious. Give such details as time, place and people involved, and end with "That's when I began to work myself up..."

_____

_____ **E**

_____

_____ Rate your anxiety on a scale of 0 to 100%: [   ] %

Step Two: The Working-Up Process

Learn about your working up process by identifying your thoughts, feelings, behaviours and bodily reactions during the event. Tick the ones that most resonate with you.

Undermining Beliefs

I fear that I have lost...
- ☐ approval
- ☐ control
- ☐ co-operation
- ☐ face
- ☐ respect
- ☐ success
- ☐ trust
- ☐ validation
- ☐ love

This event proves that I am...
- ☐ stupid
- ☐ abnormal
- ☐ incompetent
- ☐ lazy
- ☐ irresponsible
- ☐ a total failure
- ☐ undisciplined
- ☐ untogether
- ☐ useless

B

I worry that I will suffer...
- ☐ mental collapse
- ☐ illness
- ☐ financial hardship

What I want is...
- ☐ total control
- ☐ respect
- ☐ success
- ☐ perfection
- ☐ comfort
- ☐ fairness
- ☐ tranquility
- ☐ all the answers
- ☐ for life to go smoothly
- ☐ to be all things to all people

Self-destructive Behaviour

Active
- ☐ get violent
- ☐ swear
- ☐ slam doors
- ☐ run away
- ☐ overeat
- ☐ harm myself
- ☐ criticise

Passive
- ☐ take it too seriously
- ☐ give up
- ☐ wallow in self pity
- ☐ sulk
- ☐ space out
- ☐ procrastinate
- ☐ give in
- ☐ be controlled

Intense Feelings

Angry feelings
- ☐ hateful
- ☐ aggravated
- ☐ annoyed
- ☐ hostile
- ☐ outraged
- ☐ punitive
- ☐ resentful
- ☐ vengeful

Fearful feelings
- ☐ helpless
- ☐ hopeless
- ☐ disappointed
- ☐ sad

- ☐ attacked
- ☐ worn out
- ☐ rejected
- ☐ jealous
- ☐ afraid
- ☐ exploited
- ☐ lonely
- ☐ abandoned
- ☐ guilty
- ☐ insulted
- ☐ confused
- ☐ disillusioned
- ☐ misunderstood
- ☐ trapped

Bodily Reactions (Limbic System)

I am uncomfortable because I am experiencing...
- ☐ tremors
- ☐ nausea
- ☐ sweaty palms
- ☐ stomach-ache
- ☐ pounding heart
- ☐ general tension
- ☐ fatigue
- ☐ imagination on fire
- ☐ headache
- ☐ dry mouth
- ☐ jaw clenching
- ☐ shortness of breath

Continued over

B   **F**   **L**

Step Three: The Working-Down Process

Begin with, "Suddenly I realised that I was anxious and that I had choices..." This is the step of self-leadership and trust in one's ability to handle the situation.

Choose helpful thoughts:

I choose to depersonalise
There is no intention to hurt me. He is doing the best he can with the tools he has at the moment.

I choose realism over romanticism
Life presents many obstacles. I lower or raise standards as needed.

There is no right or wrong
Unless it is a moral issue, I will see it simply as a difference of opinion and/or taste.

I choose the total view of positivity
Even though this event is negative, the total view of his behaviour is positive.

I surrender control
Since I cannot change this situation, I choose to let go of it

I choose to put this event in perspective
This event is not a catastrophe because it is not life threatening. It can be viewed as a trivial life event, a normal life problem that needs to be solved not dramatised.

I choose to view this event as average, falling within the normal range
This event is not exceptional; many people have gone through this.

It's temporary - "this too shall pass"
Life is constantly changing and moving through phases and this situation will also change.

Fears or facts?
Why fear? It may not happen!

I choose to focus on this as a learning experience
Every problem that comes my way is an opportunity for me to learn about my strengths and weaknesses, others and life.

Feel soothing emotions:

I choose to feel warm, loving emotions. I do this by focusing on my heart and letting love, trust forgiveness, compassion, hope or gratitude fill my heart space.

Behave constructively:

I choose to work in part acts:
I will break the overwhelming job into manageable parts.

Do the difficult:
I will face what I fear and act with self-discipline

I choose to solutionise:
I will find a solution by taking advice or doing research.

Prioritise myself:
I will keep my life balanced by meeting friends, doing exercise or laughing.

Compartmentalise:
I will not let this event cloud my whole day; I will focus on something else now.

Utilise calming strategies:

When I:
- relax,
- breathe deeply,
- go for a run,
- shower,
- lie down,
- read,
- watch TV,
- climb into a mental helicopter
- practice mindfulness, meditation, my mind and body calm down.

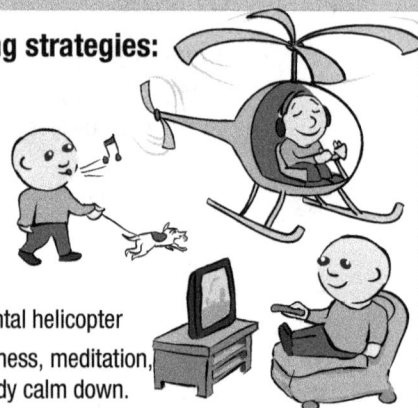

Step Four: The Self Motivation Process

Endorse yourself for any growth no matter how small.

In the past I would have...

_____

_____

But this time I...

_____

_____

Tick off the traits that you strengthened when you worked down your anxiety:

☐ generosity	☐ peacefulness
☐ kindness	☐ self-discipline
☐ compassion	☐ forgiveness
☐ consideration	☐ courage
☐ helpfulness	☐ responsibility
☐ respectfulness	☐ reliability
☐ honesty	☐ loyalty
☐ fairness	☐ love
☐ patience	☐ humility

Rate your anxiety on a scale of 0 to 100%:

_____ %

O

W

Anxiety Management Worksheet

The purpose of this worksheet is to help you to see every stressful event as an opportunity for
1. greater understanding of yourself, your anxiety and the people around you, and
2. practicing tools to manage your anxiety.

Step One: An Event

Briefly describe an event when you became anxious. Give such details as time, place and people involved, and end with "That's when I began to work myself up..."

E

Rate your anxiety on a scale of 0 to 100%: ____ %

Step Two: The Working-Up Process

Learn about your working up process by identifying your thoughts, feelings, behaviours and bodily reactions during the event. Tick the ones that most resonate with you.

Undermining Beliefs

I fear that I have lost...
- approval
- control
- co-operation
- face
- respect
- success
- trust
- validation
- love

This event proves that I am...
- stupid
- abnormal
- incompetent
- lazy
- irresponsible
- a total failure
- undisciplined
- untogether
- useless

B

I worry that I will suffer...
- mental collapse
- illness
- financial hardship

What I want is...
- total control
- respect
- success
- perfection
- comfort
- fairness
- tranquility
- all the answers
- for life to go smoothly
- to be all things to all people

Self-destructive Behaviour

Active
- get violent
- swear
- slam doors
- run away
- overeat
- harm myself
- criticise

Passive
- take it too seriously
- give up
- wallow in self pity
- sulk
- space out
- procrastinate
- give in
- be controlled

Intense Feelings

Angry feelings
- hateful
- aggravated
- annoyed
- hostile
- outraged
- punitive
- resentful
- vengeful
- attacked
- worn out
- rejected
- jealous
- afraid
- exploited
- lonely
- abandoned
- guilty
- insulted

Fearful feelings
- helpless
- hopeless
- disappointed
- sad
- confused
- disillusioned
- misunderstood
- trapped

Bodily Reactions (Limbic System)

I am uncomfortable because I am experiencing...
- tremors
- nausea
- sweaty palms
- stomach-ache
- pounding heart
- general tension
- fatigue
- imagination on fire
- headache
- dry mouth
- jaw clenching
- shortness of breath

Continued over

B   F   L

Step Three: The Working-Down Process

Begin with, "Suddenly I realised that I was anxious and that I had choices..." This is the step of self-leadership and trust in one's ability to handle the situation.

Choose helpful thoughts:

I choose to depersonalise
There is no intention to hurt me. He is doing the best he can with the tools he has at the moment.

I choose realism over romanticism
Life presents many obstacles. I lower or raise standards as needed.

There is no right or wrong
Unless it is a moral issue, I will see it simply as a difference of opinion and/or taste.

I choose the total view of positivity
Even though this event is negative, the total view of his behaviour is positive.

I surrender control
Since I cannot change this situation, I choose to let go of it

I choose to put this event in perspective
This event is not a catastrophe because it is not life threatening. It can be viewed as a trivial life event, a normal life problem that needs to be solved not dramatised.

I choose to view this event as average, falling within the normal range
This event is not exceptional; many people have gone through this.

It's temporary - "this too shall pass"
Life is constantly changing and moving through phases and this situation will also change.

Fears or facts?
Why fear? It may not happen!

I choose to focus on this as a learning experience
Every problem that comes my way is an opportunity for me to learn about my strengths and weaknesses, others and life.

Feel soothing emotions:

I choose to feel warm, loving emotions. I do this by focusing on my heart and letting love, trust forgiveness, compassion, hope or gratitude fill my heart space.

Behave constructively:

I choose to work in part acts:
I will break the overwhelming job into manageable parts.

Do the difficult:
I will face what I fear and act with self-discipline

I choose to solutionise:
I will find a solution by taking advice or doing research.

Prioritise myself:
I will keep my life balanced by meeting friends, doing exercise or laughing.

Compartmentalise:
I will not let this event cloud my whole day; I will focus on something else now.

Utilise calming strategies:

When I:
- relax,
- breathe deeply,
- go for a run,
- shower,
- lie down,
- read,
- watch TV,
- climb into a mental helicopter
- practice mindfulness, meditation, my mind and body calm down.

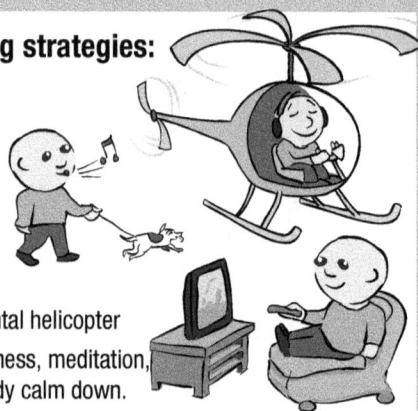

Step Four: The Self Motivation Process

Endorse yourself for any growth no matter how small.

In the past I would have...

_____

But this time I...

_____

Tick off the traits that you strengthened when you worked down your anxiety:

- ☐ generosity
- ☐ kindness
- ☐ compassion
- ☐ consideration
- ☐ helpfulness
- ☐ respectfulness
- ☐ honesty
- ☐ fairness
- ☐ patience
- ☐ peacefulness
- ☐ self-discipline
- ☐ forgiveness
- ☐ courage
- ☐ responsibility
- ☐ reliability
- ☐ loyalty
- ☐ love
- ☐ humility

Rate your anxiety on a scale of 0 to 100%:

_____ %

O

W

Anxiety Management Worksheet

The purpose of this worksheet is to help you to see every stressful event as an opportunity for
1. greater understanding of yourself, your anxiety and the people around you, and
2. practicing tools to manage your anxiety.

Step One: An Event

Briefly describe an event when you became anxious. Give such details as time, place and people involved, and end with "That's when I began to work myself up..."

_____

_____ **E**

_____

_____ Rate your anxiety on a scale of 0 to 100%: [＿＿] **%**

Step Two: The Working-Up Process

Learn about your working up process by identifying your thoughts, feelings, behaviours and bodily reactions during the event. Tick the ones that most resonate with you.

Undermining Beliefs

I fear that I have lost...

- ☐ approval
- ☐ success
- ☐ control
- ☐ trust
- ☐ co-operation
- ☐ validation
- ☐ face
- ☐ love
- ☐ respect

This event proves that I am...

- ☐ stupid
- ☐ a total failure
- ☐ abnormal
- ☐ undisciplined
- ☐ incompetent
- ☐ untogether
- ☐ lazy
- ☐ useless
- ☐ irresponsible

B

I worry that I will suffer...

- ☐ mental collapse
- ☐ illness
- ☐ financial hardship

What I want is...

- ☐ total control
- ☐ tranquility
- ☐ respect
- ☐ all the answers
- ☐ success
- ☐ for life to go smoothly
- ☐ perfection
- ☐ comfort
- ☐ to be all things to all people
- ☐ fairness

Self-destructive Behaviour

Active

- ☐ get violent
- ☐ swear
- ☐ slam doors
- ☐ run away
- ☐ overeat
- ☐ harm myself
- ☐ criticise

Passive

- ☐ take it too seriously
- ☐ give up
- ☐ wallow in self pity
- ☐ sulk
- ☐ space out
- ☐ procrastinate
- ☐ give in
- ☐ be controlled

Intense Feelings

Angry feelings

- ☐ hateful
- ☐ attacked
- ☐ aggravated
- ☐ worn out
- ☐ annoyed
- ☐ rejected
- ☐ hostile
- ☐ jealous
- ☐ outraged
- ☐ afraid
- ☐ punitive
- ☐ exploited
- ☐ resentful
- ☐ lonely
- ☐ vengeful
- ☐ abandoned
- ☐ guilty

Fearful feelings

- ☐ helpless
- ☐ insulted
- ☐ hopeless
- ☐ confused
- ☐ disappointed
- ☐ disillusioned
- ☐ sad
- ☐ misunderstood
- ☐ trapped

Bodily Reactions (Limbic System)

I am uncomfortable because I am experiencing...

- ☐ tremors
- ☐ nausea
- ☐ sweaty palms
- ☐ stomach-ache
- ☐ pounding heart
- ☐ general tension
- ☐ fatigue
- ☐ imagination on fire
- ☐ headache
- ☐ dry mouth
- ☐ jaw clenching
- ☐ shortness of breath

Continued over

B   **F**   **L**

Step Three: The Working-Down Process

Begin with, "Suddenly I realised that I was anxious and that I had choices..." This is the step of self-leadership and trust in one's ability to handle the situation.

Choose helpful thoughts:

I choose to depersonalise
There is no intention to hurt me. He is doing the best he can with the tools he has at the moment.

I choose realism over romanticism
Life presents many obstacles. I lower or raise standards as needed.

There is no right or wrong
Unless it is a moral issue, I will see it simply as a difference of opinion and/or taste.

I choose the total view of positivity
Even though this event is negative, the total view of his behaviour is positive.

I surrender control
Since I cannot change this situation, I choose to let go of it

I choose to put this event in perspective
This event is not a catastrophe because it is not life threatening. It can be viewed as a trivial life event, a normal life problem that needs to be solved not dramatised.

I choose to view this event as average, falling within the normal range
This event is not exceptional; many people have gone through this.

It's temporary - "this too shall pass"
Life is constantly changing and moving through phases and this situation will also change.

Fears or facts?
Why fear? It may not happen!

I choose to focus on this as a learning experience
Every problem that comes my way is an opportunity for me to learn about my strengths and weaknesses, others and life.

Feel soothing emotions:

I choose to feel warm, loving emotions. I do this by focusing on my heart and letting love, trust forgiveness, compassion, hope or gratitude fill my heart space.

Behave constructively:

I choose to work in part acts:
I will break the overwhelming job into manageable parts.

Do the difficult:
I will face what I fear and act with self-discipline

I choose to solutionise:
I will find a solution by taking advice or doing research.

Prioritise myself:
I will keep my life balanced by meeting friends, doing exercise or laughing.

Compartmentalise:
I will not let this event cloud my whole day; I will focus on something else now.

Utilise calming strategies:

When I:
• relax,
• breathe deeply,
• go for a run,
• shower,
• lie down,
• read,
• watch TV,
• climb into a mental helicopter
• practice mindfulness, meditation, my mind and body calm down.

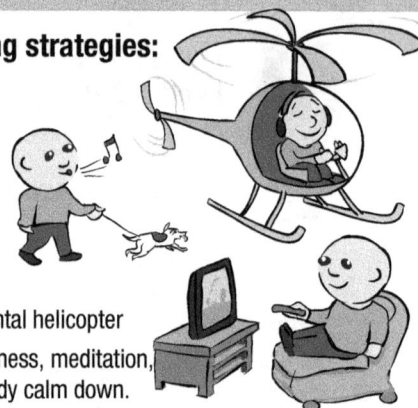

Step Four: The Self Motivation Process

Endorse yourself for any growth no matter how small.

In the past I would have...

_____

_____

But this time I...

_____

_____

Tick off the traits that you strengthened when you worked down your anxiety:

☐ generosity   ☐ peacefulness
☐ kindness   ☐ self-discipline
☐ compassion   ☐ forgiveness
☐ consideration ☐ courage
☐ helpfulness   ☐ responsibility
☐ respectfulness ☐ reliability
☐ honesty   ☐ loyalty
☐ fairness   ☐ love
☐ patience   ☐ humility

Rate your anxiety on a scale of 0 to 100%:

[____]%

O   W

Session 3

Anxiety Management Worksheet

The purpose of this worksheet is to help you to see every stressful event as an opportunity for
1. greater understanding of yourself, your anxiety and the people around you, and
2. practicing tools to manage your anxiety.

Step One: An Event

Briefly describe an event when you became anxious. Give such details as time, place and people involved, and end with "That's when I began to work myself up…"

_____

_____ E

_____

_____ Rate your anxiety on a scale of 0 to 100%: [   ] %

Step Two: The Working-Up Process

Learn about your working up process by identifying your thoughts, feelings, behaviours and bodily reactions during the event. Tick the ones that most resonate with you.

Undermining Beliefs

B

I fear that I have lost...

- ☐ approval   ☐ success
- ☐ control   ☐ trust
- ☐ co-operation   ☐ validation
- ☐ face   ☐ love
- ☐ respect

This event proves that I am...

- ☐ stupid   ☐ a total failure
- ☐ abnormal   ☐ undisciplined
- ☐ incompetent   ☐ untogether
- ☐ lazy   ☐ useless
- ☐ irresponsible

I worry that I will suffer...

- ☐ mental collapse
- ☐ illness
- ☐ financial hardship

What I want is...

- ☐ total control   ☐ tranquility
- ☐ respect   ☐ all the answers
- ☐ success   ☐ for life to go
- ☐ perfection   smoothly
- ☐ comfort   ☐ to be all things
- ☐ fairness   to all people

Self-destructive Behaviour

Active

- ☐ get violent
- ☐ swear
- ☐ slam doors
- ☐ run away
- ☐ overeat
- ☐ harm myself
- ☐ criticise

Passive

- ☐ take it too seriously
- ☐ give up
- ☐ wallow in self pity
- ☐ sulk
- ☐ space out
- ☐ procrastinate
- ☐ give in
- ☐ be controlled

Intense Feelings

Angry feelings

- ☐ hateful   ☐ attacked
- ☐ aggravated   ☐ worn out
- ☐ annoyed   ☐ rejected
- ☐ hostile   ☐ jealous
- ☐ outraged   ☐ afraid
- ☐ punitive   ☐ exploited
- ☐ resentful   ☐ lonely
- ☐ vengeful   ☐ abandoned
       ☐ guilty

Fearful feelings   ☐ insulted

- ☐ helpless   ☐ confused
- ☐ hopeless   ☐ disillusioned
- ☐ disappointed   ☐ misunderstood
- ☐ sad   ☐ trapped

Bodily Reactions (Limbic System)

I am uncomfortable because I am experiencing...

- ☐ tremors
- ☐ nausea
- ☐ sweaty palms
- ☐ stomach-ache
- ☐ pounding heart
- ☐ general tension
- ☐ fatigue
- ☐ imagination on fire
- ☐ headache
- ☐ dry mouth
- ☐ jaw clenching
- ☐ shortness of breath

Continued over

B   F   L

Page 69

Step Three: The Working-Down Process

Begin with, "Suddenly I realised that I was anxious and that I had choices..." This is the step of self-leadership and trust in one's ability to handle the situation.

Choose helpful thoughts:

I choose to depersonalise
There is no intention to hurt me. He is doing the best he can with the tools he has at the moment.

I choose realism over romanticism
Life presents many obstacles. I lower or raise standards as needed.

There is no right or wrong
Unless it is a moral issue, I will see it simply as a difference of opinion and/or taste.

I choose the total view of positivity
Even though this event is negative, the total view of his behaviour is positive.

I surrender control
Since I cannot change this situation, I choose to let go of it

I choose to put this event in perspective
This event is not a catastrophe because it is not life threatening. It can be viewed as a trivial life event, a normal life problem that needs to be solved not dramatised.

I choose to view this event as average, falling within the normal range
This event is not exceptional; many people have gone through this.

It's temporary - "this too shall pass"
Life is constantly changing and moving through phases and this situation will also change.

Fears or facts?
Why fear? It may not happen!

I choose to focus on this as a learning experience
Every problem that comes my way is an opportunity for me to learn about my strengths and weaknesses, others and life.

Feel soothing emotions:

I choose to feel warm, loving emotions. I do this by focusing on my heart and letting love, trust forgiveness, compassion, hope or gratitude fill my heart space.

Behave constructively:

I choose to work in part acts:
I will break the overwhelming job into manageable parts.

Do the difficult:
I will face what I fear and act with self-discipline

I choose to solutionise:
I will find a solution by taking advice or doing research.

Prioritise myself:
I will keep my life balanced by meeting friends, doing exercise or laughing.

Compartmentalise:
I will not let this event cloud my whole day; I will focus on something else now.

Utilise calming strategies:

When I:
• relax,
• breathe deeply,
• go for a run,
• shower,
• lie down,
• read,
• watch TV,
• climb into a mental helicopter
• practice mindfulness, meditation, my mind and body calm down.

Step Four: The Self Motivation Process

Endorse yourself for any growth no matter how small.

In the past I would have...

_____

_____

But this time I...

_____

_____

Tick off the traits that you strengthened when you worked down your anxiety:

☐ generosity   ☐ peacefulness
☐ kindness   ☐ self-discipline
☐ compassion   ☐ forgiveness
☐ consideration   ☐ courage
☐ helpfulness   ☐ responsibility
☐ respectfulness   ☐ reliability
☐ honesty   ☐ loyalty
☐ fairness   ☐ love
☐ patience   ☐ humility

Rate your anxiety on a scale of 0 to 100%:

[____]%

O   W

Anxiety Management Worksheet

The purpose of this worksheet is to help you to see every stressful event as an opportunity for
1. greater understanding of yourself, your anxiety and the people around you, and
2. practicing tools to manage your anxiety.

Step One: An Event

Briefly describe an event when you became anxious. Give such details as time, place and people involved, and end with "That's when I began to work myself up..."

_____

_____ E

_____

_____ Rate your anxiety on a scale of 0 to 100%: [   ] %

Step Two: The Working-Up Process

Learn about your working up process by identifying your thoughts, feelings, behaviours and bodily reactions during the event. Tick the ones that most resonate with you.

Undermining Beliefs

I fear that I have lost...

- ☐ approval
- ☐ control
- ☐ co-operation
- ☐ face
- ☐ respect
- ☐ success
- ☐ trust
- ☐ validation
- ☐ love

This event proves that I am...

- ☐ stupid
- ☐ abnormal
- ☐ incompetent
- ☐ lazy
- ☐ irresponsible
- ☐ a total failure
- ☐ undisciplined
- ☐ untogether
- ☐ useless

B

I worry that I will suffer...

- ☐ mental collapse
- ☐ illness
- ☐ financial hardship

What I want is...

- ☐ total control
- ☐ respect
- ☐ success
- ☐ perfection
- ☐ comfort
- ☐ fairness
- ☐ tranquility
- ☐ all the answers
- ☐ for life to go smoothly
- ☐ to be all things to all people

Self-destructive Behaviour

Active

- ☐ get violent
- ☐ swear
- ☐ slam doors
- ☐ run away
- ☐ overeat
- ☐ harm myself
- ☐ criticise

Passive

- ☐ take it too seriously
- ☐ give up
- ☐ wallow in self pity
- ☐ sulk
- ☐ space out
- ☐ procrastinate
- ☐ give in
- ☐ be controlled

Intense Feelings

Angry feelings

- ☐ hateful
- ☐ aggravated
- ☐ annoyed
- ☐ hostile
- ☐ outraged
- ☐ punitive
- ☐ resentful
- ☐ vengeful

Fearful feelings

- ☐ helpless
- ☐ hopeless
- ☐ disappointed
- ☐ sad
- ☐ attacked
- ☐ worn out
- ☐ rejected
- ☐ jealous
- ☐ afraid
- ☐ exploited
- ☐ lonely
- ☐ abandoned
- ☐ guilty
- ☐ insulted
- ☐ confused
- ☐ disillusioned
- ☐ misunderstood
- ☐ trapped

Bodily Reactions (Limbic System)

I am uncomfortable because I am experiencing...

- ☐ tremors
- ☐ nausea
- ☐ sweaty palms
- ☐ stomach-ache
- ☐ pounding heart
- ☐ general tension
- ☐ fatigue
- ☐ imagination on fire
- ☐ headache
- ☐ dry mouth
- ☐ jaw clenching
- ☐ shortness of breath

Continued over

B   F   L

Step Three: The Working-Down Process

Begin with, "Suddenly I realised that I was anxious and that I had choices..." This is the step of self-leadership and trust in one's ability to handle the situation.

Choose helpful thoughts:

I choose to depersonalise
There is no intention to hurt me. He is doing the best he can with the tools he has at the moment.

I choose realism over romanticism
Life presents many obstacles. I lower or raise standards as needed.

There is no right or wrong
Unless it is a moral issue, I will see it simply as a difference of opinion and/or taste.

I choose the total view of positivity
Even though this event is negative, the total view of his behaviour is positive.

I surrender control
Since I cannot change this situation, I choose to let go of it

I choose to put this event in perspective
This event is not a catastrophe because it is not life threatening. It can be viewed as a trivial life event, a normal life problem that needs to be solved not dramatised.

I choose to view this event as average, falling within the normal range
This event is not exceptional; many people have gone through this.

It's temporary - "this too shall pass"
Life is constantly changing and moving through phases and this situation will also change.

Fears or facts?
Why fear? It may not happen!

I choose to focus on this as a learning experience
Every problem that comes my way is an opportunity for me to learn about my strengths and weaknesses, others and life.

Feel soothing emotions:

I choose to feel warm, loving emotions. I do this by focusing on my heart and letting love, trust forgiveness, compassion, hope or gratitude fill my heart space.

Behave constructively:

I choose to work in part acts:
I will break the overwhelming job into manageable parts.

Do the difficult:
I will face what I fear and act with self-discipline

I choose to solutionise:
I will find a solution by taking advice or doing research.

Prioritise myself:
I will keep my life balanced by meeting friends, doing exercise or laughing.

Compartmentalise:
I will not let this event cloud my whole day; I will focus on something else now.

Utilise calming strategies:

When I:
- relax,
- breathe deeply,
- go for a run,
- shower,
- lie down,
- read,
- watch TV,
- climb into a mental helicopter
- practice mindfulness, meditation, my mind and body calm down.

Step Four: The Self Motivation Process

Endorse yourself for any growth no matter how small.

In the past I would have...

_____

_____

But this time I...

_____

_____

Tick off the traits that you strengthened when you worked down your anxiety:

☐ generosity   ☐ peacefulness
☐ kindness   ☐ self-discipline
☐ compassion   ☐ forgiveness
☐ consideration   ☐ courage
☐ helpfulness   ☐ responsibility
☐ respectfulness   ☐ reliability
☐ honesty   ☐ loyalty
☐ fairness   ☐ love
☐ patience   ☐ humility

Rate your anxiety on a scale of 0 to 100%:

[____]%

O   W

Anxiety Management Worksheet

The purpose of this worksheet is to help you to see every stressful event as an opportunity for
1. greater understanding of yourself, your anxiety and the people around you, and
2. practicing tools to manage your anxiety.

Step One: An Event

Briefly describe an event when you became anxious. Give such details as time, place and people involved, and end with "That's when I began to work myself up..."

_____

_____   E

_____   Rate your anxiety on a scale of 0 to 100%: [   ] %

Step Two: The Working-Up Process

Learn about your working up process by identifying your thoughts, feelings, behaviours and bodily reactions during the event. Tick the ones that most resonate with you.

Undermining Beliefs

I fear that I have lost...

- [ ] approval
- [ ] control
- [ ] co-operation
- [ ] face
- [ ] respect
- [ ] success
- [ ] trust
- [ ] validation
- [ ] love

This event proves that I am...

- [ ] stupid
- [ ] abnormal
- [ ] incompetent
- [ ] lazy
- [ ] irresponsible
- [ ] a total failure
- [ ] undisciplined
- [ ] untogether
- [ ] useless

B

I worry that I will suffer...

- [ ] mental collapse
- [ ] illness
- [ ] financial hardship

What I want is...

- [ ] total control
- [ ] respect
- [ ] success
- [ ] perfection
- [ ] comfort
- [ ] fairness
- [ ] tranquility
- [ ] all the answers
- [ ] for life to go smoothly
- [ ] to be all things to all people

Self-destructive Behaviour

Active

- [ ] get violent
- [ ] swear
- [ ] slam doors
- [ ] run away
- [ ] overeat
- [ ] harm myself
- [ ] criticise

Passive

- [ ] take it too seriously
- [ ] give up
- [ ] wallow in self pity
- [ ] sulk
- [ ] space out
- [ ] procrastinate
- [ ] give in
- [ ] be controlled

Intense Feelings

Angry feelings

- [ ] hateful
- [ ] aggravated
- [ ] annoyed
- [ ] hostile
- [ ] outraged
- [ ] punitive
- [ ] resentful
- [ ] vengeful

Fearful feelings

- [ ] helpless
- [ ] hopeless
- [ ] disappointed
- [ ] sad
- [ ] attacked
- [ ] worn out
- [ ] rejected
- [ ] jealous
- [ ] afraid
- [ ] exploited
- [ ] lonely
- [ ] abandoned
- [ ] guilty
- [ ] insulted
- [ ] confused
- [ ] disillusioned
- [ ] misunderstood
- [ ] trapped

Bodily Reactions (Limbic System)

I am uncomfortable because I am experiencing...

- [ ] tremors
- [ ] nausea
- [ ] sweaty palms
- [ ] stomach-ache
- [ ] pounding heart
- [ ] general tension
- [ ] fatigue
- [ ] imagination on fire
- [ ] headache
- [ ] dry mouth
- [ ] jaw clenching
- [ ] shortness of breath

Continued over

B   F   L

Step Three: The Working-Down Process

Begin with, "Suddenly I realised that I was anxious and that I had choices..." This is the step of self-leadership and trust in one's ability to handle the situation.

Choose helpful thoughts:

I choose to depersonalise
There is no intention to hurt me. He is doing the best he can with the tools he has at the moment.

I choose realism over romanticism
Life presents many obstacles. I lower or raise standards as needed.

There is no right or wrong
Unless it is a moral issue, I will see it simply as a difference of opinion and/or taste.

I choose the total view of positivity
Even though this event is negative, the total view of his behaviour is positive.

I surrender control
Since I cannot change this situation, I choose to let go of it

I choose to put this event in perspective
This event is not a catastrophe because it is not life threatening. It can be viewed as a trivial life event, a normal life problem that needs to be solved not dramatised.

I choose to view this event as average, falling within the normal range
This event is not exceptional; many people have gone through this.

It's temporary - "this too shall pass"
Life is constantly changing and moving through phases and this situation will also change.

Fears or facts?
Why fear? It may not happen!

I choose to focus on this as a learning experience
Every problem that comes my way is an opportunity for me to learn about my strengths and weaknesses, others and life.

Feel soothing emotions:

I choose to feel warm, loving emotions. I do this by focusing on my heart and letting love, trust forgiveness, compassion, hope or gratitude fill my heart space.

Behave constructively:

I choose to work in part acts:
I will break the overwhelming job into manageable parts.

Do the difficult:
I will face what I fear and act with self-discipline

I choose to solutionise:
I will find a solution by taking advice or doing research.

Prioritise myself:
I will keep my life balanced by meeting friends, doing exercise or laughing.

Compartmentalise:
I will not let this event cloud my whole day; I will focus on something else now.

Utilise calming strategies:

When I:
• relax,
• breathe deeply,
• go for a run,
• shower,
• lie down,
• read,
• watch TV,
• climb into a mental helicopter
• practice mindfulness, meditation, my mind and body calm down.

Step Four: The Self Motivation Process

Endorse yourself for any growth no matter how small.

In the past I would have...

_____

_____

But this time I...

_____

_____

Tick off the traits that you strengthened when you worked down your anxiety:

☐ generosity
☐ kindness
☐ compassion
☐ consideration
☐ helpfulness
☐ respectfulness
☐ honesty
☐ fairness
☐ patience

☐ peacefulness
☐ self-discipline
☐ forgiveness
☐ courage
☐ responsibility
☐ reliability
☐ loyalty
☐ love
☐ humility

Rate your anxiety on a scale of 0 to 100%:

_____%

O

W

Anxiety Management Worksheet

The purpose of this worksheet is to help you to see every stressful event as an opportunity for
1. greater understanding of yourself, your anxiety and the people around you, and
2. practicing tools to manage your anxiety.

Step One: An Event

Briefly describe an event when you became anxious. Give such details as time, place and people involved, and end with "That's when I began to work myself up..."

E

Rate your anxiety on a scale of 0 to 100%: ____ %

Step Two: The Working-Up Process

Learn about your working up process by identifying your thoughts, feelings, behaviours and bodily reactions during the event. Tick the ones that most resonate with you.

Undermining Beliefs

I fear that I have lost...
- [ ] approval
- [ ] control
- [ ] co-operation
- [ ] face
- [ ] respect
- [ ] success
- [ ] trust
- [ ] validation
- [ ] love

This event proves that I am...
- [ ] stupid
- [ ] abnormal
- [ ] incompetent
- [ ] lazy
- [ ] irresponsible
- [ ] a total failure
- [ ] undisciplined
- [ ] untogether
- [ ] useless

B

I worry that I will suffer...
- [ ] mental collapse
- [ ] illness
- [ ] financial hardship

What I want is...
- [ ] total control
- [ ] respect
- [ ] success
- [ ] perfection
- [ ] comfort
- [ ] fairness
- [ ] tranquility
- [ ] all the answers
- [ ] for life to go smoothly
- [ ] to be all things to all people

Self-destructive Behaviour

Active
- [ ] get violent
- [ ] swear
- [ ] slam doors
- [ ] run away
- [ ] overeat
- [ ] harm myself
- [ ] criticise

Passive
- [ ] take it too seriously
- [ ] give up
- [ ] wallow in self pity
- [ ] sulk
- [ ] space out
- [ ] procrastinate
- [ ] give in
- [ ] be controlled

Intense Feelings

Angry feelings
- [ ] hateful
- [ ] aggravated
- [ ] annoyed
- [ ] hostile
- [ ] outraged
- [ ] punitive
- [ ] resentful
- [ ] vengeful

Fearful feelings
- [ ] helpless
- [ ] hopeless
- [ ] disappointed
- [ ] sad
- [ ] attacked
- [ ] worn out
- [ ] rejected
- [ ] jealous
- [ ] afraid
- [ ] exploited
- [ ] lonely
- [ ] abandoned
- [ ] guilty
- [ ] insulted
- [ ] confused
- [ ] disillusioned
- [ ] misunderstood
- [ ] trapped

Bodily Reactions (Limbic System)

I am uncomfortable because I am experiencing...
- [ ] tremors
- [ ] nausea
- [ ] sweaty palms
- [ ] stomach-ache
- [ ] pounding heart
- [ ] general tension
- [ ] fatigue
- [ ] imagination on fire
- [ ] headache
- [ ] dry mouth
- [ ] jaw clenching
- [ ] shortness of breath

Continued over

B   F   L

Step Three: The Working-Down Process

Begin with, "Suddenly I realised that I was anxious and that I had choices..." This is the step of self-leadership and trust in one's ability to handle the situation.

Choose helpful thoughts:

I choose to depersonalise
There is no intention to hurt me. He is doing the best he can with the tools he has at the moment.

I choose realism over romanticism
Life presents many obstacles. I lower or raise standards as needed.

There is no right or wrong
Unless it is a moral issue, I will see it simply as a difference of opinion and/or taste.

I choose the total view of positivity
Even though this event is negative, the total view of his behaviour is positive.

I surrender control
Since I cannot change this situation, I choose to let go of it

I choose to put this event in perspective
This event is not a catastrophe because it is not life threatening. It can be viewed as a trivial life event, a normal life problem that needs to be solved not dramatised.

I choose to view this event as average, falling within the normal range
This event is not exceptional; many people have gone through this.

It's temporary - "this too shall pass"
Life is constantly changing and moving through phases and this situation will also change.

Fears or facts?
Why fear? It may not happen!

I choose to focus on this as a learning experience
Every problem that comes my way is an opportunity for me to learn about my strengths and weaknesses, others and life.

Feel soothing emotions:

I choose to feel warm, loving emotions. I do this by focusing on my heart and letting love, trust forgiveness, compassion, hope or gratitude fill my heart space.

Behave constructively:

I choose to work in part acts:
I will break the overwhelming job into manageable parts.

Do the difficult:
I will face what I fear and act with self-discipline

I choose to solutionise:
I will find a solution by taking advice or doing research.

Prioritise myself:
I will keep my life balanced by meeting friends, doing exercise or laughing.

Compartmentalise:
I will not let this event cloud my whole day; I will focus on something else now.

Utilise calming strategies:

When I:
• relax,
• breathe deeply,
• go for a run,
• shower,
• lie down,
• read,
• watch TV,
• climb into a mental helicopter
• practice mindfulness, meditation, my mind and body calm down.

Step Four: The Self Motivation Process

Endorse yourself for any growth no matter how small.

In the past I would have...

_____

_____

But this time I...

_____

_____

Tick off the traits that you strengthened when you worked down your anxiety:

☐ generosity   ☐ peacefulness
☐ kindness   ☐ self-discipline
☐ compassion   ☐ forgiveness
☐ consideration   ☐ courage
☐ helpfulness   ☐ responsibility
☐ respectfulness   ☐ reliability
☐ honesty   ☐ loyalty
☐ fairness   ☐ love
☐ patience   ☐ humility

Rate your anxiety on a scale of 0 to 100%:

☐ %

O   W

NOTES

NOTES

NOTES

Session 4

COGNITIVE TOOL: SURRENDER CONTROL

'I surrender control. Since I cannot change this situation, I choose to let go of it.'

Perseverance frequently leads to success. However, when hammering away does not bring you your desired results, it is best to surrender control and to let go. The wisdom of the serenity prayer is well known.

'God grant me the serenity to accept the things I cannot change, the courage to change the things I can, and the wisdom to know the difference'.

While most people agree with this wisdom, many find it nearly impossible to 'let go' even if they desperately want to.

Choosing to surrender control and to let go of a problem means not worrying constantly about it. It means being able to focus on other things in the here and now. It means realising that it is futile to pour endless energy, time and worry into a problem that you cannot change.

Here are a few practical suggestions of how to let go. Choose the ones that resonate with you.

- Hand your problem over to a higher power. This concept is central in Alcohol Anonymous (AA) and all the twelve step programs. These programs teach the importance of acknowledging that an addict is powerless and can only recover by 'Letting go and Letting God'.

  According to the twelve step programs, God is not necessarily defined by a religion — it is the God of your understanding. Therefore, for some, God is defined by their religion. For, others The Universe, Nature, or the group, is a higher power.

  If you relate to handing your problem over to a higher power, the way you conceptualise your higher power is totally personal and subjective.

- Utilise visualisation to assist you to let go. For instance you can imagine putting your problem in a rocket-ship and sending it, at lightning speed, out of your orbit of consciousness.

- Write down the things that are bothering you. For instance, if you are in a yucky situation like a messy divorce, write it down on some toilet paper and flush it down the toilet. It will give you huge relief.

  Or, if you cannot sleep at night, write down your thoughts and worries on a piece of paper next to your bed. This will reassure you that you can afford to switch off now, and go to sleep, because you will not forget your problems. You have recorded them which will ensure that you will be able to work on them in the morning.

- Mindfulness is a popular way of letting go (see page 81 for further information about mindfulness).

- . Relaxation and meditation can assist you to focus on stilling your mind and letting go of worrying thoughts while you are relaxing.

EXERCISE ELEVEN

Even though you now have strategies, it may be difficult for you to surrender control because you need to feel in control. The following exercise will get you to examine your need for control. There are no right or wrong answers.

Are you a person who likes to be in control?   YES/NO

If yes, do you find that you need to be in control?:   YES/NO

   a) in every aspect of your life   YES/NO

   or

   b) only in certain aspects of your life?   YES/NO

If you answered that you need to be in control in all circumstances, please elaborate further.

_____

_____

If you answered that you only need to be in control in certain circumstances, please fill in below those areas that apply to you:

- Home

- Work

- Food

- Relationships

- Other Please elaborate on your choices:

_____

_____

Does your need for control prevent you from relaxing?   YES/NO

Do you believe that your need for control helped you to reach your goals or hampered you? Please explain your answer:

_____

_____

Has your need for control ever damaged a relationship?   YES/NO

If yes, when and how?

_____

_____

Do you wish to change the manner in which you take control and if so, in which areas and how?

_____

_____

Are there any other ways of relinquishing control when appropriate that have helped you in the past?

_____

_____

_____

_____

Remember: Relinquishing control does not indicate weakness because you are not being intimidated to let go, you are CHOOSING to surrender control.

Mindfulness

A popular way of letting go is to focus your awareness and attention on the present moment (rather than the past or future), fully and completely. This is called **mindfulness.**

Being mindful is not the same as actively practicing relaxation skills because mindfulness does not require stilling your mind and calming your muscles. Mindfulness is all about being present in the moment. Having said that, a natural consequence of mindfulness is calmness, because mindfulness ensures that you are not worrying about the future or agonising about the past.

The core features of mindfulness are:

Observe: Observe your experience without being analytical. Try to directly experience your experience rather than thinking about it. Observe your thoughts, feelings and bodily sensations with a kind and gentle curiosity.

Describe: Notice the fine details of what you are observing in a very descriptive, observational manner rather than placing subjective valuations upon it.

Participate fully: Allow yourself to consider your whole experience, paying full care and attention.

Be non-judgmental: This helps to reduce emotional distress usually related to attempting to avoid or control your experience. Practice accepting the whole experience without judging it as good, bad, right or wrong.

Focus on one thing at a time: The art of 'being present' is to develop skill at paying attention to only one thing at a time, from moment to moment. By focusing your awareness to mindfully experiencing each moment you can reduce your need to follow distracting thoughts or feelings that pop up, and more easily bring your focus to the now.

Different ways of practicing mindfulness:

There are a number of ways to practice mindfulness which will assist you to focus on the present moment:

- Formal mindfulness practice
- Informal mindfulness practice
- Grounding
- Slowing down and being present

It does not matter how you go about it. The essential thing is that you keep practicing mindfulness every day. The more you incorporate these various types of mindfulness into your day to day life, the calmer you will feel.

CALMING TOOL: FORMAL MINDFULNESS

One type of mindfulness is called formal mindfulness and is similar to meditating. Just like when you meditate, it is important to sit in a quiet space and to focus on something that is ongoing, such as your breath

Find a quiet spot and commit fifteen or twenty minutes to this practice. Observe your breath entering your lungs and then emptying out. Sooner or later you will lose focus. You will start to think of other things or feel different sensations in your body. Make no judgements. Just gently bring your attention back to your breath. The more you practice this process, the better you will be at sustaining attention and being non-judgmental.

EXERCISE TWELVE

Are you able to commit to regular sessions of formal mindfulness? YES/NO

If no, why not?

_____

_____

_____

_____

If yes, commit to it now. (Fill out your name and the regular sessions you are committing to.)

_____

commit to practicing formal mindfulness _____ times a day/week/month,

starting from _____

CALMING TOOL: GROUNDING

Grounding is a form of mindfulness that utilises your five senses to help you notice what is happening right here, right now.

In any given situation, ask yourself:

What am I seeing?

What am I hearing?

What am I touching?

What am I smelling?

What am I tasting?

Grounding helps you to stop, think and take in the moment.

Illustration

Let's say you are washing dishes. Take a moment to ask yourself:

What am I seeing — soapy suds.

What am I hearing — the water splash.

What am I touching — warm soapy water.

What am I smelling — the lemon of the soap.

What am I tasting — the steak from dinner.

All through the day, there are opportunities for grounding. When you cook, dress, shower, or sit on the train…the list is endless.

EXERCISE THIRTEEN

Stop right now and ground yourself by asking and answering:

What am I seeing?

_____

What am I hearing?

_____

What am I touching?

_____

What am I smelling?

_____

What am I tasting?

_____

CALMING TOOL: INFORMAL MINDFULNESS

Informal mindfulness practice can be done anywhere and at any time. The aim is to make you aware of how you think and act as well as what is happening in the present moment. You do not need to take time out of your regular daily activities to be mindful in this way. Nor do you need a special room or space to do it. All you need to do is simply become more aware of what you are doing in the moment.

Everyday activities provide excellent opportunities to practice informal mindfulness including sitting on the train, walking or closing a door:

- When you close a door, for example, be mindful of closing it with intention. This may mean making sure it does not slam or create any noise or, on the contrary, you deliberately slam it.

- When you cook, be mindful of how you spice the food. Think about the taste you are trying to create.

- When you are sitting at your desk be mindful of your posture. If your posture is poor, mindfully correct it.

EXERCISE FOURTEEN

As you are reading this page now, become aware of how you are reading. Are you reading slowly and with concentration or are you skimming through? Do you understand the content or do you feel confused? How are you sitting? Where are your hands? Write down your observations.

_____

_____

_____

_____

CALMING TOOL: SLOWING DOWN

Simply slowing down in your day, and becoming more aware of what is happening around you, is a form of mindfulness.

Do you know the expression: 'Stop and smell the roses'? Well that is exactly what slowing down is. The next time you have a break, instead of checking your emails, spend ten minutes looking around you and appreciating what surrounds you. Consider taking a walk around your neighbourhood at half speed. Take this opportunity to look around and notice as many details as possible. Take note especially of any detail you may have missed previously when you walked at a faster pace.

EXERCISE FIFTEEN

Think about times in your day where you could slow down. Write them down:

_____

_____

_____

_____

From today make a conscious effort to slow down where possible.

DAILY MONITORING DIARY

WEEK ENDING _____

Day	M	T	W	T	F	S	S
Overall Anxiety Rating for the day (0-10)							

1. EXERCISE

	M	T	W	T	F	S	S
How long?							
Anxiety level before (0-10)							
Anxiety level after (0-10)							

2. BREATHING & RELAXATION

	M	T	W	T	F	S	S
How long?							
Anxiety level before (0-10)							
Anxiety level after (0-10)							

3. CATASTROPHIC THINKING

	M	T	W	T	F	S	S
How often this type of thought occurred							
Belief in thoughts before challenging (0-10)							
Belief in thoughts after challenging (0-10)							

4. FEARS NOT FACTS

	M	T	W	T	F	S	S
How often this type of thought occurred							
Belief in thoughts before challenging (0-10)							
Belief in thoughts after challenging (0-10)							

5. PERVASIVE PESSIMISTIC THINKING

	M	T	W	T	F	S	S
How often this type of thought occurred							
Belief in thoughts before challenging (0-10)							
Belief in thoughts after challenging (0-10)							

6. PERMANENT PESSIMISTIC THINKING

	M	T	W	T	F	S	S
How often this type of thought occurred							
Belief in thoughts before challenging (0-10)							
Belief in thoughts after challenging (0-10)							

7. MINDFULNESS (FORMAL, GROUNDING, INFORMAL MINDFULNESS)

	M	T	W	T	F	S	S
How long?							
Anxiety level before (0-10)							
Anxiety level after (0-10)							

Session 4

Anxiety Management Worksheet

The purpose of this worksheet is to help you to see every stressful event as an opportunity for
1. greater understanding of yourself, your anxiety and the people around you, and
2. practicing tools to manage your anxiety.

Step One: An Event

Briefly describe an event when you became anxious. Give such details as time, place and people involved, and end with "That's when I began to work myself up..."

E

Rate your anxiety on a scale of 0 to 100%: ___ %

Step Two: The Working-Up Process

Learn about your working up process by identifying your thoughts, feelings, behaviours and bodily reactions during the event. Tick the ones that most resonate with you.

Undermining Beliefs

I fear that I have lost...
- [ ] approval
- [ ] control
- [ ] co-operation
- [ ] face
- [ ] respect
- [ ] success
- [ ] trust
- [ ] validation
- [ ] love

This event proves that I am...
- [ ] stupid
- [ ] abnormal
- [ ] incompetent
- [ ] lazy
- [ ] irresponsible
- [ ] a total failure
- [ ] undisciplined
- [ ] untogether
- [ ] useless

B

I worry that I will suffer...
- [ ] mental collapse
- [ ] illness
- [ ] financial hardship

What I want is...
- [ ] total control
- [ ] respect
- [ ] success
- [ ] perfection
- [ ] comfort
- [ ] fairness
- [ ] tranquility
- [ ] all the answers
- [ ] for life to go smoothly
- [ ] to be all things to all people

Self-destructive Behaviour

Active
- [ ] get violent
- [ ] swear
- [ ] slam doors
- [ ] run away
- [ ] overeat
- [ ] harm myself
- [ ] criticise

Passive
- [ ] take it too seriously
- [ ] give up
- [ ] wallow in self pity
- [ ] sulk
- [ ] space out
- [ ] procrastinate
- [ ] give in
- [ ] be controlled

Intense Feelings

Angry feelings
- [ ] hateful
- [ ] aggravated
- [ ] annoyed
- [ ] hostile
- [ ] outraged
- [ ] punitive
- [ ] resentful
- [ ] vengeful

Fearful feelings
- [ ] helpless
- [ ] hopeless
- [ ] disappointed
- [ ] sad
- [ ] attacked
- [ ] worn out
- [ ] rejected
- [ ] jealous
- [ ] afraid
- [ ] exploited
- [ ] lonely
- [ ] abandoned
- [ ] guilty
- [ ] insulted
- [ ] confused
- [ ] disillusioned
- [ ] misunderstood
- [ ] trapped

Bodily Reactions (Limbic System)

I am uncomfortable because I am experiencing...
- [ ] tremors
- [ ] nausea
- [ ] sweaty palms
- [ ] stomach-ache
- [ ] pounding heart
- [ ] general tension
- [ ] fatigue
- [ ] imagination on fire
- [ ] headache
- [ ] dry mouth
- [ ] jaw clenching
- [ ] shortness of breath

Continued over

B　　　　F　　　　L

Step Three: The Working-Down Process

Begin with, "Suddenly I realised that I was anxious and that I had choices..." This is the step of self-leadership and trust in one's ability to handle the situation.

Choose helpful thoughts:

I choose to depersonalise
There is no intention to hurt me. He is doing the best he can with the tools he has at the moment.

I choose realism over romanticism
Life presents many obstacles. I lower or raise standards as needed.

There is no right or wrong
Unless it is a moral issue, I will see it simply as a difference of opinion and/or taste.

I choose the total view of positivity
Even though this event is negative, the total view of his behaviour is positive.

I surrender control
Since I cannot change this situation, I choose to let go of it

I choose to put this event in perspective
This event is not a catastrophe because it is not life threatening. It can be viewed as a trivial life event, a normal life problem that needs to be solved not dramatised.

I choose to view this event as average, falling within the normal range
This event is not exceptional; many people have gone through this.

It's temporary - "this too shall pass"
Life is constantly changing and moving through phases and this situation will also change.

Fears or facts?
Why fear? It may not happen!

I choose to focus on this as a learning experience
Every problem that comes my way is an opportunity for me to learn about my strengths and weaknesses, others and life.

Feel soothing emotions:

I choose to feel warm, loving emotions. I do this by focusing on my heart and letting love, trust forgiveness, compassion, hope or gratitude fill my heart space.

Behave constructively:

I choose to work in part acts:
I will break the overwhelming job into manageable parts.

Do the difficult:
I will face what I fear and act with self-discipline

I choose to solutionise:
I will find a solution by taking advice or doing research.

Prioritise myself:
I will keep my life balanced by meeting friends, doing exercise or laughing.

Compartmentalise:
I will not let this event cloud my whole day; I will focus on something else now.

Utilise calming strategies:

When I:
- relax,
- breathe deeply,
- go for a run,
- shower,
- lie down,
- read,
- watch TV,
- climb into a mental helicopter
- practice mindfulness, meditation, my mind and body calm down.

Step Four: The Self Motivation Process

Endorse yourself for any growth no matter how small.

In the past I would have...

_____

_____

But this time I...

_____

_____

Tick off the traits that you strengthened when you worked down your anxiety:

☐	generosity	☐	peacefulness
☐	kindness	☐	self-discipline
☐	compassion	☐	forgiveness
☐	consideration	☐	courage
☐	helpfulness	☐	responsibility
☐	respectfulness	☐	reliability
☐	honesty	☐	loyalty
☐	fairness	☐	love
☐	patience	☐	humility

Rate your anxiety on a scale of 0 to 100%:

[____]%

O

W

Session 4

Anxiety Management Worksheet

The purpose of this worksheet is to help you to see every stressful event as an opportunity for
1. greater understanding of yourself, your anxiety and the people around you, and
2. practicing tools to manage your anxiety.

Step One: An Event

Briefly describe an event when you became anxious. Give such details as time, place and people involved, and end with "That's when I began to work myself up…"

_____

_____ E

_____

_____ Rate your anxiety on a scale of 0 to 100%: [   ] %

Step Two: The Working-Up Process

Learn about your working up process by identifying your thoughts, feelings, behaviours and bodily reactions during the event. Tick the ones that most resonate with you.

Undermining Beliefs

I fear that I have lost...
- ☐ approval   ☐ success
- ☐ control   ☐ trust
- ☐ co-operation ☐ validation
- ☐ face   ☐ love
- ☐ respect

This event proves that I am...
- ☐ stupid   ☐ a total failure
- ☐ abnormal   ☐ undisciplined
- ☐ incompetent   ☐ untogether
- ☐ lazy   ☐ useless
- ☐ irresponsible

B

I worry that I will suffer...
- ☐ mental collapse
- ☐ illness
- ☐ financial hardship

What I want is...
- ☐ total control   ☐ tranquility
- ☐ respect   ☐ all the answers
- ☐ success   ☐ for life to go smoothly
- ☐ perfection   ☐ to be all things to all people
- ☐ comfort
- ☐ fairness

Self-destructive Behaviour

Active
- ☐ get violent
- ☐ swear
- ☐ slam doors
- ☐ run away
- ☐ overeat
- ☐ harm myself
- ☐ criticise

Passive
- ☐ take it too seriously
- ☐ give up
- ☐ wallow in self pity
- ☐ sulk
- ☐ space out
- ☐ procrastinate
- ☐ give in
- ☐ be controlled

Intense Feelings

Angry feelings
- ☐ hateful   ☐ attacked
- ☐ aggravated   ☐ worn out
- ☐ annoyed   ☐ rejected
- ☐ hostile   ☐ jealous
- ☐ outraged   ☐ afraid
- ☐ punitive   ☐ exploited
- ☐ resentful   ☐ lonely
- ☐ vengeful   ☐ abandoned
                  ☐ guilty
Fearful feelings ☐ insulted
- ☐ helpless   ☐ confused
- ☐ hopeless   ☐ disillusioned
- ☐ disappointed ☐ misunderstood
- ☐ sad   ☐ trapped

Bodily Reactions (Limbic System)

I am uncomfortable because I am experiencing...
- ☐ tremors
- ☐ nausea
- ☐ sweaty palms
- ☐ stomach-ache
- ☐ pounding heart
- ☐ general tension
- ☐ fatigue
- ☐ imagination on fire
- ☐ headache
- ☐ dry mouth
- ☐ jaw clenching
- ☐ shortness of breath

Continued over

B   F   L

Step Three: The Working-Down Process

Begin with, "Suddenly I realised that I was anxious and that I had choices..." This is the step of self-leadership and trust in one's ability to handle the situation.

Choose helpful thoughts:

I choose to depersonalise
There is no intention to hurt me. He is doing the best he can with the tools he has at the moment.

I choose realism over romanticism
Life presents many obstacles. I lower or raise standards as needed.

There is no right or wrong
Unless it is a moral issue, I will see it simply as a difference of opinion and/or taste.

I choose the total view of positivity
Even though this event is negative, the total view of his behaviour is positive.

I surrender control
Since I cannot change this situation, I choose to let go of it

I choose to put this event in perspective
This event is not a catastrophe because it is not life threatening. It can be viewed as a trivial life event, a normal life problem that needs to be solved not dramatised.

I choose to view this event as average, falling within the normal range
This event is not exceptional; many people have gone through this.

It's temporary - "this too shall pass"
Life is constantly changing and moving through phases and this situation will also change.

Fears or facts?
Why fear? It may not happen!

I choose to focus on this as a learning experience
Every problem that comes my way is an opportunity for me to learn about my strengths and weaknesses, others and life.

Feel soothing emotions:

I choose to feel warm, loving emotions. I do this by focusing on my heart and letting love, trust forgiveness, compassion, hope or gratitude fill my heart space.

Behave constructively:

I choose to work in part acts:
I will break the overwhelming job into manageable parts.

Do the difficult:
I will face what I fear and act with self-discipline

I choose to solutionise:
I will find a solution by taking advice or doing research.

Prioritise myself:
I will keep my life balanced by meeting friends, doing exercise or laughing.

Compartmentalise:
I will not let this event cloud my whole day; I will focus on something else now.

Utilise calming strategies:

When I:
• relax,
• breathe deeply,
• go for a run,
• shower,
• lie down,
• read,
• watch TV,
• climb into a mental helicopter
• practice mindfulness, meditation, my mind and body calm down.

Step Four: The Self Motivation Process

Endorse yourself for any growth no matter how small.

In the past I would have...

_____

_____

But this time I...

_____

_____

Tick off the traits that you strengthened when you worked down your anxiety:

☐ generosity	☐ peacefulness	Rate your anxiety on a scale of 0 to 100%:
☐ kindness	☐ self-discipline	
☐ compassion	☐ forgiveness	
☐ consideration	☐ courage	
☐ helpfulness	☐ responsibility	
☐ respectfulness	☐ reliability	
☐ honesty	☐ loyalty	
☐ fairness	☐ love	
☐ patience	☐ humility	____%

O

W

Anxiety Management Worksheet

The purpose of this worksheet is to help you to see every stressful event as an opportunity for
1. greater understanding of yourself, your anxiety and the people around you, and
2. practicing tools to manage your anxiety.

Step One: An Event

Briefly describe an event when you became anxious. Give such details as time, place and people involved, and end with "That's when I began to work myself up..."

_____

_____ E

_____

_____ Rate your anxiety on a scale of 0 to 100%: [   ] %

Step Two: The Working-Up Process

Learn about your working up process by identifying your thoughts, feelings, behaviours and bodily reactions during the event. Tick the ones that most resonate with you.

Undermining Beliefs

I fear that I have lost...
- ☐ approval
- ☐ success
- ☐ control
- ☐ trust
- ☐ co-operation
- ☐ validation
- ☐ face
- ☐ love
- ☐ respect

This event proves that I am...
- ☐ stupid
- ☐ a total failure
- ☐ abnormal
- ☐ undisciplined
- ☐ incompetent
- ☐ untogether
- ☐ lazy
- ☐ useless
- ☐ irresponsible

B

I worry that I will suffer...
- ☐ mental collapse
- ☐ illness
- ☐ financial hardship

What I want is...
- ☐ total control
- ☐ tranquility
- ☐ respect
- ☐ all the answers
- ☐ success
- ☐ for life to go smoothly
- ☐ perfection
- ☐ comfort
- ☐ to be all things to all people
- ☐ fairness

Self-destructive Behaviour

Active
- ☐ get violent
- ☐ swear
- ☐ slam doors
- ☐ run away
- ☐ overeat
- ☐ harm myself
- ☐ criticise

THWACK!

Passive
- ☐ take it too seriously
- ☐ give up
- ☐ wallow in self pity
- ☐ sulk
- ☐ space out
- ☐ procrastinate
- ☐ give in
- ☐ be controlled

Intense Feelings

Angry feelings
- ☐ hateful
- ☐ attacked
- ☐ aggravated
- ☐ worn out
- ☐ annoyed
- ☐ rejected
- ☐ hostile
- ☐ jealous
- ☐ outraged
- ☐ afraid
- ☐ punitive
- ☐ exploited
- ☐ resentful
- ☐ lonely
- ☐ vengeful
- ☐ abandoned
- ☐ guilty

Fearful feelings
- ☐ insulted
- ☐ helpless
- ☐ confused
- ☐ hopeless
- ☐ disillusioned
- ☐ disappointed
- ☐ misunderstood
- ☐ sad
- ☐ trapped

Bodily Reactions (Limbic System)

I am uncomfortable because I am experiencing...
- ☐ tremors
- ☐ nausea
- ☐ sweaty palms
- ☐ stomach-ache
- ☐ pounding heart
- ☐ general tension
- ☐ fatigue
- ☐ imagination on fire
- ☐ headache
- ☐ dry mouth
- ☐ jaw clenching
- ☐ shortness of breath

Continued over

B   F   L

Step Three: The Working-Down Process

Begin with, "Suddenly I realised that I was anxious and that I had choices..." This is the step of self-leadership and trust in one's ability to handle the situation.

Choose helpful thoughts:

I choose to depersonalise
There is no intention to hurt me. He is doing the best he can with the tools he has at the moment.

I choose realism over romanticism
Life presents many obstacles. I lower or raise standards as needed.

There is no right or wrong
Unless it is a moral issue, I will see it simply as a difference of opinion and/or taste.

I choose the total view of positivity
Even though this event is negative, the total view of his behaviour is positive.

I surrender control
Since I cannot change this situation, I choose to let go of it

I choose to put this event in perspective
This event is not a catastrophe because it is not life threatening. It can be viewed as a trivial life event, a normal life problem that needs to be solved not dramatised.

I choose to view this event as average, falling within the normal range
This event is not exceptional; many people have gone through this.

It's temporary - "this too shall pass"
Life is constantly changing and moving through phases and this situation will also change.

Fears or facts?
Why fear? It may not happen!

I choose to focus on this as a learning experience
Every problem that comes my way is an opportunity for me to learn about my strengths and weaknesses, others and life.

Feel soothing emotions:

I choose to feel warm, loving emotions. I do this by focusing on my heart and letting love, trust forgiveness, compassion, hope or gratitude fill my heart space.

Behave constructively:

I choose to work in part acts:
I will break the overwhelming job into manageable parts.

Do the difficult:
I will face what I fear and act with self-discipline

I choose to solutionise:
I will find a solution by taking advice or doing research.

Prioritise myself:
I will keep my life balanced by meeting friends, doing exercise or laughing.

Compartmentalise:
I will not let this event cloud my whole day; I will focus on something else now.

Utilise calming strategies:

When I:
- relax,
- breathe deeply,
- go for a run,
- shower,
- lie down,
- read,
- watch TV,
- climb into a mental helicopter
- practice mindfulness, meditation, my mind and body calm down.

Step Four: The Self Motivation Process

Endorse yourself for any growth no matter how small.

In the past I would have...

_____

_____

But this time I...

_____

_____

Tick off the traits that you strengthened when you worked down your anxiety:

- ☐ generosity
- ☐ kindness
- ☐ compassion
- ☐ consideration
- ☐ helpfulness
- ☐ respectfulness
- ☐ honesty
- ☐ fairness
- ☐ patience
- ☐ peacefulness
- ☐ self-discipline
- ☐ forgiveness
- ☐ courage
- ☐ responsibility
- ☐ reliability
- ☐ loyalty
- ☐ love
- ☐ humility

Rate your anxiety on a scale of 0 to 100%:

[ ]%

O

W

Anxiety Management Worksheet

The purpose of this worksheet is to help you to see every stressful event as an opportunity for
1. greater understanding of yourself, your anxiety and the people around you, and
2. practicing tools to manage your anxiety.

Step One: An Event

Briefly describe an event when you became anxious. Give such details as time, place and people involved, and end with "That's when I began to work myself up..."

_____

_____ E

_____

_____ Rate your anxiety on a scale of 0 to 100%: [   ] %

Step Two: The Working-Up Process

Learn about your working up process by identifying your thoughts, feelings, behaviours and bodily reactions during the event. Tick the ones that most resonate with you.

Undermining Beliefs

B

I fear that I have lost...
- ☐ approval
- ☐ control
- ☐ co-operation
- ☐ face
- ☐ respect
- ☐ success
- ☐ trust
- ☐ validation
- ☐ love

This event proves that I am...
- ☐ stupid
- ☐ abnormal
- ☐ incompetent
- ☐ lazy
- ☐ irresponsible
- ☐ a total failure
- ☐ undisciplined
- ☐ untogether
- ☐ useless

I worry that I will suffer...
- ☐ mental collapse
- ☐ illness
- ☐ financial hardship

What I want is...
- ☐ total control
- ☐ respect
- ☐ success
- ☐ perfection
- ☐ comfort
- ☐ fairness
- ☐ tranquility
- ☐ all the answers
- ☐ for life to go smoothly
- ☐ to be all things to all people

Self-destructive Behaviour

Active
- ☐ get violent
- ☐ swear
- ☐ slam doors
- ☐ run away
- ☐ overeat
- ☐ harm myself
- ☐ criticise

Passive
- ☐ take it too seriously
- ☐ give up
- ☐ wallow in self pity
- ☐ sulk
- ☐ space out
- ☐ procrastinate
- ☐ give in
- ☐ be controlled

Intense Feelings

Angry feelings
- ☐ hateful
- ☐ aggravated
- ☐ annoyed
- ☐ hostile
- ☐ outraged
- ☐ punitive
- ☐ resentful
- ☐ vengeful

Fearful feelings
- ☐ helpless
- ☐ hopeless
- ☐ disappointed
- ☐ sad
- ☐ attacked
- ☐ worn out
- ☐ rejected
- ☐ jealous
- ☐ afraid
- ☐ exploited
- ☐ lonely
- ☐ abandoned
- ☐ guilty
- ☐ insulted
- ☐ confused
- ☐ disillusioned
- ☐ misunderstood
- ☐ trapped

Bodily Reactions (Limbic System)

I am uncomfortable because I am experiencing...
- ☐ tremors
- ☐ nausea
- ☐ sweaty palms
- ☐ stomach-ache
- ☐ pounding heart
- ☐ general tension
- ☐ fatigue
- ☐ imagination on fire
- ☐ headache
- ☐ dry mouth
- ☐ jaw clenching
- ☐ shortness of breath

B   F   L

Continued over

Step Three: The Working-Down Process

Begin with, "Suddenly I realised that I was anxious and that I had choices..." This is the step of self-leadership and trust in one's ability to handle the situation.

Choose helpful thoughts:

I choose to depersonalise
There is no intention to hurt me. He is doing the best he can with the tools he has at the moment.

I choose realism over romanticism
Life presents many obstacles. I lower or raise standards as needed.

There is no right or wrong
Unless it is a moral issue, I will see it simply as a difference of opinion and/or taste.

I choose the total view of positivity
Even though this event is negative, the total view of his behaviour is positive.

I surrender control
Since I cannot change this situation, I choose to let go of it

I choose to put this event in perspective
This event is not a catastrophe because it is not life threatening. It can be viewed as a trivial life event, a normal life problem that needs to be solved not dramatised.

I choose to view this event as average, falling within the normal range
This event is not exceptional; many people have gone through this.

It's temporary - "this too shall pass"
Life is constantly changing and moving through phases and this situation will also change.

Fears or facts?
Why fear? It may not happen!

I choose to focus on this as a learning experience
Every problem that comes my way is an opportunity for me to learn about my strengths and weaknesses, others and life.

Feel soothing emotions:

I choose to feel warm, loving emotions. I do this by focusing on my heart and letting love, trust forgiveness, compassion, hope or gratitude fill my heart space.

Behave constructively:

I choose to work in part acts:
I will break the overwhelming job into manageable parts.

Do the difficult:
I will face what I fear and act with self-discipline

I choose to solutionise:
I will find a solution by taking advice or doing research.

Prioritise myself:
I will keep my life balanced by meeting friends, doing exercise or laughing.

Compartmentalise:
I will not let this event cloud my whole day; I will focus on something else now.

Utilise calming strategies:

When I:
• relax,
• breathe deeply,
• go for a run,
• shower,
• lie down,
• read,
• watch TV,
• climb into a mental helicopter
• practice mindfulness, meditation, my mind and body calm down.

Step Four: The Self Motivation Process

Endorse yourself for any growth no matter how small.

In the past I would have...

_____

_____

But this time I...

_____

_____

Tick off the traits that you strengthened when you worked down your anxiety:

☐ generosity
☐ kindness
☐ compassion
☐ consideration
☐ helpfulness
☐ respectfulness
☐ honesty
☐ fairness
☐ patience

☐ peacefulness
☐ self-discipline
☐ forgiveness
☐ courage
☐ responsibility
☐ reliability
☐ loyalty
☐ love
☐ humility

Rate your anxiety on a scale of 0 to 100%:

☐ %

O   W

Session 4

Anxiety Management Worksheet

The purpose of this worksheet is to help you to see every stressful event as an opportunity for
1. greater understanding of yourself, your anxiety and the people around you, and
2. practicing tools to manage your anxiety.

Step One: An Event

Briefly describe an event when you became anxious. Give such details as time, place and people involved, and end with "That's when I began to work myself up..."

_____

_____ E

_____

_____ Rate your anxiety on a scale of 0 to 100%: [   ] %

Step Two: The Working-Up Process

Learn about your working up process by identifying your thoughts, feelings, behaviours and bodily reactions during the event. Tick the ones that most resonate with you.

Undermining Beliefs

I fear that I have lost...
- ☐ approval
- ☐ success
- ☐ control
- ☐ trust
- ☐ co-operation
- ☐ validation
- ☐ face
- ☐ love
- ☐ respect

This event proves that I am...
- ☐ stupid
- ☐ a total failure
- ☐ abnormal
- ☐ undisciplined
- ☐ incompetent
- ☐ untogether
- ☐ lazy
- ☐ useless
- ☐ irresponsible

B

I worry that I will suffer...
- ☐ mental collapse
- ☐ illness
- ☐ financial hardship

What I want is...
- ☐ total control
- ☐ tranquility
- ☐ respect
- ☐ all the answers
- ☐ success
- ☐ for life to go smoothly
- ☐ perfection
- ☐ comfort
- ☐ to be all things to all people
- ☐ fairness

Self-destructive Behaviour

Active
- ☐ get violent
- ☐ swear
- ☐ slam doors
- ☐ run away
- ☐ overeat
- ☐ harm myself
- ☐ criticise

Passive
- ☐ take it too seriously
- ☐ give up
- ☐ wallow in self pity
- ☐ sulk
- ☐ space out
- ☐ procrastinate
- ☐ give in
- ☐ be controlled

Intense Feelings

Angry feelings
- ☐ hateful
- ☐ aggravated
- ☐ annoyed
- ☐ hostile
- ☐ outraged
- ☐ punitive
- ☐ resentful
- ☐ vengeful

Fearful feelings
- ☐ helpless
- ☐ hopeless
- ☐ disappointed
- ☐ sad

- ☐ attacked
- ☐ worn out
- ☐ rejected
- ☐ jealous
- ☐ afraid
- ☐ exploited
- ☐ lonely
- ☐ abandoned
- ☐ guilty
- ☐ insulted
- ☐ confused
- ☐ disillusioned
- ☐ misunderstood
- ☐ trapped

Bodily Reactions (Limbic System)

I am uncomfortable because I am experiencing...
- ☐ tremors
- ☐ nausea
- ☐ sweaty palms
- ☐ stomach-ache
- ☐ pounding heart
- ☐ general tension
- ☐ fatigue
- ☐ imagination on fire
- ☐ headache
- ☐ dry mouth
- ☐ jaw clenching
- ☐ shortness of breath

Continued over

B   F   L

Step Three: The Working-Down Process

Begin with, "Suddenly I realised that I was anxious and that I had choices…" This is the step of self-leadership and trust in one's ability to handle the situation.

Choose helpful thoughts:

I choose to depersonalise
There is no intention to hurt me. He is doing the best he can with the tools he has at the moment.

I choose realism over romanticism
Life presents many obstacles. I lower or raise standards as needed.

There is no right or wrong
Unless it is a moral issue, I will see it simply as a difference of opinion and/or taste.

I choose the total view of positivity
Even though this event is negative, the total view of his behaviour is positive.

I surrender control
Since I cannot change this situation, I choose to let go of it

I choose to put this event in perspective
This event is not a catastrophe because it is not life threatening. It can be viewed as a trivial life event, a normal life problem that needs to be solved not dramatised.

I choose to view this event as average, falling within the normal range
This event is not exceptional; many people have gone through this.

It's temporary - "this too shall pass"
Life is constantly changing and moving through phases and this situation will also change.

Fears or facts?
Why fear? It may not happen!

I choose to focus on this as a learning experience
Every problem that comes my way is an opportunity for me to learn about my strengths and weaknesses, others and life.

Feel soothing emotions:

I choose to feel warm, loving emotions. I do this by focusing on my heart and letting love, trust forgiveness, compassion, hope or gratitude fill my heart space.

Behave constructively:

I choose to work in part acts:
I will break the overwhelming job into manageable parts.

Do the difficult:
I will face what I fear and act with self-discipline

I choose to solutionise:
I will find a solution by taking advice or doing research.

Prioritise myself:
I will keep my life balanced by meeting friends, doing exercise or laughing.

Compartmentalise:
I will not let this event cloud my whole day; I will focus on something else now.

Utilise calming strategies:

When I:
- relax,
- breathe deeply,
- go for a run,
- shower,
- lie down,
- read,
- watch TV,
- climb into a mental helicopter
- practice mindfulness, meditation, my mind and body calm down.

Step Four: The Self Motivation Process

Endorse yourself for any growth no matter how small.

In the past I would have...

_____

_____

But this time I...

_____

_____

Tick off the traits that you strengthened when you worked down your anxiety:

☐ generosity	☐ peacefulness
☐ kindness	☐ self-discipline
☐ compassion	☐ forgiveness
☐ consideration	☐ courage
☐ helpfulness	☐ responsibility
☐ respectfulness	☐ reliability
☐ honesty	☐ loyalty
☐ fairness	☐ love
☐ patience	☐ humility

Rate your anxiety on a scale of 0 to 100%:

☐ %

O

W

Anxiety Management Worksheet

The purpose of this worksheet is to help you to see every stressful event as an opportunity for
1. greater understanding of yourself, your anxiety and the people around you, and
2. practicing tools to manage your anxiety.

Step One: An Event

Briefly describe an event when you became anxious. Give such details as time, place and people involved, and end with "That's when I began to work myself up..."

_____

_____ E

_____

Rate your anxiety on a scale of 0 to 100%: [   ] %

Step Two: The Working-Up Process

Learn about your working up process by identifying your thoughts, feelings, behaviours and bodily reactions during the event. Tick the ones that most resonate with you.

Undermining Beliefs

I fear that I have lost...
- [ ] approval
- [ ] control
- [ ] co-operation
- [ ] face
- [ ] respect
- [ ] success
- [ ] trust
- [ ] validation
- [ ] love

This event proves that I am...
- [ ] stupid
- [ ] abnormal
- [ ] incompetent
- [ ] lazy
- [ ] irresponsible
- [ ] a total failure
- [ ] undisciplined
- [ ] untogether
- [ ] useless

B

I worry that I will suffer...
- [ ] mental collapse
- [ ] illness
- [ ] financial hardship

What I want is...
- [ ] total control
- [ ] respect
- [ ] success
- [ ] perfection
- [ ] comfort
- [ ] fairness
- [ ] tranquility
- [ ] all the answers
- [ ] for life to go smoothly
- [ ] to be all things to all people

Self-destructive Behaviour

Active
- [ ] get violent
- [ ] swear
- [ ] slam doors
- [ ] run away
- [ ] overeat
- [ ] harm myself
- [ ] criticise

Passive
- [ ] take it too seriously
- [ ] give up
- [ ] wallow in self pity
- [ ] sulk
- [ ] space out
- [ ] procrastinate
- [ ] give in
- [ ] be controlled

Intense Feelings

Angry feelings
- [ ] hateful
- [ ] aggravated
- [ ] annoyed
- [ ] hostile
- [ ] outraged
- [ ] punitive
- [ ] resentful
- [ ] vengeful

Fearful feelings
- [ ] helpless
- [ ] hopeless
- [ ] disappointed
- [ ] sad
- [ ] attacked
- [ ] worn out
- [ ] rejected
- [ ] jealous
- [ ] afraid
- [ ] exploited
- [ ] lonely
- [ ] abandoned
- [ ] guilty
- [ ] insulted
- [ ] confused
- [ ] disillusioned
- [ ] misunderstood
- [ ] trapped

Bodily Reactions (Limbic System)

I am uncomfortable because I am experiencing...
- [ ] tremors
- [ ] nausea
- [ ] sweaty palms
- [ ] stomach-ache
- [ ] pounding heart
- [ ] general tension
- [ ] fatigue
- [ ] imagination on fire
- [ ] headache
- [ ] dry mouth
- [ ] jaw clenching
- [ ] shortness of breath

Continued over

B   F   L

Step Three: The Working-Down Process

Begin with, "Suddenly I realised that I was anxious and that I had choices..." This is the step of self-leadership and trust in one's ability to handle the situation.

Choose helpful thoughts:

I choose to depersonalise
There is no intention to hurt me. He is doing the best he can with the tools he has at the moment.

I choose realism over romanticism
Life presents many obstacles. I lower or raise standards as needed.

There is no right or wrong
Unless it is a moral issue, I will see it simply as a difference of opinion and/or taste.

I choose the total view of positivity
Even though this event is negative, the total view of his behaviour is positive.

I surrender control
Since I cannot change this situation, I choose to let go of it

I choose to put this event in perspective
This event is not a catastrophe because it is not life threatening. It can be viewed as a trivial life event, a normal life problem that needs to be solved not dramatised.

I choose to view this event as average, falling within the normal range
This event is not exceptional; many people have gone through this.

It's temporary - "this too shall pass"
Life is constantly changing and moving through phases and this situation will also change.

Fears or facts?
Why fear? It may not happen!

I choose to focus on this as a learning experience
Every problem that comes my way is an opportunity for me to learn about my strengths and weaknesses, others and life.

Feel soothing emotions:

I choose to feel warm, loving emotions. I do this by focusing on my heart and letting love, trust forgiveness, compassion, hope or gratitude fill my heart space.

Behave constructively:

I choose to work in part acts:
I will break the overwhelming job into manageable parts.

Do the difficult:
I will face what I fear and act with self-discipline

I choose to solutionise:
I will find a solution by taking advice or doing research.

Prioritise myself:
I will keep my life balanced by meeting friends, doing exercise or laughing.

Compartmentalise:
I will not let this event cloud my whole day; I will focus on something else now.

Utilise calming strategies:

When I:
- relax,
- breathe deeply,
- go for a run,
- shower,
- lie down,
- read,
- watch TV,
- climb into a mental helicopter
- practice mindfulness, meditation, my mind and body calm down.

Step Four: The Self Motivation Process

Endorse yourself for any growth no matter how small.

In the past I would have...

_____

_____

But this time I...

_____

_____

Tick off the traits that you strengthened when you worked down your anxiety:

☐ generosity	☐ peacefulness	
☐ kindness	☐ self-discipline	
☐ compassion	☐ forgiveness	
☐ consideration	☐ courage	
☐ helpfulness	☐ responsibility	
☐ respectfulness	☐ reliability	
☐ honesty	☐ loyalty	
☐ fairness	☐ love	
☐ patience	☐ humility	

Rate your anxiety on a scale of 0 to 100%:

[____]%

O   W

Session 4

Anxiety Management Worksheet

The purpose of this worksheet is to help you to see every stressful event as an opportunity for
1. greater understanding of yourself, your anxiety and the people around you, and
2. practicing tools to manage your anxiety.

Step One: An Event

Briefly describe an event when you became anxious. Give such details as time, place and people involved, and end with "That's when I began to work myself up..."

_____

_____ E

_____

_____ Rate your anxiety on a scale of 0 to 100%: [   ] %

Step Two: The Working-Up Process

Learn about your working up process by identifying your thoughts, feelings, behaviours and bodily reactions during the event. Tick the ones that most resonate with you.

Undermining Beliefs

I fear that I have lost...
- approval
- control
- co-operation
- face
- respect
- success
- trust
- validation
- love

This event proves that I am...
- stupid
- abnormal
- incompetent
- lazy
- irresponsible
- a total failure
- undisciplined
- untogether
- useless

B

I worry that I will suffer...
- mental collapse
- illness
- financial hardship

What I want is...
- total control
- respect
- success
- perfection
- comfort
- fairness
- tranquility
- all the answers
- for life to go smoothly
- to be all things to all people

Self-destructive Behaviour

Active
- get violent
- swear
- slam doors
- run away
- overeat
- harm myself
- criticise

Passive
- take it too seriously
- give up
- wallow in self pity
- sulk
- space out
- procrastinate
- give in
- be controlled

Intense Feelings

Angry feelings
- hateful
- aggravated
- annoyed
- hostile
- outraged
- punitive
- resentful
- vengeful

Fearful feelings
- helpless
- hopeless
- disappointed
- sad
- attacked
- worn out
- rejected
- jealous
- afraid
- exploited
- lonely
- abandoned
- guilty
- insulted
- confused
- disillusioned
- misunderstood
- trapped

Bodily Reactions (Limbic System)

I am uncomfortable because I am experiencing...
- tremors
- nausea
- sweaty palms
- stomach-ache
- pounding heart
- general tension
- fatigue
- imagination on fire
- headache
- dry mouth
- jaw clenching
- shortness of breath

Continued over

B   F   L

Step Three: The Working-Down Process

Begin with, "Suddenly I realised that I was anxious and that I had choices..." This is the step of self-leadership and trust in one's ability to handle the situation.

Choose helpful thoughts:

I choose to depersonalise
There is no intention to hurt me. He is doing the best he can with the tools he has at the moment.

I choose realism over romanticism
Life presents many obstacles. I lower or raise standards as needed.

There is no right or wrong
Unless it is a moral issue, I will see it simply as a difference of opinion and/or taste.

I choose the total view of positivity
Even though this event is negative, the total view of his behaviour is positive.

I surrender control
Since I cannot change this situation, I choose to let go of it

I choose to put this event in perspective
This event is not a catastrophe because it is not life threatening. It can be viewed as a trivial life event, a normal life problem that needs to be solved not dramatised.

I choose to view this event as average, falling within the normal range
This event is not exceptional; many people have gone through this.

It's temporary - "this too shall pass"
Life is constantly changing and moving through phases and this situation will also change.

Fears or facts?
Why fear? It may not happen!

I choose to focus on this as a learning experience
Every problem that comes my way is an opportunity for me to learn about my strengths and weaknesses, others and life.

Feel soothing emotions:

I choose to feel warm, loving emotions. I do this by focusing on my heart and letting love, trust forgiveness, compassion, hope or gratitude fill my heart space.

Behave constructively:

I choose to work in part acts:
I will break the overwhelming job into manageable parts.

Do the difficult:
I will face what I fear and act with self-discipline

I choose to solutionise:
I will find a solution by taking advice or doing research.

Prioritise myself:
I will keep my life balanced by meeting friends, doing exercise or laughing.

Compartmentalise:
I will not let this event cloud my whole day; I will focus on something else now.

Utilise calming strategies:

When I:
• relax,
• breathe deeply,
• go for a run,
• shower,
• lie down,
• read,
• watch TV,
• climb into a mental helicopter
• practice mindfulness, meditation, my mind and body calm down.

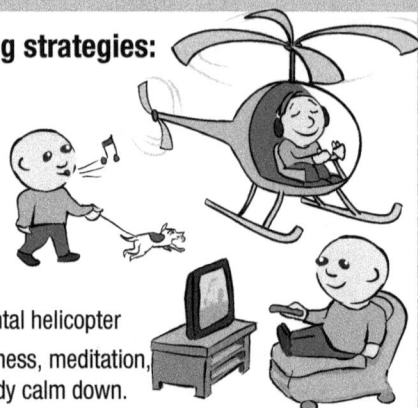

Step Four: The Self Motivation Process

Endorse yourself for any growth no matter how small.

In the past I would have...

_____

_____

But this time I...

_____

_____

Tick off the traits that you strengthened when you worked down your anxiety:

☐ generosity
☐ kindness
☐ compassion
☐ consideration
☐ helpfulness
☐ respectfulness
☐ honesty
☐ fairness
☐ patience

☐ peacefulness
☐ self-discipline
☐ forgiveness
☐ courage
☐ responsibility
☐ reliability
☐ loyalty
☐ love
☐ humility

Rate your anxiety on a scale of 0 to 100%:

[____]%

O   W

NOTES

NOTES

Session 5

COGNITIVE TOOL: OCCURRENCE IS NOT EXCEPTIONAL

'I choose to view this event as average, falling within the normal range. This event is not exceptional; many people have gone through this'.

Please fill out the exercise below. This will assist you to identify whether or not you feel exceptional. After working through this chapter and understanding the tool you will have the opportunity to re-evaluate.

EXERCISE SIXTEEN

Do you ever feel that you are different to other people?   YES/NO

If yes, in what ways?

_____

_____

_____

Do you ever think that your work/home/relationship situation is exceptionally bad (i.e. worse than most other people's)?   YES/NO

If yes, in what ways?

_____

_____

_____

For the purposes of this tool, there are two options. The first is that you feel normal, part of the human race, like everybody else. The second option is that you feel exceptional, an exception to the rule. Exceptional means that you feel different in some way.

When you believe that you are the exception, it will result in you feeling different, misunderstood, alone, helpless or abnormal. Conversely, when you know that what you are going through is a common problem, you no longer feel different or alone. Moreover you can turn to people who have been through the same thing for support and solutions.

This is a major strength in group therapy or supportive groups. For example, there are groups for mums with new babies, dads recently divorced, people trying to lose weight, alcoholics, step-mothers and any other human experience you could think of. Hospitals run groups for patients who are suffering from the same illness. Cancer Councils train volunteers who have recovered to go out and visit and support others living with cancer. Today the web is filled with forums made up of people from all over the world who share their experiences.

What a relief it is to discover then that you are not the only new mum who gets angry when the baby will not settle OR that you are not the only divorced dad who feels bereft at leaving his children.

When you have a problem that is bad enough and you need to work through it, for instance, if you are a father who moved out of the family home, you may feel sad and lost. It will take time and emotional work to move forward. Without this tool, your problems will multiply. Thinking you are the only person going through this life adjustment creates a second problem. You now additionally feel sorry for yourself, lonely, misunderstood and guilty. However, when you meet a group of fathers who are going through the identical issues, the second problem falls away and you only have the first one to deal with.

Even when an incident is exceptional, there will always be a group who has experienced the same thing. For instance, let us say you require a mastectomy. Nobody in your circle has had one. The problem (mastectomy) may be exceptional at this moment among your family and friends but, rest assured, many other women have had a mastectomy and felt very similar to the way you feel now.

The best way to explain this tool is to use something called *the bell curve*. Understanding the bell curve will help you see that even if you are 'different', 'eccentric' or 'out of the box', you are still part of the normal human race. 'Normal' covers a huge range.

A bell curve is a simple graph that can be applied to a wide range of human characteristics. Below is a diagram of a bell curve of intelligence or IQ. It shows the range of scores people gain on a popular intelligence test called the Wechsler Adult Intelligence Scale.

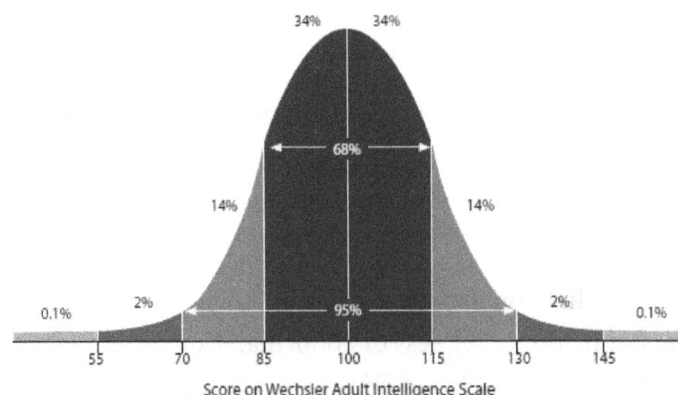

Score on Wechsler Adult Intelligence Scale

The range of IQ scores is large, 0–150. Most people are likely to score between 85 points and 115 points (68% of people). The range of very high and very low scores however, is small. Little more than 2% of people score above 130 points or below an IQ score of 70. This demonstrates that 96% of us fall within the normal range.

If we were to do a bell curve of height, it would look identical. Most people fall within the blue section. A very short person, may fall into the brown section, the second percentile, but would not be classified a dwarf. In other words, a very short person still falls within the normal range. Similarly a person of 6'8' feet may be classified as very tall, but will still be within the normal range and is not a 'giant'.

Dwarfs and giants do actually exist of course. They have a medical diagnosis and their height is always associated with other signs and symptoms. They would fall on the beige end of the curve. The bell curve, therefore also shows that it is 'normal' to have a small number of people experience something unusual.

The bell curve in this case is being used to explain a concept, namely, that you fit in to the human race. It is important that you think you are normal and that your problems fit into a normal range. If you believe that you are alone, abnormal, or a freak, you will feel much, much worse.

This tool also teaches you to view your problem as a normal life event that could, and does happen, to many other people.

Rest assured, the bell curve does not remove individuality. As explained, very short and very tall people (plus every height in between) exist. No two people are alike. However, whatever your height, know that you fall within the normal range.

Similarly, events that happen to you will have individual variations but will belong in the normal range of events. Except in extremely rare circumstances, we all have experiences that are universal and fall within the normal range.

Self-Esteem

People with low self-esteem typically compare themselves to others. When you compare yourself, you will frequently feel inferior because there will always be somebody who is better/smarter/richer/thinner than you.

One common suggestion made to help with these comparisons is to only look at those people who are less smart, less rich and fatter than you. My recommendation instead is that you use the bell curve to feel better about yourself. The bell curve graph shows that each individual occupies a different place (or percentile). Work on accepting that you have a unique place, a unique purpose and a unique destiny in the world that only you can fulfill. Once you do this, your self-esteem will rise.

The composition of an orchestra illustrates this point clearly. An orchestra makes beautiful music because many different instruments contribute their unique and distinctive sounds. The piano sounds different to the violins, which sound different to the wind instruments and cymbals.

The violinists may appear to be more 'important' than the cymbals because they work much harder. However, the symphony would not have been complete without the clashing of the cymbals. In other words, every instrument is vital in order to produce a complete and wonderful sound.

An orchestra is analogous to a society of people. Each of us makes a unique contribution to the world. You may be the busy violinist or the occasional cymbal clasher. You have that function because of your unique blend of height and weight and intelligence and age and musical expertise. There is no use comparing yourself to anybody else. Whether you are the violinist, or the percussionist, you will be on bell curve.

When you embrace your individuality and strive to be the best cymbal clasher ever, you will feel good about yourself, less anxious and happier.

Arrogance

Some arrogant individuals like to believe that they are exceptional. When somebody boasts that they are smartest, the tallest or the richest, their arrogance is obvious. However, their arrogance is less obvious when they boast about negative things.

Common arrogant expressions are:

- You think you have it hard? My work is more back breaking than yours.
- You do not know what pain is. When I get a headache I cannot move for three days.
- My husband is the most uncommunicative man in the world.
- My son is, for sure, the wildest boy in his age group.

Do you like to think that you are exceptional? Whatever your motivation to holding on to feeling exceptional, I encourage you to let go of it. You will feel much happier and calmer when you accept that you fit in the normal range and that your life is following the natural path.

EXERCISE SEVENTEEN

Having learned this tool, do you still think that you are exceptional?
YES/NO

If yes, please elaborate:

_____

_____

Do you still think that your anxiety-provoking situation is exceptional?
YES/NO

If yes, please elaborate:

_____

_____

If you have answered yes to either of the above, then this tool is not applicable to your situation. Can you think of another tool you have learned in this program so far that would be better suited to your predicament?

_____

_____

_____

Is it possible that you are holding on to believing that you/your situation is exceptional because it makes you feel good?

_____

_____

_____

This tool is only applicable when an occurrence is not exceptional but you **believe** that it is, and the belief is causing you stress.

When a situation is indeed exceptional (e.g. an abusive situation), measures must be taken immediately to change/stop/move away from the situation.

You might need the advice of a friend or objective third party to clarify whether or not the situation is indeed exceptional.

FEELING TOOL: FEEL SOOTHING EMOTIONS

Just like you can only think one thought at a time, you can only feel one feeling at a time. When you substitute soothing emotions for distressing emotions, you will feel calmer.

Intense negative feelings include angry feelings (fight) and fearful feelings (flight). Soothing emotions include love, trust, forgiveness, compassion and gratitude.

In order to move from distressing feelings to soothing feelings, you need to focus on the area where the emotion is felt. This area is called your **heart space** and it is located literally in your chest around your heart.

You can fill your heart space with a positive feeling by imagining a positive interaction you have had — just like watching a video of a past event in your life.

Examples of moving from distressing feelings to soothing feelings

1. Let us say you are furious with your child. You want to become loving instead. Take a minute and focus on the area around your heart. Now focus on your breathing and imagine you are breathing from your heart. Do this for 5 breaths. Think of a loving moment you had with your child in the past. Feel that love fill your heart space. There is no room for any other emotion besides love when you do this. Your anger will dissipate. The more you do this the easier it becomes and the less angry you will be.

2. Let us say you are fearful for the future. You are worried that you will not get a job. You would prefer to trust in the future. Take a minute and focus on the area around your heart. Now focus on your breathing and imagine that you are breathing from your heart. Do this for 5 breaths. Think of previous times in your life when you found a job after a job loss. Feel feelings of trust fill your heart space. There is no room for any other emotion than trust when you do this. Your fear will decrease. Keep practicing this to sustain the trust long term.

3. Let's imagine that you are not coping well at work because your mother is ill. At first you are critical of yourself, disappointed that you are not able to work perfectly all the time. Suddenly you realise that you deserve to feel compassion for your difficult circumstances. Imagine a friend is in your exact position. You feel compassion for her because her life is tough right now. Her mother is sick and she needs to keep working. Experience compassion, fill your heart space. Then direct the compassion towards yourself. There is no longer any room for criticism. All you feel is compassion.

EXERCISE EIGHTEEN

Name a specific negative emotion you wish to replace.

_____

_____

_____

Name the emotion that you wish to replace it with. Think of a situation that happened in the past where you felt the positive emotion you wish to feel.

_____

_____

_____

Take a minute and focus on the area around your heart. Now focus on your breathing and imagine you are breathing from your heart. Do this for 5 breaths.

Now imagine the situation you wrote about as if it was a movie. Feel the positive emotion fill your heart space.

DAILY MONITORING DIARY

WEEK ENDING _____

Day	M	T	W	T	F	S	S
Overall Anxiety Rating for the day (0-10)							

1. EXERCISE

	M	T	W	T	F	S	S
How long?							
Anxiety level before (0-10)							
Anxiety level after (0-10)							

2. BREATHING & RELAXATION

	M	T	W	T	F	S	S
How long?							
Anxiety level before (0-10)							
Anxiety level after (0-10)							

3. CATASTROPHIC THINKING

	M	T	W	T	F	S	S
How often this type of thought occurred							
Belief in thoughts before challenging (0-10)							
Belief in thoughts after challenging (0-10)							

4. FEARS NOT FACTS

	M	T	W	T	F	S	S
How often this type of thought occurred							
Belief in thoughts before challenging (0-10)							
Belief in thoughts after challenging (0-10)							

5. PERVASIVE PESSIMISTIC THINKING

	M	T	W	T	F	S	S
How often this type of thought occurred							
Belief in thoughts before challenging (0-10)							
Belief in thoughts after challenging (0-10)							

6. PERMANENT PESSIMISTIC THINKING

	M	T	W	T	F	S	S
How often this type of thought occurred							
Belief in thoughts before challenging (0-10)							
Belief in thoughts after challenging (0-10)							

7. MINDFULNESS (FORMAL, GROUNDING, INFORMAL MINDFULNESS)

	M	T	W	T	F	S	S
How long?							
Anxiety level before (0-10)							
Anxiety level after (0-10)							

8. EXCEPTIONAL THINKING

	M	T	W	T	F	S	S
How often this type of thought occurred							
Belief in thoughts before challenging (0-10)							
Belief in thoughts after challenging (0-10)							

Anxiety Management Worksheet

The purpose of this worksheet is to help you to see every stressful event as an opportunity for
1. greater understanding of yourself, your anxiety and the people around you, and
2. practicing tools to manage your anxiety.

Step One: An Event

Briefly describe an event when you became anxious. Give such details as time, place and people involved, and end with "That's when I began to work myself up..."

_____

_____ E

_____

Rate your anxiety on a scale of 0 to 100%: [   ] %

Step Two: The Working-Up Process

Learn about your working up process by identifying your thoughts, feelings, behaviours and bodily reactions during the event. Tick the ones that most resonate with you.

Undermining Beliefs

I fear that I have lost...
- ☐ approval
- ☐ control
- ☐ co-operation
- ☐ face
- ☐ respect
- ☐ success
- ☐ trust
- ☐ validation
- ☐ love

This event proves that I am...
- ☐ stupid
- ☐ abnormal
- ☐ incompetent
- ☐ lazy
- ☐ irresponsible
- ☐ a total failure
- ☐ undisciplined
- ☐ untogether
- ☐ useless

B

I worry that I will suffer...
- ☐ mental collapse
- ☐ illness
- ☐ financial hardship

What I want is...
- ☐ total control
- ☐ respect
- ☐ success
- ☐ perfection
- ☐ comfort
- ☐ fairness
- ☐ tranquility
- ☐ all the answers
- ☐ for life to go smoothly
- ☐ to be all things to all people

Self-destructive Behaviour

Active
- ☐ get violent
- ☐ swear
- ☐ slam doors
- ☐ run away
- ☐ overeat
- ☐ harm myself
- ☐ criticise

Passive
- ☐ take it too seriously
- ☐ give up
- ☐ wallow in self pity
- ☐ sulk
- ☐ space out
- ☐ procrastinate
- ☐ give in
- ☐ be controlled

Intense Feelings

Angry feelings
- ☐ hateful
- ☐ aggravated
- ☐ annoyed
- ☐ hostile
- ☐ outraged
- ☐ punitive
- ☐ resentful
- ☐ vengeful

Fearful feelings
- ☐ helpless
- ☐ hopeless
- ☐ disappointed
- ☐ sad
- ☐ attacked
- ☐ worn out
- ☐ rejected
- ☐ jealous
- ☐ afraid
- ☐ exploited
- ☐ lonely
- ☐ abandoned
- ☐ guilty
- ☐ insulted
- ☐ confused
- ☐ disillusioned
- ☐ misunderstood
- ☐ trapped

Bodily Reactions (Limbic System)

I am uncomfortable because I am experiencing...
- ☐ tremors
- ☐ nausea
- ☐ sweaty palms
- ☐ stomach-ache
- ☐ pounding heart
- ☐ general tension
- ☐ fatigue
- ☐ imagination on fire
- ☐ headache
- ☐ dry mouth
- ☐ jaw clenching
- ☐ shortness of breath

Continued over

B   F   L

Step Three: The Working-Down Process

Begin with, "Suddenly I realised that I was anxious and that I had choices..." This is the step of self-leadership and trust in one's ability to handle the situation.

Choose helpful thoughts:

I choose to depersonalise
There is no intention to hurt me. He is doing the best he can with the tools he has at the moment.

I choose realism over romanticism
Life presents many obstacles. I lower or raise standards as needed.

There is no right or wrong
Unless it is a moral issue, I will see it simply as a difference of opinion and/or taste.

I choose the total view of positivity
Even though this event is negative, the total view of his behaviour is positive.

I surrender control
Since I cannot change this situation, I choose to let go of it

I choose to put this event in perspective
This event is not a catastrophe because it is not life threatening. It can be viewed as a trivial life event, a normal life problem that needs to be solved not dramatised.

I choose to view this event as average, falling within the normal range
This event is not exceptional; many people have gone through this.

It's temporary - "this too shall pass"
Life is constantly changing and moving through phases and this situation will also change.

Fears or facts?
Why fear? It may not happen!

I choose to focus on this as a learning experience
Every problem that comes my way is an opportunity for me to learn about my strengths and weaknesses, others and life.

Feel soothing emotions:

I choose to feel warm, loving emotions. I do this by focusing on my heart and letting love, trust forgiveness, compassion, hope or gratitude fill my heart space.

Behave constructively:

I choose to work in part acts:
I will break the overwhelming job into manageable parts.

Do the difficult:
I will face what I fear and act with self-discipline

I choose to solutionise:
I will find a solution by taking advice or doing research.

Prioritise myself:
I will keep my life balanced by meeting friends, doing exercise or laughing.

Compartmentalise:
I will not let this event cloud my whole day; I will focus on something else now.

Utilise calming strategies:

When I:
- relax,
- breathe deeply,
- go for a run,
- shower,
- lie down,
- read,
- watch TV,
- climb into a mental helicopter
- practice mindfulness, meditation, my mind and body calm down.

Step Four: The Self Motivation Process

Endorse yourself for any growth no matter how small.

In the past I would have...

_____

_____

But this time I...

_____

_____

Tick off the traits that you strengthened when you worked down your anxiety:

☐ generosity ☐ peacefulness
☐ kindness ☐ self-discipline
☐ compassion ☐ forgiveness
☐ consideration ☐ courage
☐ helpfulness ☐ responsibility
☐ respectfulness ☐ reliability
☐ honesty ☐ loyalty
☐ fairness ☐ love
☐ patience ☐ humility

Rate your anxiety on a scale of 0 to 100%:

☐ %

O

W

Anxiety Management Worksheet

ANXIETY
SOLUTIONS**CBT**
Psychology Practice

The purpose of this worksheet is to help you to see every stressful event as an opportunity for
1. greater understanding of yourself, your anxiety and the people around you, and
2. practicing tools to manage your anxiety.

Step One: An Event

Briefly describe an event when you became anxious. Give such details as time, place and people involved, and end with
"That's when I began to work myself up..."

_____

_____ **E**

_____

_____ Rate your anxiety on a scale of 0 to 100%: [   ] **%**

Step Two: The Working-Up Process

Learn about your working up process by identifying your thoughts, feelings, behaviours and bodily reactions during the event.
Tick the ones that most resonate with you.

Undermining Beliefs

I fear that I have lost...
- ☐ approval
- ☐ success
- ☐ control
- ☐ trust
- ☐ co-operation
- ☐ validation
- ☐ face
- ☐ love
- ☐ respect

This event proves that I am...
- ☐ stupid
- ☐ a total failure
- ☐ abnormal
- ☐ undisciplined
- ☐ incompetent
- ☐ untogether
- ☐ lazy
- ☐ useless
- ☐ irresponsible

B

I worry that I will suffer...
- ☐ mental collapse
- ☐ illness
- ☐ financial hardship

What I want is...
- ☐ total control
- ☐ tranquility
- ☐ respect
- ☐ all the answers
- ☐ success
- ☐ for life to go
- ☐ perfection   smoothly
- ☐ comfort
- ☐ to be all things
- ☐ fairness   to all people

Self-destructive Behaviour

Active
- ☐ get violent
- ☐ swear
- ☐ slam doors
- ☐ run away
- ☐ overeat
- ☐ harm myself
- ☐ criticise

Passive
- ☐ take it too seriously
- ☐ give up
- ☐ wallow in self pity
- ☐ sulk
- ☐ space out
- ☐ procrastinate
- ☐ give in
- ☐ be controlled

Intense Feelings

Angry feelings
- ☐ hateful
- ☐ attacked
- ☐ aggravated
- ☐ worn out
- ☐ annoyed
- ☐ rejected
- ☐ hostile
- ☐ jealous
- ☐ outraged
- ☐ afraid
- ☐ punitive
- ☐ exploited
- ☐ resentful
- ☐ lonely
- ☐ vengeful
- ☐ abandoned
- ☐ guilty

Fearful feelings
- ☐ insulted
- ☐ helpless
- ☐ confused
- ☐ hopeless
- ☐ disillusioned
- ☐ disappointed
- ☐ misunderstood
- ☐ sad
- ☐ trapped

Bodily Reactions (Limbic System)

I am uncomfortable because I am experiencing...
- ☐ tremors
- ☐ nausea
- ☐ sweaty palms
- ☐ stomach-ache
- ☐ pounding heart
- ☐ general tension
- ☐ fatigue
- ☐ imagination on fire
- ☐ headache
- ☐ dry mouth
- ☐ jaw clenching
- ☐ shortness of breath

Continued over

B   **F**   **L**

Step Three: The Working-Down Process

Begin with, "Suddenly I realised that I was anxious and that I had choices..." This is the step of self-leadership and trust in one's ability to handle the situation.

Choose helpful thoughts:

I choose to depersonalise
There is no intention to hurt me. He is doing the best he can with the tools he has at the moment.

I choose realism over romanticism
Life presents many obstacles. I lower or raise standards as needed.

There is no right or wrong
Unless it is a moral issue, I will see it simply as a difference of opinion and/or taste.

I choose the total view of positivity
Even though this event is negative, the total view of his behaviour is positive.

I surrender control
Since I cannot change this situation, I choose to let go of it

I choose to put this event in perspective
This event is not a catastrophe because it is not life threatening. It can be viewed as a trivial life event, a normal life problem that needs to be solved not dramatised.

I choose to view this event as average, falling within the normal range
This event is not exceptional; many people have gone through this.

It's temporary - "this too shall pass"
Life is constantly changing and moving through phases and this situation will also change.

Fears or facts?
Why fear? It may not happen!

I choose to focus on this as a learning experience
Every problem that comes my way is an opportunity for me to learn about my strengths and weaknesses, others and life.

Feel soothing emotions:

I choose to feel warm, loving emotions. I do this by focusing on my heart and letting love, trust forgiveness, compassion, hope or gratitude fill my heart space.

Behave constructively:

I choose to work in part acts:
I will break the overwhelming job into manageable parts.

Do the difficult:
I will face what I fear and act with self-discipline

I choose to solutionise:
I will find a solution by taking advice or doing research.

Prioritise myself:
I will keep my life balanced by meeting friends, doing exercise or laughing.

Compartmentalise:
I will not let this event cloud my whole day; I will focus on something else now.

Utilise calming strategies:

When I:
- relax,
- breathe deeply,
- go for a run,
- shower,
- lie down,
- read,
- watch TV,
- climb into a mental helicopter
- practice mindfulness, meditation, my mind and body calm down.

Step Four: The Self Motivation Process

Endorse yourself for any growth no matter how small.

In the past I would have...
_____
_____

But this time I...
_____
_____

Tick off the traits that you strengthened when you worked down your anxiety:

☐ generosity	☐ peacefulness
☐ kindness	☐ self-discipline
☐ compassion	☐ forgiveness
☐ consideration	☐ courage
☐ helpfulness	☐ responsibility
☐ respectfulness	☐ reliability
☐ honesty	☐ loyalty
☐ fairness	☐ love
☐ patience	☐ humility

Rate your anxiety on a scale of 0 to 100%:

[____]%

O   W

Anxiety Management Worksheet

The purpose of this worksheet is to help you to see every stressful event as an opportunity for
1. greater understanding of yourself, your anxiety and the people around you, and
2. practicing tools to manage your anxiety.

Step One: An Event

Briefly describe an event when you became anxious. Give such details as time, place and people involved, and end with "That's when I began to work myself up..."

_____

_____   E

_____

_____ Rate your anxiety on a scale of 0 to 100%: [   ] %

Step Two: The Working-Up Process

Learn about your working up process by identifying your thoughts, feelings, behaviours and bodily reactions during the event. Tick the ones that most resonate with you.

Undermining Beliefs

I fear that I have lost...
- ☐ approval
- ☐ control
- ☐ co-operation
- ☐ face
- ☐ respect
- ☐ success
- ☐ trust
- ☐ validation
- ☐ love

This event proves that I am...   B
- ☐ stupid
- ☐ abnormal
- ☐ incompetent
- ☐ lazy
- ☐ irresponsible
- ☐ a total failure
- ☐ undisciplined
- ☐ untogether
- ☐ useless

I worry that I will suffer...
- ☐ mental collapse
- ☐ illness
- ☐ financial hardship

What I want is...
- ☐ total control
- ☐ respect
- ☐ success
- ☐ perfection
- ☐ comfort
- ☐ fairness
- ☐ tranquility
- ☐ all the answers
- ☐ for life to go smoothly
- ☐ to be all things to all people

Self-destructive Behaviour

Active
- ☐ get violent
- ☐ swear
- ☐ slam doors
- ☐ run away
- ☐ overeat
- ☐ harm myself
- ☐ criticise

Passive
- ☐ take it too seriously
- ☐ give up
- ☐ wallow in self pity
- ☐ sulk
- ☐ space out
- ☐ procrastinate
- ☐ give in
- ☐ be controlled

Intense Feelings

Angry feelings
- ☐ hateful
- ☐ aggravated
- ☐ annoyed
- ☐ hostile
- ☐ outraged
- ☐ punitive
- ☐ resentful
- ☐ vengeful

Fearful feelings
- ☐ helpless
- ☐ hopeless
- ☐ disappointed
- ☐ sad

- ☐ attacked
- ☐ worn out
- ☐ rejected
- ☐ jealous
- ☐ afraid
- ☐ exploited
- ☐ lonely
- ☐ abandoned
- ☐ guilty
- ☐ insulted
- ☐ confused
- ☐ disillusioned
- ☐ misunderstood
- ☐ trapped

Bodily Reactions (Limbic System)

I am uncomfortable because I am experiencing...
- ☐ tremors
- ☐ nausea
- ☐ sweaty palms
- ☐ stomach-ache
- ☐ pounding heart
- ☐ general tension
- ☐ fatigue
- ☐ imagination on fire
- ☐ headache
- ☐ dry mouth
- ☐ jaw clenching
- ☐ shortness of breath

Continued over

B   F   L

Step Three: The Working-Down Process

Begin with, "Suddenly I realised that I was anxious and that I had choices..." This is the step of self-leadership and trust in one's ability to handle the situation.

Choose helpful thoughts:

I choose to depersonalise
There is no intention to hurt me. He is doing the best he can with the tools he has at the moment.

I choose realism over romanticism
Life presents many obstacles. I lower or raise standards as needed.

There is no right or wrong
Unless it is a moral issue, I will see it simply as a difference of opinion and/or taste.

I choose the total view of positivity
Even though this event is negative, the total view of his behaviour is positive.

I surrender control
Since I cannot change this situation, I choose to let go of it

I choose to put this event in perspective
This event is not a catastrophe because it is not life threatening. It can be viewed as a trivial life event, a normal life problem that needs to be solved not dramatised.

I choose to view this event as average, falling within the normal range
This event is not exceptional; many people have gone through this.

It's temporary - "this too shall pass"
Life is constantly changing and moving through phases and this situation will also change.

Fears or facts?
Why fear? It may not happen!

I choose to focus on this as a learning experience
Every problem that comes my way is an opportunity for me to learn about my strengths and weaknesses, others and life.

Feel soothing emotions:

I choose to feel warm, loving emotions. I do this by focusing on my heart and letting love, trust forgiveness, compassion, hope or gratitude fill my heart space.

Behave constructively:

I choose to work in part acts:
I will break the overwhelming job into manageable parts.

Do the difficult:
I will face what I fear and act with self-discipline

I choose to solutionise:
I will find a solution by taking advice or doing research.

Prioritise myself:
I will keep my life balanced by meeting friends, doing exercise or laughing.

Compartmentalise:
I will not let this event cloud my whole day; I will focus on something else now.

Utilise calming strategies:

When I:
- relax,
- breathe deeply,
- go for a run,
- shower,
- lie down,
- read,
- watch TV,
- climb into a mental helicopter
- practice mindfulness, meditation, my mind and body calm down.

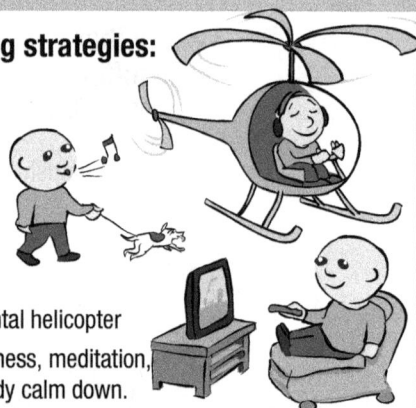

Step Four: The Self Motivation Process

Endorse yourself for any growth no matter how small.

In the past I would have...

_____

_____

But this time I...

_____

_____

Tick off the traits that you strengthened when you worked down your anxiety:

☐ generosity	☐ peacefulness
☐ kindness	☐ self-discipline
☐ compassion	☐ forgiveness
☐ consideration	☐ courage
☐ helpfulness	☐ responsibility
☐ respectfulness	☐ reliability
☐ honesty	☐ loyalty
☐ fairness	☐ love
☐ patience	☐ humility

Rate your anxiety on a scale of 0 to 100%:

☐ %

O

W

Anxiety Management Worksheet

The purpose of this worksheet is to help you to see every stressful event as an opportunity for
1. greater understanding of yourself, your anxiety and the people around you, and
2. practicing tools to manage your anxiety.

Step One: An Event

Briefly describe an event when you became anxious. Give such details as time, place and people involved, and end with "That's when I began to work myself up..."

E

Rate your anxiety on a scale of 0 to 100%: ____ %

Step Two: The Working-Up Process

Learn about your working up process by identifying your thoughts, feelings, behaviours and bodily reactions during the event. Tick the ones that most resonate with you.

Undermining Beliefs

I fear that I have lost...
- approval
- control
- co-operation
- face
- respect
- success
- trust
- validation
- love

This event proves that I am...
- stupid
- abnormal
- incompetent
- lazy
- irresponsible
- a total failure
- undisciplined
- untogether
- useless

B

I worry that I will suffer...
- mental collapse
- illness
- financial hardship

What I want is...
- total control
- respect
- success
- perfection
- comfort
- fairness
- tranquility
- all the answers
- for life to go smoothly
- to be all things to all people

Self-destructive Behaviour

Active
- get violent
- swear
- slam doors
- run away
- overeat
- harm myself
- criticise

Passive
- take it too seriously
- give up
- wallow in self pity
- sulk
- space out
- procrastinate
- give in
- be controlled

Intense Feelings

Angry feelings
- hateful
- aggravated
- annoyed
- hostile
- outraged
- punitive
- resentful
- vengeful

Fearful feelings
- helpless
- hopeless
- disappointed
- sad
- attacked
- worn out
- rejected
- jealous
- afraid
- exploited
- lonely
- abandoned
- guilty
- insulted
- confused
- disillusioned
- misunderstood
- trapped

Bodily Reactions (Limbic System)

I am uncomfortable because I am experiencing...
- tremors
- nausea
- sweaty palms
- stomach-ache
- pounding heart
- general tension
- fatigue
- imagination on fire
- headache
- dry mouth
- jaw clenching
- shortness of breath

Continued over

B   F   L

Step Three: The Working-Down Process

Begin with, "Suddenly I realised that I was anxious and that I had choices..." This is the step of self-leadership and trust in one's ability to handle the situation.

Choose helpful thoughts:

I choose to depersonalise
There is no intention to hurt me. He is doing the best he can with the tools he has at the moment.

I choose realism over romanticism
Life presents many obstacles. I lower or raise standards as needed.

There is no right or wrong
Unless it is a moral issue, I will see it simply as a difference of opinion and/or taste.

I choose the total view of positivity
Even though this event is negative, the total view of his behaviour is positive.

I surrender control
Since I cannot change this situation, I choose to let go of it

I choose to put this event in perspective
This event is not a catastrophe because it is not life threatening. It can be viewed as a trivial life event, a normal life problem that needs to be solved not dramatised.

I choose to view this event as average, falling within the normal range
This event is not exceptional; many people have gone through this.

It's temporary - "this too shall pass"
Life is constantly changing and moving through phases and this situation will also change.

Fears or facts?
Why fear? It may not happen!

I choose to focus on this as a learning experience
Every problem that comes my way is an opportunity for me to learn about my strengths and weaknesses, others and life.

Feel soothing emotions:

I choose to feel warm, loving emotions. I do this by focusing on my heart and letting love, trust forgiveness, compassion, hope or gratitude fill my heart space.

Behave constructively:

I choose to work in part acts:
I will break the overwhelming job into manageable parts.

Do the difficult:
I will face what I fear and act with self-discipline

I choose to solutionise:
I will find a solution by taking advice or doing research.

Prioritise myself:
I will keep my life balanced by meeting friends, doing exercise or laughing.

Compartmentalise:
I will not let this event cloud my whole day; I will focus on something else now.

Utilise calming strategies:

When I:
• relax,
• breathe deeply,
• go for a run,
• shower,
• lie down,
• read,
• watch TV,
• climb into a mental helicopter
• practice mindfulness, meditation, my mind and body calm down.

Step Four: The Self Motivation Process

Endorse yourself for any growth no matter how small.

In the past I would have...

_____

_____

But this time I...

_____

_____

Tick off the traits that you strengthened when you worked down your anxiety:

☐ generosity
☐ kindness
☐ compassion
☐ consideration
☐ helpfulness
☐ respectfulness
☐ honesty
☐ fairness
☐ patience

☐ peacefulness
☐ self-discipline
☐ forgiveness
☐ courage
☐ responsibility
☐ reliability
☐ loyalty
☐ love
☐ humility

Rate your anxiety on a scale of 0 to 100%:

☐ %

O

W

Session 5

Anxiety Management Worksheet

The purpose of this worksheet is to help you to see every stressful event as an opportunity for
1. greater understanding of yourself, your anxiety and the people around you, and
2. practicing tools to manage your anxiety.

Step One: An Event

Briefly describe an event when you became anxious. Give such details as time, place and people involved, and end with "That's when I began to work myself up..."

_____

_____ E

_____

_____ Rate your anxiety on a scale of 0 to 100%: [   ] %

Step Two: The Working-Up Process

Learn about your working up process by identifying your thoughts, feelings, behaviours and bodily reactions during the event. Tick the ones that most resonate with you.

Undermining Beliefs

I fear that I have lost...
- ☐ approval
- ☐ control
- ☐ co-operation
- ☐ face
- ☐ respect
- ☐ success
- ☐ trust
- ☐ validation
- ☐ love

This event proves that I am...
- ☐ stupid
- ☐ abnormal
- ☐ incompetent
- ☐ lazy
- ☐ irresponsible
- ☐ a total failure
- ☐ undisciplined
- ☐ untogether
- ☐ useless

B

I worry that I will suffer...
- ☐ mental collapse
- ☐ illness
- ☐ financial hardship

What I want is...
- ☐ total control
- ☐ respect
- ☐ success
- ☐ perfection
- ☐ comfort
- ☐ fairness
- ☐ tranquility
- ☐ all the answers
- ☐ for life to go smoothly
- ☐ to be all things to all people

Self-destructive Behaviour

Active
- ☐ get violent
- ☐ swear
- ☐ slam doors
- ☐ run away
- ☐ overeat
- ☐ harm myself
- ☐ criticise

Passive
- ☐ take it too seriously
- ☐ give up
- ☐ wallow in self pity
- ☐ sulk
- ☐ space out
- ☐ procrastinate
- ☐ give in
- ☐ be controlled

Intense Feelings

Angry feelings
- ☐ hateful
- ☐ aggravated
- ☐ annoyed
- ☐ hostile
- ☐ outraged
- ☐ punitive
- ☐ resentful
- ☐ vengeful

Fearful feelings
- ☐ helpless
- ☐ hopeless
- ☐ disappointed
- ☐ sad

- ☐ attacked
- ☐ worn out
- ☐ rejected
- ☐ jealous
- ☐ afraid
- ☐ exploited
- ☐ lonely
- ☐ abandoned
- ☐ guilty
- ☐ insulted
- ☐ confused
- ☐ disillusioned
- ☐ misunderstood
- ☐ trapped

Bodily Reactions (Limbic System)

I am uncomfortable because I am experiencing...
- ☐ tremors
- ☐ nausea
- ☐ sweaty palms
- ☐ stomach-ache
- ☐ pounding heart
- ☐ general tension
- ☐ fatigue
- ☐ imagination on fire
- ☐ headache
- ☐ dry mouth
- ☐ jaw clenching
- ☐ shortness of breath

Continued over

B   F   L

Step Three: The Working-Down Process

Begin with, "Suddenly I realised that I was anxious and that I had choices..." This is the step of self-leadership and trust in one's ability to handle the situation.

Choose helpful thoughts:

I choose to depersonalise
There is no intention to hurt me. He is doing the best he can with the tools he has at the moment.

I choose realism over romanticism
Life presents many obstacles. I lower or raise standards as needed.

There is no right or wrong
Unless it is a moral issue, I will see it simply as a difference of opinion and/or taste.

I choose the total view of positivity
Even though this event is negative, the total view of his behaviour is positive.

I surrender control
Since I cannot change this situation, I choose to let go of it

I choose to put this event in perspective
This event is not a catastrophe because it is not life threatening. It can be viewed as a trivial life event, a normal life problem that needs to be solved not dramatised.

I choose to view this event as average, falling within the normal range
This event is not exceptional; many people have gone through this.

It's temporary - "this too shall pass"
Life is constantly changing and moving through phases and this situation will also change.

Fears or facts?
Why fear? It may not happen!

I choose to focus on this as a learning experience
Every problem that comes my way is an opportunity for me to learn about my strengths and weaknesses, others and life.

Feel soothing emotions:

I choose to feel warm, loving emotions. I do this by focusing on my heart and letting love, trust forgiveness, compassion, hope or gratitude fill my heart space.

Behave constructively:

I choose to work in part acts:
I will break the overwhelming job into manageable parts.

Do the difficult:
I will face what I fear and act with self-discipline

I choose to solutionise:
I will find a solution by taking advice or doing research.

Prioritise myself:
I will keep my life balanced by meeting friends, doing exercise or laughing.

Compartmentalise:
I will not let this event cloud my whole day; I will focus on something else now.

Utilise calming strategies:

When I:
• relax,
• breathe deeply,
• go for a run,
• shower,
• lie down,
• read,
• watch TV,
• climb into a mental helicopter
• practice mindfulness, meditation, my mind and body calm down.

Step Four: The Self Motivation Process

Endorse yourself for any growth no matter how small.

In the past I would have...

_____

_____

But this time I...

_____

_____

Tick off the traits that you strengthened when you worked down your anxiety:

☐ generosity   ☐ peacefulness
☐ kindness   ☐ self-discipline
☐ compassion   ☐ forgiveness
☐ consideration   ☐ courage
☐ helpfulness   ☐ responsibility
☐ respectfulness   ☐ reliability
☐ honesty   ☐ loyalty
☐ fairness   ☐ love
☐ patience   ☐ humility

Rate your anxiety on a scale of 0 to 100%:

[____]%

O   W

Session 5

Anxiety Management Worksheet

The purpose of this worksheet is to help you to see every stressful event as an opportunity for
1. greater understanding of yourself, your anxiety and the people around you, and
2. practicing tools to manage your anxiety.

Step One: An Event

Briefly describe an event when you became anxious. Give such details as time, place and people involved, and end with "That's when I began to work myself up..."

_____

_____ E

_____

Rate your anxiety on a scale of 0 to 100%: [   ] %

Step Two: The Working-Up Process

Learn about your working up process by identifying your thoughts, feelings, behaviours and bodily reactions during the event. Tick the ones that most resonate with you.

Undermining Beliefs

I fear that I have lost...
- ☐ approval
- ☐ control
- ☐ co-operation
- ☐ face
- ☐ respect
- ☐ success
- ☐ trust
- ☐ validation
- ☐ love

This event proves that I am...
- ☐ stupid
- ☐ abnormal
- ☐ incompetent
- ☐ lazy
- ☐ irresponsible
- ☐ a total failure
- ☐ undisciplined
- ☐ untogether
- ☐ useless

B

I worry that I will suffer...
- ☐ mental collapse
- ☐ illness
- ☐ financial hardship

What I want is...
- ☐ total control
- ☐ respect
- ☐ success
- ☐ perfection
- ☐ comfort
- ☐ fairness
- ☐ tranquility
- ☐ all the answers
- ☐ for life to go smoothly
- ☐ to be all things to all people

Self-destructive Behaviour

Active
- ☐ get violent
- ☐ swear
- ☐ slam doors
- ☐ run away
- ☐ overeat
- ☐ harm myself
- ☐ criticise

Passive
- ☐ take it too seriously
- ☐ give up
- ☐ wallow in self pity
- ☐ sulk
- ☐ space out
- ☐ procrastinate
- ☐ give in
- ☐ be controlled

Intense Feelings

Angry feelings
- ☐ hateful
- ☐ aggravated
- ☐ annoyed
- ☐ hostile
- ☐ outraged
- ☐ punitive
- ☐ resentful
- ☐ vengeful

Fearful feelings
- ☐ helpless
- ☐ hopeless
- ☐ disappointed
- ☐ sad

- ☐ attacked
- ☐ worn out
- ☐ rejected
- ☐ jealous
- ☐ afraid
- ☐ exploited
- ☐ lonely
- ☐ abandoned
- ☐ guilty
- ☐ insulted
- ☐ confused
- ☐ disillusioned
- ☐ misunderstood
- ☐ trapped

Bodily Reactions (Limbic System)

I am uncomfortable because I am experiencing...
- ☐ tremors
- ☐ nausea
- ☐ sweaty palms
- ☐ stomach-ache
- ☐ pounding heart
- ☐ general tension
- ☐ fatigue
- ☐ imagination on fire
- ☐ headache
- ☐ dry mouth
- ☐ jaw clenching
- ☐ shortness of breath

Continued over

B   F   L

Step Three: The Working-Down Process

Begin with, "Suddenly I realised that I was anxious and that I had choices..." This is the step of self-leadership and trust in one's ability to handle the situation.

Choose helpful thoughts:

I choose to depersonalise
There is no intention to hurt me. He is doing the best he can with the tools he has at the moment.

I choose realism over romanticism
Life presents many obstacles. I lower or raise standards as needed.

There is no right or wrong
Unless it is a moral issue, I will see it simply as a difference of opinion and/or taste.

I choose the total view of positivity
Even though this event is negative, the total view of his behaviour is positive.

I surrender control
Since I cannot change this situation, I choose to let go of it

I choose to put this event in perspective
This event is not a catastrophe because it is not life threatening. It can be viewed as a trivial life event, a normal life problem that needs to be solved not dramatised.

I choose to view this event as average, falling within the normal range
This event is not exceptional; many people have gone through this.

It's temporary - "this too shall pass"
Life is constantly changing and moving through phases and this situation will also change.

Fears or facts?
Why fear? It may not happen!

I choose to focus on this as a learning experience
Every problem that comes my way is an opportunity for me to learn about my strengths and weaknesses, others and life.

Feel soothing emotions:

I choose to feel warm, loving emotions. I do this by focusing on my heart and letting love, trust forgiveness, compassion, hope or gratitude fill my heart space.

Behave constructively:

I choose to work in part acts:
I will break the overwhelming job into manageable parts.

Do the difficult:
I will face what I fear and act with self-discipline

I choose to solutionise:
I will find a solution by taking advice or doing research.

Prioritise myself:
I will keep my life balanced by meeting friends, doing exercise or laughing.

Compartmentalise:
I will not let this event cloud my whole day; I will focus on something else now.

Utilise calming strategies:

When I:
• relax,
• breathe deeply,
• go for a run,
• shower,
• lie down,
• read,
• watch TV,
• climb into a mental helicopter
• practice mindfulness, meditation, my mind and body calm down.

Step Four: The Self Motivation Process

Endorse yourself for any growth no matter how small.

In the past I would have...

_____

_____

But this time I...

_____

_____

Tick off the traits that you strengthened when you worked down your anxiety:

☐ generosity   ☐ peacefulness
☐ kindness   ☐ self-discipline
☐ compassion   ☐ forgiveness
☐ consideration   ☐ courage
☐ helpfulness   ☐ responsibility
☐ respectfulness   ☐ reliability
☐ honesty   ☐ loyalty
☐ fairness   ☐ love
☐ patience   ☐ humility

Rate your anxiety on a scale of 0 to 100%:

[ ] %

O   W

Anxiety Management Worksheet

The purpose of this worksheet is to help you to see every stressful event as an opportunity for
1. greater understanding of yourself, your anxiety and the people around you, and
2. practicing tools to manage your anxiety.

Step One: An Event

Briefly describe an event when you became anxious. Give such details as time, place and people involved, and end with "That's when I began to work myself up..."

E

Rate your anxiety on a scale of 0 to 100%: [   ] %

Step Two: The Working-Up Process

Learn about your working up process by identifying your thoughts, feelings, behaviours and bodily reactions during the event. Tick the ones that most resonate with you.

Undermining Beliefs

I fear that I have lost...
- approval
- control
- co-operation
- face
- respect
- success
- trust
- validation
- love

This event proves that I am...
- stupid
- abnormal
- incompetent
- lazy
- irresponsible
- a total failure
- undisciplined
- untogether
- useless

B

I worry that I will suffer...
- mental collapse
- illness
- financial hardship

What I want is...
- total control
- respect
- success
- perfection
- comfort
- fairness
- tranquility
- all the answers
- for life to go smoothly
- to be all things to all people

Self-destructive Behaviour

Active
- get violent
- swear
- slam doors
- run away
- overeat
- harm myself
- criticise

Passive
- take it too seriously
- give up
- wallow in self pity
- sulk
- space out
- procrastinate
- give in
- be controlled

Intense Feelings

Angry feelings
- hateful
- aggravated
- annoyed
- hostile
- outraged
- punitive
- resentful
- vengeful

Fearful feelings
- helpless
- hopeless
- disappointed
- sad
- attacked
- worn out
- rejected
- jealous
- afraid
- exploited
- lonely
- abandoned
- guilty
- insulted
- confused
- disillusioned
- misunderstood
- trapped

Bodily Reactions (Limbic System)

I am uncomfortable because I am experiencing...
- tremors
- nausea
- sweaty palms
- stomach-ache
- pounding heart
- general tension
- fatigue
- imagination on fire
- headache
- dry mouth
- jaw clenching
- shortness of breath

Continued over

B   F   L

Step Three: The Working-Down Process

Begin with, "Suddenly I realised that I was anxious and that I had choices…" This is the step of self-leadership and trust in one's ability to handle the situation.

Choose helpful thoughts:

I choose to depersonalise
There is no intention to hurt me. He is doing the best he can with the tools he has at the moment.

I choose realism over romanticism
Life presents many obstacles. I lower or raise standards as needed.

There is no right or wrong
Unless it is a moral issue, I will see it simply as a difference of opinion and/or taste.

I choose the total view of positivity
Even though this event is negative, the total view of his behaviour is positive.

I surrender control
Since I cannot change this situation, I choose to let go of it

I choose to put this event in perspective
This event is not a catastrophe because it is not life threatening. It can be viewed as a trivial life event, a normal life problem that needs to be solved not dramatised.

I choose to view this event as average, falling within the normal range
This event is not exceptional; many people have gone through this.

It's temporary - "this too shall pass"
Life is constantly changing and moving through phases and this situation will also change.

Fears or facts?
Why fear? It may not happen!

I choose to focus on this as a learning experience
Every problem that comes my way is an opportunity for me to learn about my strengths and weaknesses, others and life.

Feel soothing emotions:

I choose to feel warm, loving emotions. I do this by focusing on my heart and letting love, trust forgiveness, compassion, hope or gratitude fill my heart space.

Behave constructively:

I choose to work in part acts:
I will break the overwhelming job into manageable parts.

Do the difficult:
I will face what I fear and act with self-discipline

I choose to solutionise:
I will find a solution by taking advice or doing research.

Prioritise myself:
I will keep my life balanced by meeting friends, doing exercise or laughing.

Compartmentalise:
I will not let this event cloud my whole day; I will focus on something else now.

Utilise calming strategies:

When I:
- relax,
- breathe deeply,
- go for a run,
- shower,
- lie down,
- read,
- watch TV,
- climb into a mental helicopter
- practice mindfulness, meditation, my mind and body calm down.

Step Four: The Self Motivation Process

Endorse yourself for any growth no matter how small.

In the past I would have…

_____

_____

But this time I…

_____

_____

Tick off the traits that you strengthened when you worked down your anxiety:

☐ generosity	☐ peacefulness
☐ kindness	☐ self-discipline
☐ compassion	☐ forgiveness
☐ consideration	☐ courage
☐ helpfulness	☐ responsibility
☐ respectfulness	☐ reliability
☐ honesty	☐ loyalty
☐ fairness	☐ love
☐ patience	☐ humility

Rate your anxiety on a scale of 0 to 100%:

☐ %

O

W

NOTES

NOTES

Session 6

BEHAVIOURAL TOOL: COMPARTMENTALISE

'I will not let this incident cloud my whole day: I will focus on something else now.'

Anxious thinking, and ruminating, can ruin your whole day and serve no real purpose. It is best to *fix it or ignore it*. How to ignore it? By distracting yourself with something else.

Distraction is not about trying to avoid reality. You are simply making a choice to intentionally focus on something else. You are fully in the moment, and being productive, but with an activity that is affirming rather than negating. When you distract yourself, your anxiety will subside.

There are hundreds of ways that you can distract yourself from your anxious feelings or persistent worry. Here is a sample:

- Doodling on a piece of paper.

- Flipping through a magazine.

- Playing a game, including electronic games.

- Spending time connecting on Facebook.

- Going to a movie, watching TV or a video, listening to a lecture.

- Focusing on anything that interests you such as playing the piano, reading a gripping novel, painting, gardening, sewing, and scrapbooking.

- Putting all your energies into a new project.

- In fact, doing any activity that you enjoy will work to calm you down and soothe your anxiety levels.

Crafts and creative pursuits soothe the soul. However, crafts and hobbies seem to have lost their appeal with the advent of technology. I would like to encourage you to bring a hobby into your life as an effective tool to manage anxiety.

A hobby can be used in a curative manner. For instance, when you feel anxious and go outside to garden, you will calm down.

Being engaged in an ongoing hobby can also be preventative. For instance, people who garden regularly, derive immense satisfaction, wellbeing and purpose from gardening, which goes a long way to reducing anxiety in the long term.

EXERCISE NINETEEN

Complete this exercise to help you think about your hobbies and interests. Hobbies include crafts, creative endeavors or collections. They do not include sport or exercise.

What are your hobbies?

_____

_____

_____

Which ones are constantly accessible? (e.g. reading)

_____

_____

_____

Which ones are only accessible at times?

_____

_____

_____

Do you think you could use any of the above listed hobbies to distract yourself from your worries?

_____

_____

_____

Can you think of any other hobbies that could work for you in the future?

_____

_____

_____

How could you go about incorporating these new hobbies into your life?

_____

_____

_____

Session 6

BEHAVIOURAL TOOL: PRIORITISE MYSELF

'I will keep my life balanced by meeting friends, doing exercise or laughing.'

We live in a world where we have forgotten how to prioritise ourselves. The focus in the Western world is success at work and material wealth. This usually translates into working long and hard and neglecting other parts of our life.

Over the years, I have said to clients that overwork: 'No matter how important a situation is, your physical and mental health should take top priority.' One common response I get is: 'Isn't it indulgent to put yourself first?' Another common response is: 'But I have to make a living and cannot take time off for myself'.

The story about a woodcutter (per Stephen Covey) demonstrates the need to prioritise yourself. This woodcutter was in a large forest, attempting to saw down a tree but not getting very far because his saw was blunt. An observant passer-by stopped to point out that the saw was blunt and needed sharpening. The woodcutter angrily replied *'Do you think I am stupid? Do you think that I do not know that the saw is blunt? Can you see how large this forest is and how many trees I still have to cut? I simply do not have time to sharpen the saw!'*

In the story, the saw is a metaphor for you. You may believe that you have so much to get through every day that you have no time to sharpen the saw, that is, to replenish yourself. This belief is foolhardy because a blunt saw is ineffective. If the woodcutter had taken time to sharpen the saw, he would have completed his job in the forest much faster and more efficiently.

Similarly, if you take the time to keep mentally and physically fit, you will achieve much more in the long-term. You would also feel less anxious.

To sharpen the saw, every week you need to 'feed' the following five dimensions:

1. Physical
2. Spiritual
3. Mental
4. Social
5. Emotional

The Physical Dimension

This relates to eating, sleeping and exercise.

Do you eat a healthy balanced diet?   YES/NO

Do you get enough sleep?   YES/NO

Do you exercise regularly?   YES/NO

If you answered no to any of the above, please make a commitment to change here. Write down your plan of how you will make that change.

_____

_____

_____

_____

_____

_____

_____

The Spiritual Dimension

This relates to any religious or spiritual practice that 'feeds your soul'. It includes praying, participating at a house of worship, basking in nature, listening to music, meditating, and yoga.

Do you practice any of the above in a consistent manner? YES/NO

If no, make a commitment here to bring a spiritual practice into your daily life.

_____

_____

_____

_____

_____

_____

_____

The Mental Dimension

Mental refers to any activity which stimulates your brain but is different to your work. Even if you are a professor in math, you need to do some pleasurable mental task that will activate other parts of your brain.

Some suggestions are reading non-fiction, playing bridge, working out puzzles, learning to play a musical instrument or learning another language.

Do you enjoy stimulating mental activities outside of your work? YES/NO

If no, commit now to incorporating some into your weekly schedule.

_____

_____

_____

_____

_____

_____

_____

The Social Dimension

Meeting with friends and generally socialising is a very important tool. Mental health professionals recognise that social interactions are central to the treatment of anxiety and depression. The Black Dog Institute has 'socialising time' as a category on a par with bed time and exercise on its social and biological rhythms monitoring timetable, an adaption of which is listed here on page 135).

The main benefits of socialising can be summarised as:

- Socialising with others serves as a distraction. When you are busy chatting to friends, you forget your woes and can be quite animated.

- Socialising can force you to leave home and venture out to a different venue. This is therapeutic.

- Mixing with friends serves to help you to feel better about yourself. When you are anxious, you can be consumed with devaluing, negative self-talk. Your friends will remind you that you are a lovable human being.

- Friends understand us in a way that parents, siblings and family members cannot. We choose our friends and they choose us. They see value in us even when we mess up. We share good times and bad, and there is a wonderful acceptance of each other.

- Socialising is affirming because it reminds you that you do not only have a fearful, anxious side. You have many different facets. Your whole worth, therefore, cannot be measured by your anxious habits and thoughts.

- Much of anxiety centres on fear. Being with friends can reduce the fear. You do not feel alone in facing your problems. You receive support, advice, help and comfort.

In order to gain the maximum benefit from this tool, socialising needs to be built into the fabric of your life and seen as valuable for your mental wellbeing. Do not wait for plans to be made spontaneously. Make plans conscientiously every week. Filling in the social and biological rhythms monitoring timetable on page 135 will help you to do this.

Remember also, do not rely on others to take the lead. Be proactive and ensure that you are creating situations that will benefit you.

On those occasions that you do not feel like mixing with others, just DO IT anyway. Force yourself, drag yourself, do whatever it takes to get to the meeting point. After a few minutes, you will be so glad that you did. You will discover that socialising is much better than moping about alone in your river of anxieties at home.

An Illustration

A common experience is what happened to Jo. She was feeling very anxious and just wanted to be left alone. When her friend Daisy called, and insisted Jo join her for a coffee with friends, it was the last thing Jo felt like doing. However, she forced herself to go because she did not want Daisy to know how awful she felt.

Once she arrived however, and got caught up in the camaraderie, Jo's mood lifted. Her anxiety symptoms faded and she felt great.

EXERCISE TWENTY

Would you describe yourself as a loner?   YES/NO

If no, do you prioritise your social life?   YES/NO

If not, why not?

_____

_____

_____

How could you improve your social life?

_____

_____

_____

Name those friends that are fun to hang out with.

_____

_____

_____

Name those friends that you can confide in and ask for support.

_____

_____

_____

Do you feel that anxiety has interfered with your social life? If so, how could you remedy that? (This is not referring to social anxiety. This refers to anxiety about other things that interfere with you being social).

_____

_____

_____

Unless you are a true loner, a person who has no need for others, then socialising is vital for your mental health. Getting out of the house and mixing with others is part of your treatment.

Just like you plan to exercise and have meals, you need to plan to socialise.

Social Anxiety

It is common for individuals suffering from generalised anxiety or phobias to reduce their socialising because they do not feel good about themselves. However, it is an entirely different thing if you suffer from social anxiety. Social anxiety is when the source of your fear is mixing with others.

Do you suffer from social anxiety?   YES/NO

If yes, then it will be difficult to prioritise your social life until that anxiety is managed. The most effective way of doing it is to **gradually** expose yourself to social situations. This method of reducing anxiety levels is explained in detail in the section _Do the Difficult_ in Session 7.

Do you meet with any friends outside of work?   YES/NO

If no, make a commitment to start socialising more from today.

_____

_____

The Emotional Dimension

Emotional 'food' is a vital part of a stress free life. This means making time to share quality time with your partner and family. Sometimes it includes seeking help from a therapist.

Do you have a regular date night with your partner?   YES/NO

Do you make time for intimacy?   YES/NO

Do you have quality time with your kids?   YES/NO

Are you seeking emotional help if you are suffering from anxiety, depression or relationship issues?   YES/NO

If you said no to any of the above, please make a plan to do so right here and commit to starting right away.

Remember to prioritise your physical and mental health every single day. Do not let anyone or anything else convince you otherwise. When you feel well, healthy and energised, then the rest of your life is easier to deal with.

Set Your Biological Rhythms

Human beings have social and biological rhythms. This means we have a 'body clock' that switches functions on and off at different times. When your life has a regular rhythm, your body clock will run efficiently and you will feel good.

Sleep is an excellent example of this. You have natural chemical neurotransmitters in your brain that help you to fall asleep and others that help you to wake up and be alert. When you stick to regular bedtimes and wake up times, you will feel sleepy just before bedtime and alert at wake up time.

However, if you have no routine, your neurotransmitters have no idea what to do. Should they activate or de-activate? Are you expecting to be sleepy or to be alert? This confusion explains why sleeping for a longer time than usual often results in you feeling groggy rather than awake.

Similarly, when you eat at regular times, your digestive system will become active just before a meal, preparing your body for the digestion required. This is hunger. However, when you eat at random times, you may not be sure when you are hungry and you may crave food at odd times.

The Black Dog Institute discovered that when patients with depression lived their lives according to regular routines, their moods tended to be more stable. In fact, overall feelings of wellbeing improved. Many individuals who suffer from anxiety have found routines helpful too.

EXERCISE TWENTY-ONE

The timetable below was compiled by The Black Dog Institute to help patients decide on suitable routines and then monitor the benefits of sticking to the allocated time. Variations in mood frequently occur when routines are not consistent.

If you feel 'out of whack', then please fill in the timetable below. Choose times that fit into your lifestyle and that you are most likely to maintain.

Social and Biological Rhythms Monitoring Timetable adapted from Black Dog Institute

		Mon	Tues	Wed	Thurs	Fri	Sat	Sun	
Bed time	earlier								Usual/optimal time
	later								
Main meal time	earlier								Usual/optimal time
	later								
Socialising time	earlier								Usual/optimal time
	later								
Exercise time	earlier								Usual/optimal time
	later								
Time of leaving home to go out	earlier								Usual/optimal time
	later								
Waking up time	earlier								Usual/optimal time
	later								
Anxiety level									

Choose an optimum time for each of the following:

- Bed time
- Main meal time
- Wake up time
- Socialising time
- Exercising time

Below is an example of how the timetable will look when you fill it in.

		Mon	Tues	Wed	Thurs	Fri	Sat	Sun	
Bed time 11:00pm	Earlier X	X	X		X				Usual/optimal time
	later			X		X	X	
Main meal time 6:00pm	earlier X	X	X		X				Usual/optimal time
	later			X		X		
Socialising time 3:00pm	earlier X	X	X	X		X	X		Usual/optimal time
	later				X			
Exercise time 9:00am	earlier X		X		X				Usual/optimal time
	later							
Time of leaving home to go out 11:00am	earlier X	X	X	X	X	X			Usual/optimal time
	later						X	
Waking up time 7:00am	earlier X	X	X	X	X				Usual/optimal time
	later						X	
Anxiety level	1	3	1	4	3	7	8	

Begin following the timetable you constructed and continue to rate your anxiety on a daily basis on the daily monitoring diary. Observe if, and how much, inconsistency exacerbates your anxiety. If after a month, you find no difference, then by all means drop the routine. However, most people find that their overall mood improves and their anxiety lessens with regular routines.

BEHAVIOURAL TOOL: LAUGHTER

'A good joke is the best medicine.'

Laughing is therapeutic. When you laugh, certain hormones and neurotransmitters are released which lead to positive feelings and increased immunity. When you laugh regularly, your mood lifts and you feel calmer.

Moreover, when you can see the humour in difficult situations, it signifies mental resilience. For instance, let's say your shoe breaks and you are forced to walk in a public place with one shoe off. You feel ridiculous. But if you can see the humour in it, and realise how funny you must look, it indicates resilience.

Resilience can be defined as bouncing up, in the face of a difficult situation.

Some people laugh more easily than others it is true. But like any skill, you can train yourself to see humour in situations. You can also train yourself to laugh long and hard — what is called a belly laugh.

As a tool to lower your anxiety, ensure that you laugh regularly, long and hard. Read joke books, watch sitcoms and full-length comedies. Find the style of humour that appeals to you and indulge. Build having a good laugh into your daily schedule.

EXERCISE TWENTY-TWO

What types of humour do you enjoy?

_____

_____

_____

Where do you source it?

_____

_____

_____

Have you ever thought about consciously seeking out laughter?   YES/NO.
Describe how you might do this.

_____

_____

_____

_____

Write a plan of how you can incorporate laughter into your daily life.

_____

_____

_____

_____

DAILY MONITORING DIARY

WEEK ENDING _____

Day	M	T	W	T	F	S	S
Overall Anxiety Rating for the day (0-10)							

1. EXERCISE

	M	T	W	T	F	S	S
How long?							
Anxiety level before (0-10)							
Anxiety level after (0-10)							

2. BREATHING & RELAXATION

	M	T	W	T	F	S	S
How long?							
Anxiety level before (0-10)							
Anxiety level after (0-10)							

3. CATASTROPHIC THINKING

	M	T	W	T	F	S	S
How often this type of thought occurred							
Belief in thoughts before challenging (0-10)							
Belief in thoughts after challenging (0-10)							

4. FEARS NOT FACTS

	M	T	W	T	F	S	S
How often this type of thought occurred							
Belief in thoughts before challenging (0-10)							
Belief in thoughts after challenging (0-10)							

5. PERVASIVE PESSIMISTIC THINKING

	M	T	W	T	F	S	S
How often this type of thought occurred							
Belief in thoughts before challenging (0-10)							
Belief in thoughts after challenging (0-10)							

6. PERMANENT PESSIMISTIC THINKING

	M	T	W	T	F	S	S
How often this type of thought occurred							
Belief in thoughts before challenging (0-10)							
Belief in thoughts after challenging (0-10)							

7. MINDFULNESS (FORMAL, GROUNDING, INFORMAL MINDFULNESS)

	M	T	W	T	F	S	S
How long?							
Anxiety level before (0-10)							
Anxiety level after (0-10)							

8. EXCEPTIONAL THINKING

	M	T	W	T	F	S	S
How often this type of thought occurred							
Belief in thoughts before challenging (0-10)							
Belief in thoughts after challenging (0-10)							

Anxiety Management Worksheet

The purpose of this worksheet is to help you to see every stressful event as an opportunity for
1. greater understanding of yourself, your anxiety and the people around you, and
2. practicing tools to manage your anxiety.

Step One: An Event

Briefly describe an event when you became anxious. Give such details as time, place and people involved, and end with "That's when I began to work myself up..."

_____

_____ E

_____

_____ Rate your anxiety on a scale of 0 to 100%: [＿＿＿] %

Step Two: The Working-Up Process

Learn about your working up process by identifying your thoughts, feelings, behaviours and bodily reactions during the event. Tick the ones that most resonate with you.

Undermining Beliefs

I fear that I have lost...
- ☐ approval
- ☐ control
- ☐ co-operation
- ☐ face
- ☐ respect
- ☐ success
- ☐ trust
- ☐ validation
- ☐ love

This event proves that I am...
- ☐ stupid
- ☐ abnormal
- ☐ incompetent
- ☐ lazy
- ☐ irresponsible
- ☐ a total failure
- ☐ undisciplined
- ☐ untogether
- ☐ useless

B

I worry that I will suffer...
- ☐ mental collapse
- ☐ illness
- ☐ financial hardship

What I want is...
- ☐ total control
- ☐ respect
- ☐ success
- ☐ perfection
- ☐ comfort
- ☐ fairness
- ☐ tranquility
- ☐ all the answers
- ☐ for life to go smoothly
- ☐ to be all things to all people

Self-destructive Behaviour

Active
- ☐ get violent
- ☐ swear
- ☐ slam doors
- ☐ run away
- ☐ overeat
- ☐ harm myself
- ☐ criticise

Passive
- ☐ take it too seriously
- ☐ give up
- ☐ wallow in self pity
- ☐ sulk
- ☐ space out
- ☐ procrastinate
- ☐ give in
- ☐ be controlled

Intense Feelings

Angry feelings
- ☐ hateful
- ☐ aggravated
- ☐ annoyed
- ☐ hostile
- ☐ outraged
- ☐ punitive
- ☐ resentful
- ☐ vengeful

Fearful feelings
- ☐ helpless
- ☐ hopeless
- ☐ disappointed
- ☐ sad

- ☐ attacked
- ☐ worn out
- ☐ rejected
- ☐ jealous
- ☐ afraid
- ☐ exploited
- ☐ lonely
- ☐ abandoned
- ☐ guilty
- ☐ insulted
- ☐ confused
- ☐ disillusioned
- ☐ misunderstood
- ☐ trapped

Bodily Reactions (Limbic System)

I am uncomfortable because I am experiencing...
- ☐ tremors
- ☐ nausea
- ☐ sweaty palms
- ☐ stomach-ache
- ☐ pounding heart
- ☐ general tension
- ☐ fatigue
- ☐ imagination on fire
- ☐ headache
- ☐ dry mouth
- ☐ jaw clenching
- ☐ shortness of breath

Continued over

B   F   L

Step Three: The Working-Down Process

Begin with, "Suddenly I realised that I was anxious and that I had choices..." This is the step of self-leadership and trust in one's ability to handle the situation.

Choose helpful thoughts:

I choose to depersonalise
There is no intention to hurt me. He is doing the best he can with the tools he has at the moment.

I choose realism over romanticism
Life presents many obstacles. I lower or raise standards as needed.

There is no right or wrong
Unless it is a moral issue, I will see it simply as a difference of opinion and/or taste.

I choose the total view of positivity
Even though this event is negative, the total view of his behaviour is positive.

I surrender control
Since I cannot change this situation, I choose to let go of it

I choose to put this event in perspective
This event is not a catastrophe because it is not life threatening. It can be viewed as a trivial life event, a normal life problem that needs to be solved not dramatised.

I choose to view this event as average, falling within the normal range
This event is not exceptional; many people have gone through this.

It's temporary - "this too shall pass"
Life is constantly changing and moving through phases and this situation will also change.

Fears or facts?
Why fear? It may not happen!

I choose to focus on this as a learning experience
Every problem that comes my way is an opportunity for me to learn about my strengths and weaknesses, others and life.

Feel soothing emotions:

I choose to feel warm, loving emotions. I do this by focusing on my heart and letting love, trust forgiveness, compassion, hope or gratitude fill my heart space.

Behave constructively:

I choose to work in part acts:
I will break the overwhelming job into manageable parts.

Do the difficult:
I will face what I fear and act with self-discipline

I choose to solutionise:
I will find a solution by taking advice or doing research.

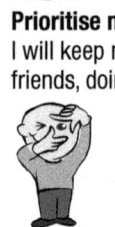

Prioritise myself:
I will keep my life balanced by meeting friends, doing exercise or laughing.

Compartmentalise:
I will not let this event cloud my whole day; I will focus on something else now.

Utilise calming strategies:

When I:
• relax,
• breathe deeply,
• go for a run,
• shower,
• lie down,
• read,
• watch TV,
• climb into a mental helicopter
• practice mindfulness, meditation, my mind and body calm down.

Step Four: The Self Motivation Process

Endorse yourself for any growth no matter how small.

In the past I would have...

_____

_____

But this time I...

_____

_____

Tick off the traits that you strengthened when you worked down your anxiety:

☐ generosity	☐ peacefulness
☐ kindness	☐ self-discipline
☐ compassion	☐ forgiveness
☐ consideration	☐ courage
☐ helpfulness	☐ responsibility
☐ respectfulness	☐ reliability
☐ honesty	☐ loyalty
☐ fairness	☐ love
☐ patience	☐ humility

Rate your anxiety on a scale of 0 to 100%:

[____]%

O   W

Anxiety Management Worksheet

The purpose of this worksheet is to help you to see every stressful event as an opportunity for
1. greater understanding of yourself, your anxiety and the people around you, and
2. practicing tools to manage your anxiety.

Step One: An Event

Briefly describe an event when you became anxious. Give such details as time, place and people involved, and end with "That's when I began to work myself up..."

E

Rate your anxiety on a scale of 0 to 100%: ____ %

Step Two: The Working-Up Process

Learn about your working up process by identifying your thoughts, feelings, behaviours and bodily reactions during the event. Tick the ones that most resonate with you.

Undermining Beliefs

I fear that I have lost...
- [ ] approval
- [ ] control
- [ ] co-operation
- [ ] face
- [ ] respect
- [ ] success
- [ ] trust
- [ ] validation
- [ ] love

This event proves that I am...
- [ ] stupid
- [ ] abnormal
- [ ] incompetent
- [ ] lazy
- [ ] irresponsible
- [ ] a total failure
- [ ] undisciplined
- [ ] untogether
- [ ] useless

B

I worry that I will suffer...
- [ ] mental collapse
- [ ] illness
- [ ] financial hardship

What I want is...
- [ ] total control
- [ ] respect
- [ ] success
- [ ] perfection
- [ ] comfort
- [ ] fairness
- [ ] tranquility
- [ ] all the answers
- [ ] for life to go smoothly
- [ ] to be all things to all people

Self-destructive Behaviour

Active
- [ ] get violent
- [ ] swear
- [ ] slam doors
- [ ] run away
- [ ] overeat
- [ ] harm myself
- [ ] criticise

Passive
- [ ] take it too seriously
- [ ] give up
- [ ] wallow in self pity
- [ ] sulk
- [ ] space out
- [ ] procrastinate
- [ ] give in
- [ ] be controlled

Intense Feelings

Angry feelings
- [ ] hateful
- [ ] aggravated
- [ ] annoyed
- [ ] hostile
- [ ] outraged
- [ ] punitive
- [ ] resentful
- [ ] vengeful

Fearful feelings
- [ ] helpless
- [ ] hopeless
- [ ] disappointed
- [ ] sad

- [ ] attacked
- [ ] worn out
- [ ] rejected
- [ ] jealous
- [ ] afraid
- [ ] exploited
- [ ] lonely
- [ ] abandoned
- [ ] guilty
- [ ] insulted
- [ ] confused
- [ ] disillusioned
- [ ] misunderstood
- [ ] trapped

Bodily Reactions (Limbic System)

I am uncomfortable because I am experiencing...
- [ ] tremors
- [ ] nausea
- [ ] sweaty palms
- [ ] stomach-ache
- [ ] pounding heart
- [ ] general tension
- [ ] fatigue
- [ ] imagination on fire
- [ ] headache
- [ ] dry mouth
- [ ] jaw clenching
- [ ] shortness of breath

Continued over

B   F   L

Step Three: The Working-Down Process

Begin with, "Suddenly I realised that I was anxious and that I had choices..." This is the step of self-leadership and trust in one's ability to handle the situation.

Choose helpful thoughts:

I choose to depersonalise
There is no intention to hurt me. He is doing the best he can with the tools he has at the moment.

I choose realism over romanticism
Life presents many obstacles. I lower or raise standards as needed.

There is no right or wrong
Unless it is a moral issue, I will see it simply as a difference of opinion and/or taste.

I choose the total view of positivity
Even though this event is negative, the total view of his behaviour is positive.

I surrender control
Since I cannot change this situation, I choose to let go of it

I choose to put this event in perspective
This event is not a catastrophe because it is not life threatening. It can be viewed as a trivial life event, a normal life problem that needs to be solved not dramatised.

I choose to view this event as average, falling within the normal range
This event is not exceptional; many people have gone through this.

It's temporary - "this too shall pass"
Life is constantly changing and moving through phases and this situation will also change.

Fears or facts?
Why fear? It may not happen!

I choose to focus on this as a learning experience
Every problem that comes my way is an opportunity for me to learn about my strengths and weaknesses, others and life.

Feel soothing emotions:

I choose to feel warm, loving emotions. I do this by focusing on my heart and letting love, trust forgiveness, compassion, hope or gratitude fill my heart space.

Behave constructively:

I choose to work in part acts:
I will break the overwhelming job into manageable parts.

Do the difficult:
I will face what I fear and act with self-discipline

I choose to solutionise:
I will find a solution by taking advice or doing research.

Prioritise myself:
I will keep my life balanced by meeting friends, doing exercise or laughing.

Compartmentalise:
I will not let this event cloud my whole day; I will focus on something else now.

Utilise calming strategies:

When I:
- relax,
- breathe deeply,
- go for a run,
- shower,
- lie down,
- read,
- watch TV,
- climb into a mental helicopter
- practice mindfulness, meditation, my mind and body calm down.

Step Four: The Self Motivation Process

Endorse yourself for any growth no matter how small.

In the past I would have...

_____

_____

But this time I...

_____

_____

Tick off the traits that you strengthened when you worked down your anxiety:

☐	generosity	☐	peacefulness
☐	kindness	☐	self-discipline
☐	compassion	☐	forgiveness
☐	consideration	☐	courage
☐	helpfulness	☐	responsibility
☐	respectfulness	☐	reliability
☐	honesty	☐	loyalty
☐	fairness	☐	love
☐	patience	☐	humility

Rate your anxiety on a scale of 0 to 100%:

_____%

O

W

Anxiety Management Worksheet

The purpose of this worksheet is to help you to see every stressful event as an opportunity for
1. greater understanding of yourself, your anxiety and the people around you, and
2. practicing tools to manage your anxiety.

Step One: An Event

Briefly describe an event when you became anxious. Give such details as time, place and people involved, and end with "That's when I began to work myself up..."

_____

_____ E

_____

_____ Rate your anxiety on a scale of 0 to 100%: [   ] %

Step Two: The Working-Up Process

Learn about your working up process by identifying your thoughts, feelings, behaviours and bodily reactions during the event. Tick the ones that most resonate with you.

Undermining Beliefs

I fear that I have lost...
- ☐ approval
- ☐ control
- ☐ co-operation
- ☐ face
- ☐ respect
- ☐ success
- ☐ trust
- ☐ validation
- ☐ love

This event proves that I am...
- ☐ stupid
- ☐ abnormal
- ☐ incompetent
- ☐ lazy
- ☐ irresponsible
- ☐ a total failure
- ☐ undisciplined
- ☐ untogether
- ☐ useless

B

I worry that I will suffer...
- ☐ mental collapse
- ☐ illness
- ☐ financial hardship

What I want is...
- ☐ total control
- ☐ respect
- ☐ success
- ☐ perfection
- ☐ comfort
- ☐ fairness
- ☐ tranquility
- ☐ all the answers
- ☐ for life to go smoothly
- ☐ to be all things to all people

Self-destructive Behaviour

Active
- ☐ get violent
- ☐ swear
- ☐ slam doors
- ☐ run away
- ☐ overeat
- ☐ harm myself
- ☐ criticise

Passive
- ☐ take it too seriously
- ☐ give up
- ☐ wallow in self pity
- ☐ sulk
- ☐ space out
- ☐ procrastinate
- ☐ give in
- ☐ be controlled

Intense Feelings

Angry feelings
- ☐ hateful
- ☐ aggravated
- ☐ annoyed
- ☐ hostile
- ☐ outraged
- ☐ punitive
- ☐ resentful
- ☐ vengeful

Fearful feelings
- ☐ helpless
- ☐ hopeless
- ☐ disappointed
- ☐ sad

- ☐ attacked
- ☐ worn out
- ☐ rejected
- ☐ jealous
- ☐ afraid
- ☐ exploited
- ☐ lonely
- ☐ abandoned
- ☐ guilty
- ☐ insulted
- ☐ confused
- ☐ disillusioned
- ☐ misunderstood
- ☐ trapped

Bodily Reactions (Limbic System)

I am uncomfortable because I am experiencing...
- ☐ tremors
- ☐ nausea
- ☐ sweaty palms
- ☐ stomach-ache
- ☐ pounding heart
- ☐ general tension
- ☐ fatigue
- ☐ imagination on fire
- ☐ headache
- ☐ dry mouth
- ☐ jaw clenching
- ☐ shortness of breath

Continued over

B   F   L

Step Three: The Working-Down Process

Begin with, "Suddenly I realised that I was anxious and that I had choices..." This is the step of self-leadership and trust in one's ability to handle the situation.

Choose helpful thoughts:

I choose to depersonalise
There is no intention to hurt me. He is doing the best he can with the tools he has at the moment.

I choose realism over romanticism
Life presents many obstacles. I lower or raise standards as needed.

There is no right or wrong
Unless it is a moral issue, I will see it simply as a difference of opinion and/or taste.

I choose the total view of positivity
Even though this event is negative, the total view of his behaviour is positive.

I surrender control
Since I cannot change this situation, I choose to let go of it

I choose to put this event in perspective
This event is not a catastrophe because it is not life threatening. It can be viewed as a trivial life event, a normal life problem that needs to be solved not dramatised.

I choose to view this event as average, falling within the normal range
This event is not exceptional; many people have gone through this.

It's temporary - "this too shall pass"
Life is constantly changing and moving through phases and this situation will also change.

Fears or facts?
Why fear? It may not happen!

I choose to focus on this as a learning experience
Every problem that comes my way is an opportunity for me to learn about my strengths and weaknesses, others and life.

Feel soothing emotions:

I choose to feel warm, loving emotions. I do this by focusing on my heart and letting love, trust forgiveness, compassion, hope or gratitude fill my heart space.

Behave constructively:

I choose to work in part acts:
I will break the overwhelming job into manageable parts.

Do the difficult:
I will face what I fear and act with self-discipline

I choose to solutionise:
I will find a solution by taking advice or doing research.

Prioritise myself:
I will keep my life balanced by meeting friends, doing exercise or laughing.

Compartmentalise:
I will not let this event cloud my whole day; I will focus on something else now.

Utilise calming strategies:

When I:
• relax,
• breathe deeply,
• go for a run,
• shower,
• lie down,
• read,
• watch TV,
• climb into a mental helicopter
• practice mindfulness, meditation, my mind and body calm down.

Step Four: The Self Motivation Process

Endorse yourself for any growth no matter how small.

In the past I would have...

_____

_____

But this time I...

_____

_____

Tick off the traits that you strengthened when you worked down your anxiety:

☐ generosity	☐ peacefulness
☐ kindness	☐ self-discipline
☐ compassion	☐ forgiveness
☐ consideration	☐ courage
☐ helpfulness	☐ responsibility
☐ respectfulness	☐ reliability
☐ honesty	☐ loyalty
☐ fairness	☐ love
☐ patience	☐ humility

Rate your anxiety on a scale of 0 to 100%:

[_____]%

0

W

Session 6

Anxiety Management Worksheet

The purpose of this worksheet is to help you to see every stressful event as an opportunity for
1. greater understanding of yourself, your anxiety and the people around you, and
2. practicing tools to manage your anxiety.

Step One: An Event

Briefly describe an event when you became anxious. Give such details as time, place and people involved, and end with "That's when I began to work myself up..."

_____

_____   E

_____

_____ Rate your anxiety on a scale of 0 to 100%: [   ] %

Step Two: The Working-Up Process

Learn about your working up process by identifying your thoughts, feelings, behaviours and bodily reactions during the event. Tick the ones that most resonate with you.

Undermining Beliefs

I fear that I have lost...
- ☐ approval
- ☐ control
- ☐ co-operation
- ☐ face
- ☐ respect
- ☐ success
- ☐ trust
- ☐ validation
- ☐ love

This event proves that I am...
- ☐ stupid
- ☐ abnormal
- ☐ incompetent
- ☐ lazy
- ☐ irresponsible
- ☐ a total failure
- ☐ undisciplined
- ☐ untogether
- ☐ useless

B

I worry that I will suffer...
- ☐ mental collapse
- ☐ illness
- ☐ financial hardship

What I want is...
- ☐ total control
- ☐ respect
- ☐ success
- ☐ perfection
- ☐ comfort
- ☐ fairness
- ☐ tranquility
- ☐ all the answers
- ☐ for life to go smoothly
- ☐ to be all things to all people

Self-destructive Behaviour

Active
- ☐ get violent
- ☐ swear
- ☐ slam doors
- ☐ run away
- ☐ overeat
- ☐ harm myself
- ☐ criticise

Passive
- ☐ take it too seriously
- ☐ give up
- ☐ wallow in self pity
- ☐ sulk
- ☐ space out
- ☐ procrastinate
- ☐ give in
- ☐ be controlled

Intense Feelings

Angry feelings
- ☐ hateful
- ☐ aggravated
- ☐ annoyed
- ☐ hostile
- ☐ outraged
- ☐ punitive
- ☐ resentful
- ☐ vengeful

Fearful feelings
- ☐ helpless
- ☐ hopeless
- ☐ disappointed
- ☐ sad
- ☐ attacked
- ☐ worn out
- ☐ rejected
- ☐ jealous
- ☐ afraid
- ☐ exploited
- ☐ lonely
- ☐ abandoned
- ☐ guilty
- ☐ insulted
- ☐ confused
- ☐ disillusioned
- ☐ misunderstood
- ☐ trapped

Bodily Reactions (Limbic System)

I am uncomfortable because I am experiencing...
- ☐ tremors
- ☐ nausea
- ☐ sweaty palms
- ☐ stomach-ache
- ☐ pounding heart
- ☐ general tension
- ☐ fatigue
- ☐ imagination on fire
- ☐ headache
- ☐ dry mouth
- ☐ jaw clenching
- ☐ shortness of breath

Continued over

B   F   L

Step Three: The Working-Down Process

Begin with, "Suddenly I realised that I was anxious and that I had choices..." This is the step of self-leadership and trust in one's ability to handle the situation.

Choose helpful thoughts:

I choose to depersonalise
There is no intention to hurt me. He is doing the best he can with the tools he has at the moment.

I choose realism over romanticism
Life presents many obstacles. I lower or raise standards as needed.

There is no right or wrong
Unless it is a moral issue, I will see it simply as a difference of opinion and/or taste.

I choose the total view of positivity
Even though this event is negative, the total view of his behaviour is positive.

I surrender control
Since I cannot change this situation, I choose to let go of it

I choose to put this event in perspective
This event is not a catastrophe because it is not life threatening. It can be viewed as a trivial life event, a normal life problem that needs to be solved not dramatised.

I choose to view this event as average, falling within the normal range
This event is not exceptional; many people have gone through this.

It's temporary - "this too shall pass"
Life is constantly changing and moving through phases and this situation will also change.

Fears or facts?
Why fear? It may not happen!

I choose to focus on this as a learning experience
Every problem that comes my way is an opportunity for me to learn about my strengths and weaknesses, others and life.

Feel soothing emotions:

I choose to feel warm, loving emotions. I do this by focusing on my heart and letting love, trust forgiveness, compassion, hope or gratitude fill my heart space.

Behave constructively:

I choose to work in part acts:
I will break the overwhelming job into manageable parts.

Do the difficult:
I will face what I fear and act with self-discipline

I choose to solutionise:
I will find a solution by taking advice or doing research.

Prioritise myself:
I will keep my life balanced by meeting friends, doing exercise or laughing.

Compartmentalise:
I will not let this event cloud my whole day; I will focus on something else now.

Utilise calming strategies:

When I:
• relax,
• breathe deeply,
• go for a run,
• shower,
• lie down,
• read,
• watch TV,
• climb into a mental helicopter
• practice mindfulness, meditation, my mind and body calm down.

Step Four: The Self Motivation Process

Endorse yourself for any growth no matter how small.

In the past I would have...

_____

_____

But this time I...

_____

_____

Tick off the traits that you strengthened when you worked down your anxiety:

☐ generosity	☐ peacefulness	
☐ kindness	☐ self-discipline	
☐ compassion	☐ forgiveness	
☐ consideration	☐ courage	
☐ helpfulness	☐ responsibility	
☐ respectfulness	☐ reliability	
☐ honesty	☐ loyalty	
☐ fairness	☐ love	
☐ patience	☐ humility	

Rate your anxiety on a scale of 0 to 100%:

☐ %

O   W

Session 6

Anxiety Management Worksheet

The purpose of this worksheet is to help you to see every stressful event as an opportunity for
1. greater understanding of yourself, your anxiety and the people around you, and
2. practicing tools to manage your anxiety.

Step One: An Event

Briefly describe an event when you became anxious. Give such details as time, place and people involved, and end with "That's when I began to work myself up..."

_____

_____ E

_____

_____ Rate your anxiety on a scale of 0 to 100%: [   ] %

Step Two: The Working-Up Process

Learn about your working up process by identifying your thoughts, feelings, behaviours and bodily reactions during the event. Tick the ones that most resonate with you.

Undermining Beliefs

I fear that I have lost...
- ☐ approval
- ☐ success
- ☐ control
- ☐ trust
- ☐ co-operation
- ☐ validation
- ☐ face
- ☐ love
- ☐ respect

This event proves that I am...
- ☐ stupid
- ☐ a total failure
- ☐ abnormal
- ☐ undisciplined
- ☐ incompetent
- ☐ untogether
- ☐ lazy
- ☐ useless
- ☐ irresponsible

B

I worry that I will suffer...
- ☐ mental collapse
- ☐ illness
- ☐ financial hardship

What I want is...
- ☐ total control
- ☐ tranquility
- ☐ respect
- ☐ all the answers
- ☐ success
- ☐ for life to go smoothly
- ☐ perfection
- ☐ comfort
- ☐ to be all things to all people
- ☐ fairness

Self-destructive Behaviour

Active
- ☐ get violent
- ☐ swear
- ☐ slam doors
- ☐ run away
- ☐ overeat
- ☐ harm myself
- ☐ criticise

Passive
- ☐ take it too seriously
- ☐ give up
- ☐ wallow in self pity
- ☐ sulk
- ☐ space out
- ☐ procrastinate
- ☐ give in
- ☐ be controlled

Intense Feelings

Angry feelings
- ☐ hateful
- ☐ attacked
- ☐ aggravated
- ☐ worn out
- ☐ annoyed
- ☐ rejected
- ☐ hostile
- ☐ jealous
- ☐ outraged
- ☐ afraid
- ☐ punitive
- ☐ exploited
- ☐ resentful
- ☐ lonely
- ☐ vengeful
- ☐ abandoned
- ☐ guilty

Fearful feelings
- ☐ insulted
- ☐ helpless
- ☐ confused
- ☐ hopeless
- ☐ disillusioned
- ☐ disappointed
- ☐ misunderstood
- ☐ sad
- ☐ trapped

Bodily Reactions (Limbic System)

I am uncomfortable because I am experiencing...
- ☐ tremors
- ☐ nausea
- ☐ sweaty palms
- ☐ stomach-ache
- ☐ pounding heart
- ☐ general tension
- ☐ fatigue
- ☐ imagination on fire
- ☐ headache
- ☐ dry mouth
- ☐ jaw clenching
- ☐ shortness of breath

Continued over

B   F   L

Page 147

Step Three: The Working-Down Process

Begin with, "Suddenly I realised that I was anxious and that I had choices..." This is the step of self-leadership and trust in one's ability to handle the situation.

Choose helpful thoughts:

I choose to depersonalise
There is no intention to hurt me. He is doing the best he can with the tools he has at the moment.

I choose realism over romanticism
Life presents many obstacles. I lower or raise standards as needed.

There is no right or wrong
Unless it is a moral issue, I will see it simply as a difference of opinion and/or taste.

I choose the total view of positivity
Even though this event is negative, the total view of his behaviour is positive.

I surrender control
Since I cannot change this situation, I choose to let go of it

I choose to put this event in perspective
This event is not a catastrophe because it is not life threatening. It can be viewed as a trivial life event, a normal life problem that needs to be solved not dramatised.

I choose to view this event as average, falling within the normal range
This event is not exceptional; many people have gone through this.

It's temporary - "this too shall pass"
Life is constantly changing and moving through phases and this situation will also change.

Fears or facts?
Why fear? It may not happen!

I choose to focus on this as a learning experience
Every problem that comes my way is an opportunity for me to learn about my strengths and weaknesses, others and life.

Feel soothing emotions:

I choose to feel warm, loving emotions. I do this by focusing on my heart and letting love, trust forgiveness, compassion, hope or gratitude fill my heart space.

Behave constructively:

I choose to work in part acts:
I will break the overwhelming job into manageable parts.

Do the difficult:
I will face what I fear and act with self-discipline

I choose to solutionise:
I will find a solution by taking advice or doing research.

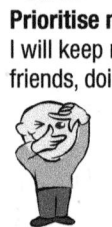

Prioritise myself:
I will keep my life balanced by meeting friends, doing exercise or laughing.

Compartmentalise:
I will not let this event cloud my whole day; I will focus on something else now.

Utilise calming strategies:

When I:
- relax,
- breathe deeply,
- go for a run,
- shower,
- lie down,
- read,
- watch TV,
- climb into a mental helicopter
- practice mindfulness, meditation, my mind and body calm down.

Step Four: The Self Motivation Process

Endorse yourself for any growth no matter how small.

In the past I would have...

_____

_____

But this time I...

_____

_____

Tick off the traits that you strengthened when you worked down your anxiety:

☐ generosity	☐ peacefulness
☐ kindness	☐ self-discipline
☐ compassion	☐ forgiveness
☐ consideration	☐ courage
☐ helpfulness	☐ responsibility
☐ respectfulness	☐ reliability
☐ honesty	☐ loyalty
☐ fairness	☐ love
☐ patience	☐ humility

Rate your anxiety on a scale of 0 to 100%:

[____]%

O

W

Session 6

Anxiety Management Worksheet

The purpose of this worksheet is to help you to see every stressful event as an opportunity for
1. greater understanding of yourself, your anxiety and the people around you, and
2. practicing tools to manage your anxiety.

Step One: An Event

Briefly describe an event when you became anxious. Give such details as time, place and people involved, and end with "That's when I began to work myself up..."

_____

_____ E

_____

_____ Rate your anxiety on a scale of 0 to 100%: [＿＿＿] %

Step Two: The Working-Up Process

Learn about your working up process by identifying your thoughts, feelings, behaviours and bodily reactions during the event. Tick the ones that most resonate with you.

Undermining Beliefs

I fear that I have lost...
- ☐ approval
- ☐ control
- ☐ co-operation
- ☐ face
- ☐ respect
- ☐ success
- ☐ trust
- ☐ validation
- ☐ love

This event proves that I am...
- ☐ stupid
- ☐ abnormal
- ☐ incompetent
- ☐ lazy
- ☐ irresponsible
- ☐ a total failure
- ☐ undisciplined
- ☐ untogether
- ☐ useless

B

I worry that I will suffer...
- ☐ mental collapse
- ☐ illness
- ☐ financial hardship

What I want is...
- ☐ total control
- ☐ respect
- ☐ success
- ☐ perfection
- ☐ comfort
- ☐ fairness
- ☐ tranquility
- ☐ all the answers
- ☐ for life to go smoothly
- ☐ to be all things to all people

Self-destructive Behaviour

Active
- ☐ get violent
- ☐ swear
- ☐ slam doors
- ☐ run away
- ☐ overeat
- ☐ harm myself
- ☐ criticise

Passive
- ☐ take it too seriously
- ☐ give up
- ☐ wallow in self pity
- ☐ sulk
- ☐ space out
- ☐ procrastinate
- ☐ give in
- ☐ be controlled

Intense Feelings

Angry feelings
- ☐ hateful
- ☐ aggravated
- ☐ annoyed
- ☐ hostile
- ☐ outraged
- ☐ punitive
- ☐ resentful
- ☐ vengeful

Fearful feelings
- ☐ helpless
- ☐ hopeless
- ☐ disappointed
- ☐ sad
- ☐ attacked
- ☐ worn out
- ☐ rejected
- ☐ jealous
- ☐ afraid
- ☐ exploited
- ☐ lonely
- ☐ abandoned
- ☐ guilty
- ☐ insulted
- ☐ confused
- ☐ disillusioned
- ☐ misunderstood
- ☐ trapped

Bodily Reactions (Limbic System)

I am uncomfortable because I am experiencing...
- ☐ tremors
- ☐ nausea
- ☐ sweaty palms
- ☐ stomach-ache
- ☐ pounding heart
- ☐ general tension
- ☐ fatigue
- ☐ imagination on fire
- ☐ headache
- ☐ dry mouth
- ☐ jaw clenching
- ☐ shortness of breath

Continued over

B   F   L

Step Three: The Working-Down Process

Begin with, "Suddenly I realised that I was anxious and that I had choices..." This is the step of self-leadership and trust in one's ability to handle the situation.

Choose helpful thoughts:

I choose to depersonalise
There is no intention to hurt me. He is doing the best he can with the tools he has at the moment.

I choose realism over romanticism
Life presents many obstacles. I lower or raise standards as needed.

There is no right or wrong
Unless it is a moral issue, I will see it simply as a difference of opinion and/or taste.

I choose the total view of positivity
Even though this event is negative, the total view of his behaviour is positive.

I surrender control
Since I cannot change this situation, I choose to let go of it

I choose to put this event in perspective
This event is not a catastrophe because it is not life threatening. It can be viewed as a trivial life event, a normal life problem that needs to be solved not dramatised.

I choose to view this event as average, falling within the normal range
This event is not exceptional; many people have gone through this.

It's temporary - "this too shall pass"
Life is constantly changing and moving through phases and this situation will also change.

Fears or facts?
Why fear? It may not happen!

I choose to focus on this as a learning experience
Every problem that comes my way is an opportunity for me to learn about my strengths and weaknesses, others and life.

Feel soothing emotions:

I choose to feel warm, loving emotions. I do this by focusing on my heart and letting love, trust forgiveness, compassion, hope or gratitude fill my heart space.

Behave constructively:

I choose to work in part acts:
I will break the overwhelming job into manageable parts.

Do the difficult:
I will face what I fear and act with self-discipline

I choose to solutionise:
I will find a solution by taking advice or doing research.

Prioritise myself:
I will keep my life balanced by meeting friends, doing exercise or laughing.

Compartmentalise:
I will not let this event cloud my whole day; I will focus on something else now.

Utilise calming strategies:

When I:
- relax,
- breathe deeply,
- go for a run,
- shower,
- lie down,
- read,
- watch TV,
- climb into a mental helicopter
- practice mindfulness, meditation, my mind and body calm down.

Step Four: The Self Motivation Process

Endorse yourself for any growth no matter how small.

In the past I would have...

_____

_____

But this time I...

_____

_____

Tick off the traits that you strengthened when you worked down your anxiety:

☐ generosity ☐ peacefulness
☐ kindness ☐ self-discipline
☐ compassion ☐ forgiveness
☐ consideration ☐ courage
☐ helpfulness ☐ responsibility
☐ respectfulness ☐ reliability
☐ honesty ☐ loyalty
☐ fairness ☐ love
☐ patience ☐ humility

Rate your anxiety on a scale of 0 to 100%:

_____%

O   W

Session 6

Anxiety Management Worksheet

The purpose of this worksheet is to help you to see every stressful event as an opportunity for
1. greater understanding of yourself, your anxiety and the people around you, and
2. practicing tools to manage your anxiety.

Step One: An Event

Briefly describe an event when you became anxious. Give such details as time, place and people involved, and end with "That's when I began to work myself up..."

_____

_____   E

_____

_____   Rate your anxiety on a scale of 0 to 100%: [   ] %

Step Two: The Working-Up Process

Learn about your working up process by identifying your thoughts, feelings, behaviours and bodily reactions during the event. Tick the ones that most resonate with you.

Undermining Beliefs

I fear that I have lost...
- ☐ approval
- ☐ control
- ☐ co-operation
- ☐ face
- ☐ respect
- ☐ success
- ☐ trust
- ☐ validation
- ☐ love

This event proves that I am...
- ☐ stupid
- ☐ abnormal
- ☐ incompetent
- ☐ lazy
- ☐ irresponsible
- ☐ a total failure
- ☐ undisciplined
- ☐ untogether
- ☐ useless

B

I worry that I will suffer...
- ☐ mental collapse
- ☐ illness
- ☐ financial hardship

What I want is...
- ☐ total control
- ☐ respect
- ☐ success
- ☐ perfection
- ☐ comfort
- ☐ fairness
- ☐ tranquility
- ☐ all the answers
- ☐ for life to go smoothly
- ☐ to be all things to all people

Self-destructive Behaviour

Active
- ☐ get violent
- ☐ swear
- ☐ slam doors
- ☐ run away
- ☐ overeat
- ☐ harm myself
- ☐ criticise

Passive
- ☐ take it too seriously
- ☐ give up
- ☐ wallow in self pity
- ☐ sulk
- ☐ space out
- ☐ procrastinate
- ☐ give in
- ☐ be controlled

Intense Feelings

Angry feelings
- ☐ hateful
- ☐ aggravated
- ☐ annoyed
- ☐ hostile
- ☐ outraged
- ☐ punitive
- ☐ resentful
- ☐ vengeful

Fearful feelings
- ☐ helpless
- ☐ hopeless
- ☐ disappointed
- ☐ sad
- ☐ attacked
- ☐ worn out
- ☐ rejected
- ☐ jealous
- ☐ afraid
- ☐ exploited
- ☐ lonely
- ☐ abandoned
- ☐ guilty
- ☐ insulted
- ☐ confused
- ☐ disillusioned
- ☐ misunderstood
- ☐ trapped

Bodily Reactions (Limbic System)

I am uncomfortable because I am experiencing...
- ☐ tremors
- ☐ nausea
- ☐ sweaty palms
- ☐ stomach-ache
- ☐ pounding heart
- ☐ general tension
- ☐ fatigue
- ☐ imagination on fire
- ☐ headache
- ☐ dry mouth
- ☐ jaw clenching
- ☐ shortness of breath

Continued over

B   F   L

Step Three: The Working-Down Process

Begin with, "Suddenly I realised that I was anxious and that I had choices..." This is the step of self-leadership and trust in one's ability to handle the situation.

Choose helpful thoughts:

I choose to depersonalise
There is no intention to hurt me. He is doing the best he can with the tools he has at the moment.

I choose realism over romanticism
Life presents many obstacles. I lower or raise standards as needed.

There is no right or wrong
Unless it is a moral issue, I will see it simply as a difference of opinion and/or taste.

I choose the total view of positivity
Even though this event is negative, the total view of his behaviour is positive.

I surrender control
Since I cannot change this situation, I choose to let go of it

I choose to put this event in perspective
This event is not a catastrophe because it is not life threatening. It can be viewed as a trivial life event, a normal life problem that needs to be solved not dramatised.

I choose to view this event as average, falling within the normal range
This event is not exceptional; many people have gone through this.

It's temporary - "this too shall pass"
Life is constantly changing and moving through phases and this situation will also change.

Fears or facts?
Why fear? It may not happen!

I choose to focus on this as a learning experience
Every problem that comes my way is an opportunity for me to learn about my strengths and weaknesses, others and life.

Feel soothing emotions:

I choose to feel warm, loving emotions. I do this by focusing on my heart and letting love, trust forgiveness, compassion, hope or gratitude fill my heart space.

Behave constructively:

I choose to work in part acts:
I will break the overwhelming job into manageable parts.

Do the difficult:
I will face what I fear and act with self-discipline

I choose to solutionise:
I will find a solution by taking advice or doing research.

Prioritise myself:
I will keep my life balanced by meeting friends, doing exercise or laughing.

Compartmentalise:
I will not let this event cloud my whole day; I will focus on something else now.

Utilise calming strategies:

When I:
• relax,
• breathe deeply,
• go for a run,
• shower,
• lie down,
• read,
• watch TV,
• climb into a mental helicopter
• practice mindfulness, meditation, my mind and body calm down.

Step Four: The Self Motivation Process

Endorse yourself for any growth no matter how small.

In the past I would have...

_____

_____

But this time I...

_____

_____

Tick off the traits that you strengthened when you worked down your anxiety:

☐ generosity ☐ peacefulness
☐ kindness ☐ self-discipline
☐ compassion ☐ forgiveness
☐ consideration ☐ courage
☐ helpfulness ☐ responsibility
☐ respectfulness ☐ reliability
☐ honesty ☐ loyalty
☐ fairness ☐ love
☐ patience ☐ humility

Rate your anxiety on a scale of 0 to 100%:

_____%

O   W

NOTES

NOTES

Session 7

BEHAVIOURAL TOOL: DO THE DIFFICULT

'I choose to do the difficult. I will face what I fear and act with self-discipline.'

'Facing what you fear' is described in several well-known idioms such as 'taking the bull by the horns' and 'getting right back on the horse after he has thrown you'. However, despite knowing this intellectually, we often do not achieve our goals because we cannot face our fears.

Facing your fears is the best way to overcome specific fears such as fear of flying, open spaces, confined spaces, crowds, spiders, dogs, snakes or lifts. Behavioural psychology teaches that being in the feared situation long enough lowers fears. Avoiding feared situations heightens fears.

Sometimes we are encouraged to tackle our biggest fear first — to 'jump in the deep end' and get it over with. However, if you try to tackle your biggest fear straight away, you may become overwhelmed and more anxious than when you started. Therefore, the preferred approach is taking it step-by-step which is less confronting and more effective. Behavioural psychologists call it *graded exposure.*

Graded exposure consists of structured and repeated exposure to anxiety-provoking situations. These are presented in levels of difficulty, starting with the situation that provokes the least amount of anxiety and moving towards more challenging situations step-by-step.

Graded exposure can be done in relation to the real object of fear or with visualisation. For example, if you are afraid of going in a lift, you will gradually work your way to getting into a lift. However, if your fear concerns snakes, your therapist may help you become deeply relaxed and then expose you to a snake in your imagination. Either way you will be exposed gradually, allowed to get used to one level, then taken on to the next level of closeness to the feared object.

This tool encourages you to face your fears in a systematic, structured way. At first, your anxiety will be high. However, when you stay in the feared situation long enough, your primitive brain realises that there is no real danger after all and your anxiety disappears.

It is important to stress that you need to stay in the anxious situation long enough so that your body adjusts your anxiety downward. After a while, these situations lose their power to evoke anxiety and you will slowly build up your confidence.

Panic Surfing

Did you know that anxiety is self-limiting? What this means is that if you do not fight your anxiety and instead 'surf' it, as you would a large wave, it will subside of its own accord. Anxiety is literally like a wave that starts big then devolves into smaller and smaller waves until it reaches the beach. This takes no more than 3–4 minutes.

In sum, when you surf the wave of fear, and do not fight it, your anxiety will limit itself in a short space of time. However, if you fight the fear, it will increase the panic and may cause it to last for hours.

EXERCISE TWENTY-THREE

Let's look at the situations that you fear.

What is one of your biggest anxieties or fears?

Example: Being in the presence of a dog.

What are you afraid might happen?

Example: The dog will jump on me.

_____

_____

_____

What is the worst case scenario — what is the worst that could happen?

Example: The dog will bite me.

_____

_____

_____

What other possible, more positive outcomes can you think of?

Example: The dog and I could become friends.

_____

_____

_____

Graded Exposure

Now you are going to develop your own ladder of graded exposure in relation to one of your major fears.

The principles to bear in mind:

1. Set SMART goals — goals that are Specific, Measureable, Achievable, Realistic and Timely. If you set goals that are unrealistic, you will not achieve them which will demotivate you.

2. Obtain support from a friend, family member or professional.

Your support person will give you confidence and ensure that you follow through with your goals.

An example Exposure Ladder

FEAR: You avoid going out to shopping malls.

GOAL: You want to be able to visit a shopping mall alone.

GOAL:	ANXIETY RATING:
Specific Measurable Achievable Realistic Timely (SMART)	(Use any number between 0 and 10 to represent how much distress you would feel in the situation)

STEP	ANXIETY RATING AT START	ANXIETY RATING AT END
1. Go to the local shopping centre on a week day afternoon (with a friend who knows about the problem), stay for 10 minutes	10	5 (after 10 minutes with breathing)
2. Go to the local shopping centre on a weekday afternoon (with a friend who knows about the problem), walk around, stay for 30 minutes	8	4 (after 30 minutes with breathing & mindfulness)
3. Go to the local shopping centre on a busy Thursday evening, stay for 10 minutes (with a friend who knows about the problem).	10	4 (after 10 minutes with breathing)
4. Go to the local shopping centre on a weekend day, stay at least 30 minutes (with a friend who knows about the problem).	7	3 (after 30 minutes with breathing & mindfulness)
5. Go to the local shopping centre on a weekend day staying for 2 hours (with a friend who knows about the problem), and walk into one shop for 5 minutes.	7	1 (after 30 minutes with breathing, mindfulness & laughter)
6. Go to the local shopping centre on a weekend day staying for 2 hours, going into a shop for 15 minutes.	5	1

EXERCISE TWENTY-FOUR

Please build an exposure ladder in relation to your biggest fear.

Name your fear:

GOAL: _____	ANXIETY RATING:
Specific Measurable Achievable Realistic Timely (SMART)	(Use any number between 0 and 10 to represent how much distress you would feel in the situation)

Fill in the steps you aim to achieve. Fill in your anxiety levels before and after you achieve your goal.

STEP	ANXIETY RATING AT START	ANXIETY RATING AT END
1.		
2.		
3.		
4.		
5.		
6.		

EXERCISE TWENTY-FIVE

Have you ever tackled a situation that you were really afraid to tackle?

YES/NO

If yes, please describe.

_____

_____

_____

How did you feel afterwards?

_____

_____

_____

Were your good feelings related to the success of your endeavour or to your feeling of self-accomplishment?

_____

_____

_____

If no, what do you think you lost by not tackling the situation?

_____

_____

_____

Now that you have tapped into the good feelings that are brought about by being bold and tackling a challenge, the next exercise will inspire you to tackle a problem you have been putting off, or avoiding, because of anxiety.

EXERCISE TWENTY-SIX

Are there any situations in your life that need to be addressed but that you have been too afraid or anxious to address?

YES/NO

If yes, what are they?

_____

_____

_____

Choose one of them and write down how you could tackle it (safely and effectively) in the very near future.

_____

_____

_____

If there are others that can be done concurrently, please explain how you will go about addressing them.

_____

_____

_____

BEHAVIOURAL TOOL: LEARNING EXPERIENCE

When you feel defeated, you will feel anxious. It seems like another person, or an event, has had the upper hand. However, if you felt victorious, then you would be calm and confident.

This tool will enable you to see every situation as one where you can be victorious. How? By believing that you have gained from the experience, no matter how difficult, complicated or negative that it seemed.

Illustration

You are stuck in traffic. You start to panic about getting to your meeting on time. You feel powerless.

As long as you feel the traffic is a negative event in your life, you will feel disempowered and frustrated. However, the minute that you believe that you gain from being stuck in traffic, you will feel empowered and less stressed.

You could say to yourself:

- 'Now is a perfect time to practice meditation as I will not have time later.'

- 'I am always rushing around. This is teaching me to learn to slow down and to plan better so that I am not so frantic. Next time I will give myself more travel time.'

- 'While I am here, I will check my emails. What difference does it make if I do it now or later in the office. In fact, doing it now is advantageous because I get them out of the way.'

Every single situation in life is an opportunity to learn something new. Sometimes it is a practical lesson like planning your travel time better. But often, the lesson pertains to personal growth. In fact, in some really difficult situations where external change is impossible, internal growth is the only place progress is possible.

When you utilise this tool in this way, it helps you to live a value based life. Life is not only about external achievement. It can also be about striving to be a better person even in a yucky situation.

Like the educator and author Stephen Covey, I believe that there are universally good values which every human being intuitively knows. These values assist you to develop a fine character and to behave in the world in an ethical, responsible manner. They include generosity, kindness, compassion, consideration, helpfulness, respectfulness, honesty, fairness, patience, peacefulness, self-discipline, forgiveness, courage, responsibility, reliability, loyalty, love and humility.

EXERCISE TWENTY-SEVEN

Example: What do you think can be gained from being stuck in traffic?

a) business arena: I will learn to pace myself better and leave more than enough time in future.

b) personal arena: I will practice the tool surrender control and strengthen patience.

What do you think can be gained from the following:

1. Having to wait in a long queue:

a) business arena _____

b) personal arena _____

2. Not getting a promotion:

a) business arena _____

b) personal arena _____

3. Losing a bargain:

a) business arena _____

b) personal arena _____

4. Having your authority overridden:

a) business arena _____

b) personal arena _____

5. Being moved to a different department:

a) business arena _____

b) personal arena _____

6. Having a neighbour scream at you:

a) business arena _____

b) personal arena _____

7. Running out of petrol on the way to an appointment:

a) business arena _____

b) personal arena _____

8. Overpaying for an article:

a) business arena _____

b) personal arena _____

DAILY MONITORING DIARY

WEEK ENDING _____

Day				M	T	W	T	F	S	S
Overall Anxiety Rating for the day (0-10)										

1. EXERCISE

		M	T	W	T	F	S	S
How long?								
Anxiety level before (0-10)								
Anxiety level after (0-10)								

2. BREATHING & RELAXATION

		M	T	W	T	F	S	S
How long?								
Anxiety level before (0-10)								
Anxiety level after (0-10)								

3. CATASTROPHIC THINKING

		M	T	W	T	F	S	S
How often this type of thought occurred								
Belief in thoughts before challenging (0-10)								
Belief in thoughts after challenging (0-10)								

4. FEARS NOT FACTS

		M	T	W	T	F	S	S
How often this type of thought occurred								
Belief in thoughts before challenging (0-10)								
Belief in thoughts after challenging (0-10)								

5. PERVASIVE PESSIMISTIC THINKING

		M	T	W	T	F	S	S
How often this type of thought occurred								
Belief in thoughts before challenging (0-10)								
Belief in thoughts after challenging (0-10)								

6. PERMANENT PESSIMISTIC THINKING

		M	T	W	T	F	S	S
How often this type of thought occurred								
Belief in thoughts before challenging (0-10)								
Belief in thoughts after challenging (0-10)								

7. MINDFULNESS (FORMAL, GROUNDING, INFORMAL MINDFULNESS)

		M	T	W	T	F	S	S
How long?								
Anxiety level before (0-10)								
Anxiety level after (0-10)								

8. EXCEPTIONAL THINKING

		M	T	W	T	F	S	S
How often this type of thought occurred								
Belief in thoughts before challenging (0-10)								
Belief in thoughts after challenging (0-10)								

Anxiety Management Worksheet

The purpose of this worksheet is to help you to see every stressful event as an opportunity for
1. greater understanding of yourself, your anxiety and the people around you, and
2. practicing tools to manage your anxiety.

Step One: An Event

Briefly describe an event when you became anxious. Give such details as time, place and people involved, and end with "That's when I began to work myself up…"

_____

_____ **E**

_____

_____ Rate your anxiety on a scale of 0 to 100%: [   ] %

Step Two: The Working-Up Process

Learn about your working up process by identifying your thoughts, feelings, behaviours and bodily reactions during the event. Tick the ones that most resonate with you.

Undermining Beliefs

I fear that I have lost…
- ☐ approval
- ☐ success
- ☐ control
- ☐ trust
- ☐ co-operation
- ☐ validation
- ☐ face
- ☐ love
- ☐ respect

This event proves that I am…
- ☐ stupid
- ☐ a total failure
- ☐ abnormal
- ☐ undisciplined
- ☐ incompetent
- ☐ untogether
- ☐ lazy
- ☐ useless
- ☐ irresponsible

B

I worry that I will suffer…
- ☐ mental collapse
- ☐ illness
- ☐ financial hardship

What I want is…
- ☐ total control
- ☐ tranquility
- ☐ respect
- ☐ all the answers
- ☐ success
- ☐ for life to go smoothly
- ☐ perfection
- ☐ comfort
- ☐ to be all things to all people
- ☐ fairness

Self-destructive Behaviour

Active
- ☐ get violent
- ☐ swear
- ☐ slam doors
- ☐ run away
- ☐ overeat
- ☐ harm myself
- ☐ criticise

Passive
- ☐ take it too seriously
- ☐ give up
- ☐ wallow in self pity
- ☐ sulk
- ☐ space out
- ☐ procrastinate
- ☐ give in
- ☐ be controlled

B

Intense Feelings

Angry feelings
- ☐ hateful
- ☐ attacked
- ☐ aggravated
- ☐ worn out
- ☐ annoyed
- ☐ rejected
- ☐ hostile
- ☐ jealous
- ☐ outraged
- ☐ afraid
- ☐ punitive
- ☐ exploited
- ☐ resentful
- ☐ lonely
- ☐ vengeful
- ☐ abandoned

Fearful feelings
- ☐ guilty
- ☐ helpless
- ☐ insulted
- ☐ hopeless
- ☐ confused
- ☐ disappointed
- ☐ disillusioned
- ☐ sad
- ☐ misunderstood
- ☐ trapped

F

Bodily Reactions (Limbic System)

I am uncomfortable because I am experiencing…
- ☐ tremors
- ☐ nausea
- ☐ sweaty palms
- ☐ stomach-ache
- ☐ pounding heart
- ☐ general tension
- ☐ fatigue
- ☐ imagination on fire
- ☐ headache
- ☐ dry mouth
- ☐ jaw clenching
- ☐ shortness of breath

Continued over

L

Step Three: The Working-Down Process

Begin with, "Suddenly I realised that I was anxious and that I had choices..." This is the step of self-leadership and trust in one's ability to handle the situation.

Choose helpful thoughts:

I choose to depersonalise
There is no intention to hurt me. He is doing the best he can with the tools he has at the moment.

I choose realism over romanticism
Life presents many obstacles. I lower or raise standards as needed.

There is no right or wrong
Unless it is a moral issue, I will see it simply as a difference of opinion and/or taste.

I choose the total view of positivity
Even though this event is negative, the total view of his behaviour is positive.

I surrender control
Since I cannot change this situation, I choose to let go of it

I choose to put this event in perspective
This event is not a catastrophe because it is not life threatening. It can be viewed as a trivial life event, a normal life problem that needs to be solved not dramatised.

I choose to view this event as average, falling within the normal range
This event is not exceptional; many people have gone through this.

It's temporary - "this too shall pass"
Life is constantly changing and moving through phases and this situation will also change.

Fears or facts?
Why fear? It may not happen!

I choose to focus on this as a learning experience
Every problem that comes my way is an opportunity for me to learn about my strengths and weaknesses, others and life.

Feel soothing emotions:

I choose to feel warm, loving emotions. I do this by focusing on my heart and letting love, trust forgiveness, compassion, hope or gratitude fill my heart space.

Behave constructively:

I choose to work in part acts:
I will break the overwhelming job into manageable parts.

Do the difficult:
I will face what I fear and act with self-discipline

I choose to solutionise:
I will find a solution by taking advice or doing research.

Prioritise myself:
I will keep my life balanced by meeting friends, doing exercise or laughing.

Compartmentalise:
I will not let this event cloud my whole day; I will focus on something else now.

Utilise calming strategies:

When I:
- relax,
- breathe deeply,
- go for a run,
- shower,
- lie down,
- read,
- watch TV,
- climb into a mental helicopter
- practice mindfulness, meditation, my mind and body calm down.

Step Four: The Self Motivation Process

Endorse yourself for any growth no matter how small.

In the past I would have...

_____

_____

But this time I...

_____

_____

Tick off the traits that you strengthened when you worked down your anxiety:

☐ generosity	☐ peacefulness
☐ kindness	☐ self-discipline
☐ compassion	☐ forgiveness
☐ consideration	☐ courage
☐ helpfulness	☐ responsibility
☐ respectfulness	☐ reliability
☐ honesty	☐ loyalty
☐ fairness	☐ love
☐ patience	☐ humility

Rate your anxiety on a scale of 0 to 100%:

_____ %

O

W

Session 7

Anxiety Management Worksheet

The purpose of this worksheet is to help you to see every stressful event as an opportunity for
1. greater understanding of yourself, your anxiety and the people around you, and
2. practicing tools to manage your anxiety.

Step One: An Event

Briefly describe an event when you became anxious. Give such details as time, place and people involved, and end with "That's when I began to work myself up..."

_____

_____ E

_____

Rate your anxiety on a scale of 0 to 100%: ☐ %

Step Two: The Working-Up Process

Learn about your working up process by identifying your thoughts, feelings, behaviours and bodily reactions during the event. Tick the ones that most resonate with you.

Undermining Beliefs

I fear that I have lost...

- ☐ approval
- ☐ success
- ☐ control
- ☐ trust
- ☐ co-operation
- ☐ validation
- ☐ face
- ☐ love
- ☐ respect

This event proves that I am...

- ☐ stupid
- ☐ a total failure
- ☐ abnormal
- ☐ undisciplined
- ☐ incompetent
- ☐ untogether
- ☐ lazy
- ☐ useless
- ☐ irresponsible

B

I worry that I will suffer...

- ☐ mental collapse
- ☐ illness
- ☐ financial hardship

What I want is...

- ☐ total control
- ☐ tranquility
- ☐ respect
- ☐ all the answers
- ☐ success
- ☐ for life to go
- ☐ perfection
- smoothly
- ☐ comfort
- ☐ to be all things
- ☐ fairness
- to all people

Self-destructive Behaviour

Active
- ☐ get violent
- ☐ swear
- ☐ slam doors
- ☐ run away
- ☐ overeat
- ☐ harm myself
- ☐ criticise

Passive
- ☐ take it too seriously
- ☐ give up
- ☐ wallow in self pity
- ☐ sulk
- ☐ space out
- ☐ procrastinate
- ☐ give in
- ☐ be controlled

Intense Feelings

Angry feelings
- ☐ hateful
- ☐ attacked
- ☐ aggravated
- ☐ worn out
- ☐ annoyed
- ☐ rejected
- ☐ hostile
- ☐ jealous
- ☐ outraged
- ☐ afraid
- ☐ punitive
- ☐ exploited
- ☐ resentful
- ☐ lonely
- ☐ vengeful
- ☐ abandoned
- ☐ guilty

Fearful feelings
- ☐ insulted
- ☐ helpless
- ☐ confused
- ☐ hopeless
- ☐ disillusioned
- ☐ disappointed
- ☐ misunderstood
- ☐ sad
- ☐ trapped

Bodily Reactions (Limbic System)

I am uncomfortable because I am experiencing...

- ☐ tremors
- ☐ nausea
- ☐ sweaty palms
- ☐ stomach-ache
- ☐ pounding heart
- ☐ general tension
- ☐ fatigue
- ☐ imagination on fire
- ☐ headache
- ☐ dry mouth
- ☐ jaw clenching
- ☐ shortness of breath

Continued over

B   F   L

Step Three: The Working-Down Process

Begin with, "Suddenly I realised that I was anxious and that I had choices..." This is the step of self-leadership and trust in one's ability to handle the situation.

Choose helpful thoughts:

I choose to depersonalise
There is no intention to hurt me. He is doing the best he can with the tools he has at the moment.

I choose realism over romanticism
Life presents many obstacles. I lower or raise standards as needed.

There is no right or wrong
Unless it is a moral issue, I will see it simply as a difference of opinion and/or taste.

I choose the total view of positivity
Even though this event is negative, the total view of his behaviour is positive.

I surrender control
Since I cannot change this situation, I choose to let go of it

I choose to put this event in perspective
This event is not a catastrophe because it is not life threatening. It can be viewed as a trivial life event, a normal life problem that needs to be solved not dramatised.

I choose to view this event as average, falling within the normal range
This event is not exceptional; many people have gone through this.

It's temporary - "this too shall pass"
Life is constantly changing and moving through phases and this situation will also change.

Fears or facts?
Why fear? It may not happen!

I choose to focus on this as a learning experience
Every problem that comes my way is an opportunity for me to learn about my strengths and weaknesses, others and life.

Feel soothing emotions:

I choose to feel warm, loving emotions. I do this by focusing on my heart and letting love, trust forgiveness, compassion, hope or gratitude fill my heart space.

Behave constructively:

I choose to work in part acts:
I will break the overwhelming job into manageable parts.

Do the difficult:
I will face what I fear and act with self-discipline

I choose to solutionise:
I will find a solution by taking advice or doing research.

Prioritise myself:
I will keep my life balanced by meeting friends, doing exercise or laughing.

Compartmentalise:
I will not let this event cloud my whole day; I will focus on something else now.

Utilise calming strategies:

When I:
- relax,
- breathe deeply,
- go for a run,
- shower,
- lie down,
- read,
- watch TV,
- climb into a mental helicopter
- practice mindfulness, meditation, my mind and body calm down.

Step Four: The Self Motivation Process

Endorse yourself for any growth no matter how small.

In the past I would have...

_____

_____

But this time I...

_____

_____

Tick off the traits that you strengthened when you worked down your anxiety:

☐ generosity	☐ peacefulness
☐ kindness	☐ self-discipline
☐ compassion	☐ forgiveness
☐ consideration	☐ courage
☐ helpfulness	☐ responsibility
☐ respectfulness	☐ reliability
☐ honesty	☐ loyalty
☐ fairness	☐ love
☐ patience	☐ humility

Rate your anxiety on a scale of 0 to 100%:

_____ %

O   W

Anxiety Management Worksheet

The purpose of this worksheet is to help you to see every stressful event as an opportunity for
1. greater understanding of yourself, your anxiety and the people around you, and
2. practicing tools to manage your anxiety.

Step One: An Event

Briefly describe an event when you became anxious. Give such details as time, place and people involved, and end with "That's when I began to work myself up..."

_____

_____   E

_____

_____ Rate your anxiety on a scale of 0 to 100%: [＿＿] %

Step Two: The Working-Up Process

Learn about your working up process by identifying your thoughts, feelings, behaviours and bodily reactions during the event. Tick the ones that most resonate with you.

Undermining Beliefs

I fear that I have lost...
- ☐ approval
- ☐ control
- ☐ co-operation
- ☐ face
- ☐ respect
- ☐ success
- ☐ trust
- ☐ validation
- ☐ love

This event proves that I am...
- ☐ stupid
- ☐ abnormal
- ☐ incompetent
- ☐ lazy
- ☐ irresponsible
- ☐ a total failure
- ☐ undisciplined
- ☐ untogether
- ☐ useless

B

I worry that I will suffer...
- ☐ mental collapse
- ☐ illness
- ☐ financial hardship

What I want is...
- ☐ total control
- ☐ respect
- ☐ success
- ☐ perfection
- ☐ comfort
- ☐ fairness
- ☐ tranquility
- ☐ all the answers
- ☐ for life to go smoothly
- ☐ to be all things to all people

Self-destructive Behaviour

Active
- ☐ get violent
- ☐ swear
- ☐ slam doors
- ☐ run away
- ☐ overeat
- ☐ harm myself
- ☐ criticise

Passive
- ☐ take it too seriously
- ☐ give up
- ☐ wallow in self pity
- ☐ sulk
- ☐ space out
- ☐ procrastinate
- ☐ give in
- ☐ be controlled

Intense Feelings

Angry feelings
- ☐ hateful
- ☐ aggravated
- ☐ annoyed
- ☐ hostile
- ☐ outraged
- ☐ punitive
- ☐ resentful
- ☐ vengeful

Fearful feelings
- ☐ helpless
- ☐ hopeless
- ☐ disappointed
- ☐ sad

- ☐ attacked
- ☐ worn out
- ☐ rejected
- ☐ jealous
- ☐ afraid
- ☐ exploited
- ☐ lonely
- ☐ abandoned
- ☐ guilty
- ☐ insulted
- ☐ confused
- ☐ disillusioned
- ☐ misunderstood
- ☐ trapped

Bodily Reactions (Limbic System)

I am uncomfortable because I am experiencing...

- ☐ tremors
- ☐ nausea
- ☐ sweaty palms
- ☐ stomach-ache
- ☐ pounding heart
- ☐ general tension
- ☐ fatigue
- ☐ imagination on fire
- ☐ headache
- ☐ dry mouth
- ☐ jaw clenching
- ☐ shortness of breath

Continued over

B   F   L

Step Three: The Working-Down Process

Begin with, "Suddenly I realised that I was anxious and that I had choices..." This is the step of self-leadership and trust in one's ability to handle the situation.

Choose helpful thoughts:

I choose to depersonalise
There is no intention to hurt me. He is doing the best he can with the tools he has at the moment.

I choose realism over romanticism
Life presents many obstacles. I lower or raise standards as needed.

There is no right or wrong
Unless it is a moral issue, I will see it simply as a difference of opinion and/or taste.

I choose the total view of positivity
Even though this event is negative, the total view of his behaviour is positive.

I surrender control
Since I cannot change this situation, I choose to let go of it

I choose to put this event in perspective
This event is not a catastrophe because it is not life threatening. It can be viewed as a trivial life event, a normal life problem that needs to be solved not dramatised.

I choose to view this event as average, falling within the normal range
This event is not exceptional; many people have gone through this.

It's temporary - "this too shall pass"
Life is constantly changing and moving through phases and this situation will also change.

Fears or facts?
Why fear? It may not happen!

I choose to focus on this as a learning experience
Every problem that comes my way is an opportunity for me to learn about my strengths and weaknesses, others and life.

Feel soothing emotions:

I choose to feel warm, loving emotions. I do this by focusing on my heart and letting love, trust forgiveness, compassion, hope or gratitude fill my heart space.

Behave constructively:

I choose to work in part acts:
I will break the overwhelming job into manageable parts.

Do the difficult:
I will face what I fear and act with self-discipline

I choose to solutionise:
I will find a solution by taking advice or doing research.

Prioritise myself:
I will keep my life balanced by meeting friends, doing exercise or laughing.

Compartmentalise:
I will not let this event cloud my whole day; I will focus on something else now.

Utilise calming strategies:

When I:
- relax,
- breathe deeply,
- go for a run,
- shower,
- lie down,
- read,
- watch TV,
- climb into a mental helicopter
- practice mindfulness, meditation, my mind and body calm down.

Step Four: The Self Motivation Process

Endorse yourself for any growth no matter how small.

In the past I would have...
_____
_____

But this time I...
_____
_____

Tick off the traits that you strengthened when you worked down your anxiety:

- □ generosity
- □ kindness
- □ compassion
- □ consideration
- □ helpfulness
- □ respectfulness
- □ honesty
- □ fairness
- □ patience
- □ peacefulness
- □ self-discipline
- □ forgiveness
- □ courage
- □ responsibility
- □ reliability
- □ loyalty
- □ love
- □ humility

Rate your anxiety on a scale of 0 to 100%:

____%

O   W

Anxiety Management Worksheet

The purpose of this worksheet is to help you to see every stressful event as an opportunity for
1. greater understanding of yourself, your anxiety and the people around you, and
2. practicing tools to manage your anxiety.

Step One: An Event

Briefly describe an event when you became anxious. Give such details as time, place and people involved, and end with "That's when I began to work myself up..."

_____

_____ E

_____

_____ Rate your anxiety on a scale of 0 to 100%: [   ] %

Step Two: The Working-Up Process

Learn about your working up process by identifying your thoughts, feelings, behaviours and bodily reactions during the event. Tick the ones that most resonate with you.

Undermining Beliefs

I fear that I have lost...
- ☐ approval
- ☐ control
- ☐ co-operation
- ☐ face
- ☐ respect
- ☐ success
- ☐ trust
- ☐ validation
- ☐ love

This event proves that I am...
- ☐ stupid
- ☐ abnormal
- ☐ incompetent
- ☐ lazy
- ☐ irresponsible
- ☐ a total failure
- ☐ undisciplined
- ☐ untogether
- ☐ useless

B

I worry that I will suffer...
- ☐ mental collapse
- ☐ illness
- ☐ financial hardship

What I want is...
- ☐ total control
- ☐ respect
- ☐ success
- ☐ perfection
- ☐ comfort
- ☐ fairness
- ☐ tranquility
- ☐ all the answers
- ☐ for life to go smoothly
- ☐ to be all things to all people

Self-destructive Behaviour

Active
- ☐ get violent
- ☐ swear
- ☐ slam doors
- ☐ run away
- ☐ overeat
- ☐ harm myself
- ☐ criticise

Passive
- ☐ take it too seriously
- ☐ give up
- ☐ wallow in self pity
- ☐ sulk
- ☐ space out
- ☐ procrastinate
- ☐ give in
- ☐ be controlled

Intense Feelings

Angry feelings
- ☐ hateful
- ☐ aggravated
- ☐ annoyed
- ☐ hostile
- ☐ outraged
- ☐ punitive
- ☐ resentful
- ☐ vengeful

Fearful feelings
- ☐ helpless
- ☐ hopeless
- ☐ disappointed
- ☐ sad
- ☐ attacked
- ☐ worn out
- ☐ rejected
- ☐ jealous
- ☐ afraid
- ☐ exploited
- ☐ lonely
- ☐ abandoned
- ☐ guilty
- ☐ insulted
- ☐ confused
- ☐ disillusioned
- ☐ misunderstood
- ☐ trapped

Bodily Reactions (Limbic System)

I am uncomfortable because I am experiencing...
- ☐ tremors
- ☐ nausea
- ☐ sweaty palms
- ☐ stomach-ache
- ☐ pounding heart
- ☐ general tension
- ☐ fatigue
- ☐ imagination on fire
- ☐ headache
- ☐ dry mouth
- ☐ jaw clenching
- ☐ shortness of breath

Continued over

B   F   L

Step Three: The Working-Down Process

Begin with, "Suddenly I realised that I was anxious and that I had choices..." This is the step of self-leadership and trust in one's ability to handle the situation.

Choose helpful thoughts:

I choose to depersonalise
There is no intention to hurt me. He is doing the best he can with the tools he has at the moment.

I choose realism over romanticism
Life presents many obstacles. I lower or raise standards as needed.

There is no right or wrong
Unless it is a moral issue, I will see it simply as a difference of opinion and/or taste.

I choose the total view of positivity
Even though this event is negative, the total view of his behaviour is positive.

I surrender control
Since I cannot change this situation, I choose to let go of it

I choose to put this event in perspective
This event is not a catastrophe because it is not life threatening. It can be viewed as a trivial life event, a normal life problem that needs to be solved not dramatised.

I choose to view this event as average, falling within the normal range
This event is not exceptional; many people have gone through this.

It's temporary - "this too shall pass"
Life is constantly changing and moving through phases and this situation will also change.

Fears or facts?
Why fear? It may not happen!

I choose to focus on this as a learning experience
Every problem that comes my way is an opportunity for me to learn about my strengths and weaknesses, others and life.

Feel soothing emotions:

I choose to feel warm, loving emotions. I do this by focusing on my heart and letting love, trust forgiveness, compassion, hope or gratitude fill my heart space.

Behave constructively:

I choose to work in part acts:
I will break the overwhelming job into manageable parts.

Do the difficult:
I will face what I fear and act with self-discipline

I choose to solutionise:
I will find a solution by taking advice or doing research.

Prioritise myself:
I will keep my life balanced by meeting friends, doing exercise or laughing.

Compartmentalise:
I will not let this event cloud my whole day; I will focus on something else now.

Utilise calming strategies:

When I:
• relax,
• breathe deeply,
• go for a run,
• shower,
• lie down,
• read,
• watch TV,
• climb into a mental helicopter
• practice mindfulness, meditation, my mind and body calm down.

Step Four: The Self Motivation Process

Endorse yourself for any growth no matter how small.

In the past I would have...

_____

But this time I...

_____

Tick off the traits that you strengthened when you worked down your anxiety:

☐ generosity   ☐ peacefulness
☐ kindness   ☐ self-discipline
☐ compassion   ☐ forgiveness
☐ consideration   ☐ courage
☐ helpfulness   ☐ responsibility
☐ respectfulness ☐ reliability
☐ honesty   ☐ loyalty
☐ fairness   ☐ love
☐ patience   ☐ humility

Rate your anxiety on a scale of 0 to 100%:

_____%

O   W

Anxiety Management Worksheet

The purpose of this worksheet is to help you to see every stressful event as an opportunity for
1. greater understanding of yourself, your anxiety and the people around you, and
2. practicing tools to manage your anxiety.

Step One: An Event

Briefly describe an event when you became anxious. Give such details as time, place and people involved, and end with "That's when I began to work myself up..."

E

Rate your anxiety on a scale of 0 to 100%: [   ] %

Step Two: The Working-Up Process

Learn about your working up process by identifying your thoughts, feelings, behaviours and bodily reactions during the event. Tick the ones that most resonate with you.

Undermining Beliefs

I fear that I have lost...
- ☐ approval
- ☐ control
- ☐ co-operation
- ☐ face
- ☐ respect
- ☐ success
- ☐ trust
- ☐ validation
- ☐ love

This event proves that I am...
- ☐ stupid
- ☐ abnormal
- ☐ incompetent
- ☐ lazy
- ☐ irresponsible
- ☐ a total failure
- ☐ undisciplined
- ☐ untogether
- ☐ useless

B

I worry that I will suffer...
- ☐ mental collapse
- ☐ illness
- ☐ financial hardship

What I want is...
- ☐ total control
- ☐ respect
- ☐ success
- ☐ perfection
- ☐ comfort
- ☐ fairness
- ☐ tranquility
- ☐ all the answers
- ☐ for life to go smoothly
- ☐ to be all things to all people

Self-destructive Behaviour

Active
- ☐ get violent
- ☐ swear
- ☐ slam doors
- ☐ run away
- ☐ overeat
- ☐ harm myself
- ☐ criticise

Passive
- ☐ take it too seriously
- ☐ give up
- ☐ wallow in self pity
- ☐ sulk
- ☐ space out
- ☐ procrastinate
- ☐ give in
- ☐ be controlled

Intense Feelings

Angry feelings
- ☐ hateful
- ☐ aggravated
- ☐ annoyed
- ☐ hostile
- ☐ outraged
- ☐ punitive
- ☐ resentful
- ☐ vengeful

Fearful feelings
- ☐ helpless
- ☐ hopeless
- ☐ disappointed
- ☐ sad
- ☐ attacked
- ☐ worn out
- ☐ rejected
- ☐ jealous
- ☐ afraid
- ☐ exploited
- ☐ lonely
- ☐ abandoned
- ☐ guilty
- ☐ insulted
- ☐ confused
- ☐ disillusioned
- ☐ misunderstood
- ☐ trapped

Bodily Reactions (Limbic System)

I am uncomfortable because I am experiencing...
- ☐ tremors
- ☐ nausea
- ☐ sweaty palms
- ☐ stomach-ache
- ☐ pounding heart
- ☐ general tension
- ☐ fatigue
- ☐ imagination on fire
- ☐ headache
- ☐ dry mouth
- ☐ jaw clenching
- ☐ shortness of breath

Continued over

B   F   L

Step Three: The Working-Down Process

Begin with, "Suddenly I realised that I was anxious and that I had choices..." This is the step of self-leadership and trust in one's ability to handle the situation.

Choose helpful thoughts:

I choose to depersonalise
There is no intention to hurt me. He is doing the best he can with the tools he has at the moment.

I choose realism over romanticism
Life presents many obstacles. I lower or raise standards as needed.

There is no right or wrong
Unless it is a moral issue, I will see it simply as a difference of opinion and/or taste.

I choose the total view of positivity
Even though this event is negative, the total view of his behaviour is positive.

I surrender control
Since I cannot change this situation, I choose to let go of it

I choose to put this event in perspective
This event is not a catastrophe because it is not life threatening. It can be viewed as a trivial life event, a normal life problem that needs to be solved not dramatised.

I choose to view this event as average, falling within the normal range
This event is not exceptional; many people have gone through this.

It's temporary - "this too shall pass"
Life is constantly changing and moving through phases and this situation will also change.

Fears or facts?
Why fear? It may not happen!

I choose to focus on this as a learning experience
Every problem that comes my way is an opportunity for me to learn about my strengths and weaknesses, others and life.

Feel soothing emotions:

I choose to feel warm, loving emotions. I do this by focusing on my heart and letting love, trust forgiveness, compassion, hope or gratitude fill my heart space.

Behave constructively:

I choose to work in part acts:
I will break the overwhelming job into manageable parts.

Do the difficult:
I will face what I fear and act with self-discipline

I choose to solutionise:
I will find a solution by taking advice or doing research.

Prioritise myself:
I will keep my life balanced by meeting friends, doing exercise or laughing.

Compartmentalise:
I will not let this event cloud my whole day; I will focus on something else now.

Utilise calming strategies:

When I:
• relax,
• breathe deeply,
• go for a run,
• shower,
• lie down,
• read,
• watch TV,
• climb into a mental helicopter
* practice mindfulness, meditation, my mind and body calm down.

Step Four: The Self Motivation Process

Endorse yourself for any growth no matter how small.

In the past I would have...
_____
_____

But this time I...
_____
_____

Tick off the traits that you strengthened when you worked down your anxiety:

☐ generosity   ☐ peacefulness
☐ kindness   ☐ self-discipline
☐ compassion   ☐ forgiveness
☐ consideration   ☐ courage
☐ helpfulness   ☐ responsibility
☐ respectfulness   ☐ reliability
☐ honesty   ☐ loyalty
☐ fairness   ☐ love
☐ patience   ☐ humility

Rate your anxiety on a scale of 0 to 100%:

[_____]%

O

W

Anxiety Management Worksheet

The purpose of this worksheet is to help you to see every stressful event as an opportunity for
1. greater understanding of yourself, your anxiety and the people around you, and
2. practicing tools to manage your anxiety.

Step One: An Event

Briefly describe an event when you became anxious. Give such details as time, place and people involved, and end with "That's when I began to work myself up..."

E

Rate your anxiety on a scale of 0 to 100%: _____ %

Step Two: The Working-Up Process

Learn about your working up process by identifying your thoughts, feelings, behaviours and bodily reactions during the event. Tick the ones that most resonate with you.

Undermining Beliefs

I fear that I have lost...
- ☐ approval
- ☐ control
- ☐ co-operation
- ☐ face
- ☐ respect
- ☐ success
- ☐ trust
- ☐ validation
- ☐ love

This event proves that I am...
- ☐ stupid
- ☐ abnormal
- ☐ incompetent
- ☐ lazy
- ☐ irresponsible
- ☐ a total failure
- ☐ undisciplined
- ☐ untogether
- ☐ useless

B

I worry that I will suffer...
- ☐ mental collapse
- ☐ illness
- ☐ financial hardship

What I want is...
- ☐ total control
- ☐ respect
- ☐ success
- ☐ perfection
- ☐ comfort
- ☐ fairness
- ☐ tranquility
- ☐ all the answers
- ☐ for life to go smoothly
- ☐ to be all things to all people

Self-destructive Behaviour

Active
- ☐ get violent
- ☐ swear
- ☐ slam doors
- ☐ run away
- ☐ overeat
- ☐ harm myself
- ☐ criticise

Passive
- ☐ take it too seriously
- ☐ give up
- ☐ wallow in self pity
- ☐ sulk
- ☐ space out
- ☐ procrastinate
- ☐ give in
- ☐ be controlled

Intense Feelings

Angry feelings
- ☐ hateful
- ☐ aggravated
- ☐ annoyed
- ☐ hostile
- ☐ outraged
- ☐ punitive
- ☐ resentful
- ☐ vengeful

Fearful feelings
- ☐ helpless
- ☐ hopeless
- ☐ disappointed
- ☐ sad
- ☐ attacked
- ☐ worn out
- ☐ rejected
- ☐ jealous
- ☐ afraid
- ☐ exploited
- ☐ lonely
- ☐ abandoned
- ☐ guilty
- ☐ insulted
- ☐ confused
- ☐ disillusioned
- ☐ misunderstood
- ☐ trapped

Bodily Reactions (Limbic System)

I am uncomfortable because I am experiencing...
- ☐ tremors
- ☐ nausea
- ☐ sweaty palms
- ☐ stomach-ache
- ☐ pounding heart
- ☐ general tension
- ☐ fatigue
- ☐ imagination on fire
- ☐ headache
- ☐ dry mouth
- ☐ jaw clenching
- ☐ shortness of breath

Continued over

B   F   L

Step Three: The Working-Down Process

Begin with, "Suddenly I realised that I was anxious and that I had choices..." This is the step of self-leadership and trust in one's ability to handle the situation.

Choose helpful thoughts:

I choose to depersonalise
There is no intention to hurt me. He is doing the best he can with the tools he has at the moment.

I choose realism over romanticism
Life presents many obstacles. I lower or raise standards as needed.

There is no right or wrong
Unless it is a moral issue, I will see it simply as a difference of opinion and/or taste.

I choose the total view of positivity
Even though this event is negative, the total view of his behaviour is positive.

I surrender control
Since I cannot change this situation, I choose to let go of it

I choose to put this event in perspective
This event is not a catastrophe because it is not life threatening. It can be viewed as a trivial life event, a normal life problem that needs to be solved not dramatised.

I choose to view this event as average, falling within the normal range
This event is not exceptional; many people have gone through this.

It's temporary - "this too shall pass"
Life is constantly changing and moving through phases and this situation will also change.

Fears or facts?
Why fear? It may not happen!

I choose to focus on this as a learning experience
Every problem that comes my way is an opportunity for me to learn about my strengths and weaknesses, others and life.

Feel soothing emotions:

I choose to feel warm, loving emotions. I do this by focusing on my heart and letting love, trust forgiveness, compassion, hope or gratitude fill my heart space.

Behave constructively:

I choose to work in part acts:
I will break the overwhelming job into manageable parts.

Do the difficult:
I will face what I fear and act with self-discipline

I choose to solutionise:
I will find a solution by taking advice or doing research.

Prioritise myself:
I will keep my life balanced by meeting friends, doing exercise or laughing.

Compartmentalise:
I will not let this event cloud my whole day; I will focus on something else now.

Utilise calming strategies:

When I:
- relax,
- breathe deeply,
- go for a run,
- shower,
- lie down,
- read,
- watch TV,
- climb into a mental helicopter
- practice mindfulness, meditation, my mind and body calm down.

Step Four: The Self Motivation Process

Endorse yourself for any growth no matter how small.

In the past I would have...

_____

_____

But this time I...

_____

_____

Tick off the traits that you strengthened when you worked down your anxiety:

☐ generosity	☐ peacefulness
☐ kindness	☐ self-discipline
☐ compassion	☐ forgiveness
☐ consideration	☐ courage
☐ helpfulness	☐ responsibility
☐ respectfulness	☐ reliability
☐ honesty	☐ loyalty
☐ fairness	☐ love
☐ patience	☐ humility

Rate your anxiety on a scale of 0 to 100%:

[____]%

O

W

Anxiety Management Worksheet

The purpose of this worksheet is to help you to see every stressful event as an opportunity for
1. greater understanding of yourself, your anxiety and the people around you, and
2. practicing tools to manage your anxiety.

Step One: An Event

Briefly describe an event when you became anxious. Give such details as time, place and people involved, and end with "That's when I began to work myself up..."

_____

_____   E

_____

_____ Rate your anxiety on a scale of 0 to 100%: [   ] %

Step Two: The Working-Up Process

Learn about your working up process by identifying your thoughts, feelings, behaviours and bodily reactions during the event. Tick the ones that most resonate with you.

Undermining Beliefs

I fear that I have lost...
- ☐ approval
- ☐ control
- ☐ co-operation
- ☐ face
- ☐ respect
- ☐ success
- ☐ trust
- ☐ validation
- ☐ love

This event proves that I am...
- ☐ stupid
- ☐ abnormal
- ☐ incompetent
- ☐ lazy
- ☐ irresponsible
- ☐ a total failure
- ☐ undisciplined
- ☐ untogether
- ☐ useless

B

I worry that I will suffer...
- ☐ mental collapse
- ☐ illness
- ☐ financial hardship

What I want is...
- ☐ total control
- ☐ respect
- ☐ success
- ☐ perfection
- ☐ comfort
- ☐ fairness
- ☐ tranquility
- ☐ all the answers
- ☐ for life to go smoothly
- ☐ to be all things to all people

Self-destructive Behaviour

Active
- ☐ get violent
- ☐ swear
- ☐ slam doors
- ☐ run away
- ☐ overeat
- ☐ harm myself
- ☐ criticise

Passive
- ☐ take it too seriously
- ☐ give up
- ☐ wallow in self pity
- ☐ sulk
- ☐ space out
- ☐ procrastinate
- ☐ give in
- ☐ be controlled

Intense Feelings

Angry feelings
- ☐ hateful
- ☐ aggravated
- ☐ annoyed
- ☐ hostile
- ☐ outraged
- ☐ punitive
- ☐ resentful
- ☐ vengeful

Fearful feelings
- ☐ helpless
- ☐ hopeless
- ☐ disappointed
- ☐ sad
- ☐ attacked
- ☐ worn out
- ☐ rejected
- ☐ jealous
- ☐ afraid
- ☐ exploited
- ☐ lonely
- ☐ abandoned
- ☐ guilty
- ☐ insulted
- ☐ confused
- ☐ disillusioned
- ☐ misunderstood
- ☐ trapped

Bodily Reactions (Limbic System)

I am uncomfortable because I am experiencing...
- ☐ tremors
- ☐ nausea
- ☐ sweaty palms
- ☐ stomach-ache
- ☐ pounding heart
- ☐ general tension
- ☐ fatigue
- ☐ imagination on fire
- ☐ headache
- ☐ dry mouth
- ☐ jaw clenching
- ☐ shortness of breath

Continued over

B   F   L

Step Three: The Working-Down Process

Begin with, "Suddenly I realised that I was anxious and that I had choices..." This is the step of self-leadership and trust in one's ability to handle the situation.

Choose helpful thoughts:

I choose to depersonalise
There is no intention to hurt me. He is doing the best he can with the tools he has at the moment.

I choose realism over romanticism
Life presents many obstacles. I lower or raise standards as needed.

There is no right or wrong
Unless it is a moral issue, I will see it simply as a difference of opinion and/or taste.

I choose the total view of positivity
Even though this event is negative, the total view of his behaviour is positive.

I surrender control
Since I cannot change this situation, I choose to let go of it

I choose to put this event in perspective
This event is not a catastrophe because it is not life threatening. It can be viewed as a trivial life event, a normal life problem that needs to be solved not dramatised.

I choose to view this event as average, falling within the normal range
This event is not exceptional; many people have gone through this.

It's temporary - "this too shall pass"
Life is constantly changing and moving through phases and this situation will also change.

Fears or facts?
Why fear? It may not happen!

I choose to focus on this as a learning experience
Every problem that comes my way is an opportunity for me to learn about my strengths and weaknesses, others and life.

Feel soothing emotions:

I choose to feel warm, loving emotions. I do this by focusing on my heart and letting love, trust forgiveness, compassion, hope or gratitude fill my heart space.

Behave constructively:

I choose to work in part acts:
I will break the overwhelming job into manageable parts.

Do the difficult:
I will face what I fear and act with self-discipline

I choose to solutionise:
I will find a solution by taking advice or doing research.

Prioritise myself:
I will keep my life balanced by meeting friends, doing exercise or laughing.

Compartmentalise:
I will not let this event cloud my whole day; I will focus on something else now.

Utilise calming strategies:

When I:
- relax,
- breathe deeply,
- go for a run,
- shower,
- lie down,
- read,
- watch TV,
- climb into a mental helicopter
- practice mindfulness, meditation, my mind and body calm down.

Step Four: The Self Motivation Process

Endorse yourself for any growth no matter how small.

In the past I would have...

_____

_____

But this time I...

_____

_____

Tick off the traits that you strengthened when you worked down your anxiety:

☐ generosity	☐ peacefulness
☐ kindness	☐ self-discipline
☐ compassion	☐ forgiveness
☐ consideration	☐ courage
☐ helpfulness	☐ responsibility
☐ respectfulness	☐ reliability
☐ honesty	☐ loyalty
☐ fairness	☐ love
☐ patience	☐ humility

Rate your anxiety on a scale of 0 to 100%:

[____]%

O

W

NOTES

NOTES

Session 8

BEHAVIOURAL TOOL: WORK IN PART ACTS

'I choose to work in part acts. I will solve the problem one step at a time'.

A major source of stress and anxiety are the projects that you feel need to be completed or problems that need to be solved. Facing a large project or problem can often lead to feelings of being overwhelmed and helpless.

This tool teaches you to tackle an overwhelming challenge one chunk at a time. As you work through each bite sized chunk, your anxiety will reduce.

Illustration

Let us say that you are moving house. When you see the large number of items that require packing, you suddenly feel overwhelmed. It is too much. You feel that no matter what you choose to do first, the job will be too big for you to complete. You begin to procrastinate and avoid the moving task ahead of you.

What you need to do is break the task into parts. That way you will feel empowered to make a start. Working in part acts, in this example, would mean packing up one room at a time, not the whole house. Or it would mean packing one box at a time, not the whole wardrobe.

There are many philosophies in life that support this value. AA (Alcoholics Anonymous) and its offshoots talk about taking it 'one day at a time'. There is a Japanese philosophy that states (this is not a direct quote): 'If a road is 1000 steps, each small step you take is one step closer to the end'.

EXERCISE TWENTY-EIGHT

How do you feel about this philosophy?

_____

_____

_____

Have you ever applied this philosophy?   Yes/No

In what situations?

_____

_____

_____

Describe how it helped reduce your anxiety?

_____

_____

_____

Write down any similar philosophies that you find useful?

_____

_____

_____

EXERCISE TWENTY-NINE

This exercise will help you to practice breaking large projects into parts. Projects can be broken up into tasks or time frames or both.

Please describe how you could break up each of the projects below into solvable, part acts.

Example: Project
You are moving house in one week.

Example: Answer
I would break the house into 6 parts (areas) and do one area per day. Example Sunday — pack up spare bedroom. Monday — pack up study. Tuesday — pack up living room. Wednesday — pack up dining room. Thursday — pack up outdoors and bathroom, except essentials. Friday — pack up my bedroom, except essentials.

1. You are planning your wedding for 100 people which is taking place in a year's time.

_____

_____

_____

2. You have been asked to write a 50 page report in a week.

_____

_____

_____

Session 8

3. You are required to plan a 4-week holiday for you and your family.

_____

_____

_____

4. You would like to renovate your home. What steps should you take to do so in the least stressful way?

_____

_____

_____

5. You have acquired a new smart phone and have no idea how it works. How will you learn to use it in the most stress free manner?

_____

_____

_____

6. You have moved to a new city and need to drive to a new location on the first day. You do not have a GPS.

_____

_____

_____

7. You are unemployed and need to find a job.

_____

_____

_____

8. You have purchased the latest microwave oven with many new features. How will you learn all the new features plus begin to use it straight away?

_____

_____

_____

COGNITIVE TOOL: DEPERSONALISE

'I choose to depersonalise. There is no intention to hurt me. He is doing the best he can with the tools he has at the moment.'

We live in a world where we are constantly interacting with others. An enormous source of our 'fight or flight' reaction is the belief that other people deliberately set out to hurt/disappoint/neglect/exclude us.

Illustration

Your partner does not wash his dinner plate but leaves it in the sink. You think 'He knows how important it is to me that he keeps the sink clean, yet he still left his dirty plate in the sink. He is so unkind.'

If you examine the thinking behind the wording, it is: 'My partner thought it through and deliberately left the sink messy. His motive was cruelty.'

No wonder you felt hurt and angry.

Here's another example. Your work colleagues go out for a drink one day when you are off sick. You think: 'They waited for me to be away so that they did not have to include me. Now I know where I stand and I will avoid being friends with them in the future.'

In this illustration, you have fearful thoughts: 'They do not like me. They plotted and planned to wait for the day that I was ill so that they could go out and have fun without me. They obviously do not want to socialise with me. I will retreat.'

Simply put, the implication in all these illustrations is that people, even those nearest and dearest, make deliberate decisions to hurt you in some way.

The reality is that:

a)   Every individual is busy with their own agenda and you are not at the centre of each person's thinking every minute of every day.

b)   Every human is imperfect, makes mistakes and is limited in various ways. This means that there are times when each one of us forgets, is lazy, careless, infantile, impulsive and pre-occupied. Moreover, when making a decision or taking action, we will be limited at that time by our level of intelligence, level of maturity, time restraints, budget, emotional capacity, needs, stresses and priorities.

So let's now reframe the above examples in a new light. Using this tool you could say: 'I choose to depersonalise. My partner left a dirty dish in the sink today. He probably got caught up in a telephone call and forgot about it.' In other words, there was no intention to hurt me. I was not even on his mind. He was doing the best he could with the time and energy at his disposal.

In the second example, it is highly unlikely that your work colleagues plotted and planned anything. It is more likely that you were not even on their radar when they decided impulsively to go out and have a drink.

Truthfully, there may be a small percentage of people who are actually 'out to get you', but the it is much less likely than the explanations given above. Always check the facts before assuming the worst. Obviously, if a person is being cruel or vindictive, using this tool would be inappropriate.

Illustration

Your friend does not invite you to her wedding. You are devastated. You call and ask her why. She tells you that she was very hurt that you did not invite her to your birthday dinner and now she wants to hurt you back.

In this case, you should not use the tool 'Depersonalise' because her actions are meant to hurt you personally. However, to move past your devastation you may need to use other tools such as 'Find a Solution' or 'Do the Difficult'.

In sum, remember that like you, the majority of people are busy with their own agendas and do not actively set out to make you unhappy. Even the most loving, successful, put-together person can make a mistake.

This tool will help you to take out the personal hurt from the equation and look at the situation in a more realistic way.

The following exercise will assist you to see situations in a less personal way from now on.

EXERCISE THIRTY

Fill out possible personalised and depersonalised thoughts for the scenarios below.

Example: A co-worker is talking loudly on the phone which prevents you from concentrating.

Personalised thought: He does not want me to be successful so he is disturbing my concentration.

Depersonalised thought: He is so excited about the deal he is closing that he is oblivious to his surroundings including me.

1. Your friend does not acknowledge your birthday.

Personalised thought:

_____

_____

Depersonalised thought:

_____

_____

2. A family member does not take you into his/her confidence.

Personalised thought:

_____

_____

Depersonalised thought:

_____

_____

3. A relative does not buy a product you are selling for work.

Personalised thought:

_____

_____

Depersonalised thought:

_____

_____

4. You are not asked by a close friend to go on holiday with them.

Personalised thought:

_____

_____

Depersonalised thought:

_____

_____

5. You did not get a raise at work.

Personalised thought:

_____

_____

Depersonalised thought:

_____

_____

6. Your spouse/partner goes out for an evening when you are sick at home.

Personalised thought:

_____

_____

Depersonalised thought:

_____

_____

DAILY MONITORING DIARY

WEEK ENDING _____

Day	M	T	W	T	F	S	S
Overall Anxiety Rating for the day (0-10)							

1. EXERCISE

How long?

Anxiety level before (0-10)

Anxiety level after (0-10)

2. BREATHING & RELAXATION

How long?

Anxiety level before (0-10)

Anxiety level after (0-10)

3. CATASTROPHIC THINKING

How often this type of thought occurred

Belief in thoughts before challenging (0-10)

Belief in thoughts after challenging (0-10)

4. FEARS NOT FACTS

How often this type of thought occurred

Belief in thoughts before challenging (0-10)

Belief in thoughts after challenging (0-10)

5. PERVASIVE PESSIMISTIC THINKING

How often this type of thought occurred

Belief in thoughts before challenging (0-10)

Belief in thoughts after challenging (0-10)

6. PERMANENT PESSIMISTIC THINKING

How often this type of thought occurred

Belief in thoughts before challenging (0-10)

Belief in thoughts after challenging (0-10)

7. MINDFULNESS (FORMAL, GROUNDING, INFORMAL MINDFULNESS)

How long?

Anxiety level before (0-10)

Anxiety level after (0-10)

8. EXCEPTIONAL THINKING

How often this type of thought occurred

Belief in thoughts before challenging (0-10)

Belief in thoughts after challenging (0-10)

9. TAKING IT PERSONALLY

How often this type of thought occurred

Belief in thoughts before challenging (0-10)

Belief in thoughts after challenging (0-10)

Anxiety Management Worksheet

The purpose of this worksheet is to help you to see every stressful event as an opportunity for
1. greater understanding of yourself, your anxiety and the people around you, and
2. practicing tools to manage your anxiety.

Step One: An Event

Briefly describe an event when you became anxious. Give such details as time, place and people involved, and end with "That's when I began to work myself up..."

_____

_____ E

_____

_____ Rate your anxiety on a scale of 0 to 100%: [   ] %

Step Two: The Working-Up Process

Learn about your working up process by identifying your thoughts, feelings, behaviours and bodily reactions during the event. Tick the ones that most resonate with you.

Undermining Beliefs

I fear that I have lost...

☐ approval   ☐ success
☐ control   ☐ trust
☐ co-operation   ☐ validation
☐ face   ☐ love
☐ respect

This event proves that I am...

☐ stupid   ☐ a total failure
☐ abnormal   ☐ undisciplined
☐ incompetent   ☐ untogether
☐ lazy   ☐ useless
☐ irresponsible

B

I worry that I will suffer...

☐ mental collapse
☐ illness
☐ financial hardship

What I want is...

☐ total control   ☐ tranquility
☐ respect   ☐ all the answers
☐ success   ☐ for life to go
☐ perfection   smoothly
☐ comfort   ☐ to be all things
☐ fairness   to all people

Self-destructive Behaviour

Active

☐ get violent
☐ swear
☐ slam doors
☐ run away
☐ overeat
☐ harm myself
☐ criticise

Passive

☐ take it too seriously
☐ give up
☐ wallow in self pity
☐ sulk
☐ space out
☐ procrastinate
☐ give in
☐ be controlled

Intense Feelings

Angry feelings
☐ hateful   ☐ attacked
☐ aggravated   ☐ worn out
☐ annoyed   ☐ rejected
☐ hostile   ☐ jealous
☐ outraged   ☐ afraid
☐ punitive   ☐ exploited
☐ resentful   ☐ lonely
☐ vengeful   ☐ abandoned
            ☐ guilty
Fearful feelings   ☐ insulted
☐ helpless   ☐ confused
☐ hopeless   ☐ disillusioned
☐ disappointed   ☐ misunderstood
☐ sad   ☐ trapped

Bodily Reactions (Limbic System)

I am uncomfortable because I am experiencing...

☐ tremors
☐ nausea
☐ sweaty palms
☐ stomach-ache
☐ pounding heart
☐ general tension
☐ fatigue
☐ imagination on fire
☐ headache
☐ dry mouth
☐ jaw clenching
☐ shortness of breath

Continued over

B   F   L

Step Three: The Working-Down Process

Begin with, "Suddenly I realised that I was anxious and that I had choices..." This is the step of self-leadership and trust in one's ability to handle the situation.

Choose helpful thoughts:

I choose to depersonalise
There is no intention to hurt me. He is doing the best he can with the tools he has at the moment.

I choose realism over romanticism
Life presents many obstacles. I lower or raise standards as needed.

There is no right or wrong
Unless it is a moral issue, I will see it simply as a difference of opinion and/or taste.

I choose the total view of positivity
Even though this event is negative, the total view of his behaviour is positive.

I surrender control
Since I cannot change this situation, I choose to let go of it

I choose to put this event in perspective
This event is not a catastrophe because it is not life threatening. It can be viewed as a trivial life event, a normal life problem that needs to be solved not dramatised.

I choose to view this event as average, falling within the normal range
This event is not exceptional; many people have gone through this.

It's temporary - "this too shall pass"
Life is constantly changing and moving through phases and this situation will also change.

Fears or facts?
Why fear? It may not happen!

I choose to focus on this as a learning experience
Every problem that comes my way is an opportunity for me to learn about my strengths and weaknesses, others and life.

Feel soothing emotions:

I choose to feel warm, loving emotions. I do this by focusing on my heart and letting love, trust forgiveness, compassion, hope or gratitude fill my heart space.

Behave constructively:

I choose to work in part acts:
I will break the overwhelming job into manageable parts.

Do the difficult:
I will face what I fear and act with self-discipline

I choose to solutionise:
I will find a solution by taking advice or doing research.

Prioritise myself:
I will keep my life balanced by meeting friends, doing exercise or laughing.

Compartmentalise:
I will not let this event cloud my whole day; I will focus on something else now.

Utilise calming strategies:

When I:
- relax,
- breathe deeply,
- go for a run,
- shower,
- lie down,
- read,
- watch TV,
- climb into a mental helicopter
- practice mindfulness, meditation, my mind and body calm down.

Step Four: The Self Motivation Process

Endorse yourself for any growth no matter how small.

In the past I would have...

_____

_____

But this time I...

_____

_____

Tick off the traits that you strengthened when you worked down your anxiety:

☐ generosity	☐ peacefulness	
☐ kindness	☐ self-discipline	
☐ compassion	☐ forgiveness	
☐ consideration	☐ courage	
☐ helpfulness	☐ responsibility	
☐ respectfulness	☐ reliability	
☐ honesty	☐ loyalty	
☐ fairness	☐ love	
☐ patience	☐ humility	

Rate your anxiety on a scale of 0 to 100%:

⬇

[____]%

O   W

Anxiety Management Worksheet

The purpose of this worksheet is to help you to see every stressful event as an opportunity for
1. greater understanding of yourself, your anxiety and the people around you, and
2. practicing tools to manage your anxiety.

Step One: An Event

Briefly describe an event when you became anxious. Give such details as time, place and people involved, and end with "That's when I began to work myself up..."

_____

_____ E

_____

_____ Rate your anxiety on a scale of 0 to 100%: [   ] %

Step Two: The Working-Up Process

Learn about your working up process by identifying your thoughts, feelings, behaviours and bodily reactions during the event. Tick the ones that most resonate with you.

Undermining Beliefs

I fear that I have lost...
- ☐ approval
- ☐ success
- ☐ control
- ☐ trust
- ☐ co-operation
- ☐ validation
- ☐ face
- ☐ love
- ☐ respect

This event proves that I am... B
- ☐ stupid
- ☐ a total failure
- ☐ abnormal
- ☐ undisciplined
- ☐ incompetent
- ☐ untogether
- ☐ lazy
- ☐ useless
- ☐ irresponsible

I worry that I will suffer...
- ☐ mental collapse
- ☐ illness
- ☐ financial hardship

What I want is...
- ☐ total control
- ☐ tranquility
- ☐ respect
- ☐ all the answers
- ☐ success
- ☐ for life to go smoothly
- ☐ perfection
- ☐ comfort
- ☐ to be all things to all people
- ☐ fairness

Self-destructive Behaviour

Active
- ☐ get violent
- ☐ swear
- ☐ slam doors
- ☐ run away
- ☐ overeat
- ☐ harm myself
- ☐ criticise

Passive
- ☐ take it too seriously
- ☐ give up
- ☐ wallow in self pity
- ☐ sulk
- ☐ space out
- ☐ procrastinate
- ☐ give in
- ☐ be controlled

Intense Feelings

Angry feelings
- ☐ hateful
- ☐ attacked
- ☐ aggravated
- ☐ worn out
- ☐ annoyed
- ☐ rejected
- ☐ hostile
- ☐ jealous
- ☐ outraged
- ☐ afraid
- ☐ punitive
- ☐ exploited
- ☐ resentful
- ☐ lonely
- ☐ vengeful
- ☐ abandoned
- ☐ guilty

Fearful feelings
- ☐ insulted
- ☐ helpless
- ☐ confused
- ☐ hopeless
- ☐ disillusioned
- ☐ disappointed
- ☐ misunderstood
- ☐ sad
- ☐ trapped

Bodily Reactions (Limbic System)

I am uncomfortable because I am experiencing...
- ☐ tremors
- ☐ nausea
- ☐ sweaty palms
- ☐ stomach-ache
- ☐ pounding heart
- ☐ general tension
- ☐ fatigue
- ☐ imagination on fire
- ☐ headache
- ☐ dry mouth
- ☐ jaw clenching
- ☐ shortness of breath

Continued over

B   F   L

Step Three: The Working-Down Process

Begin with, "Suddenly I realised that I was anxious and that I had choices..." This is the step of self-leadership and trust in one's ability to handle the situation.

Choose helpful thoughts:

I choose to depersonalise
There is no intention to hurt me. He is doing the best he can with the tools he has at the moment.

I choose realism over romanticism
Life presents many obstacles. I lower or raise standards as needed.

There is no right or wrong
Unless it is a moral issue, I will see it simply as a difference of opinion and/or taste.

I choose the total view of positivity
Even though this event is negative, the total view of his behaviour is positive.

I surrender control
Since I cannot change this situation, I choose to let go of it

I choose to put this event in perspective
This event is not a catastrophe because it is not life threatening. It can be viewed as a trivial life event, a normal life problem that needs to be solved not dramatised.

I choose to view this event as average, falling within the normal range
This event is not exceptional; many people have gone through this.

It's temporary - "this too shall pass"
Life is constantly changing and moving through phases and this situation will also change.

Fears or facts?
Why fear? It may not happen!

I choose to focus on this as a learning experience
Every problem that comes my way is an opportunity for me to learn about my strengths and weaknesses, others and life.

Feel soothing emotions:

I choose to feel warm, loving emotions. I do this by focusing on my heart and letting love, trust forgiveness, compassion, hope or gratitude fill my heart space.

Behave constructively:

I choose to work in part acts:
I will break the overwhelming job into manageable parts.

Do the difficult:
I will face what I fear and act with self-discipline

I choose to solutionise:
I will find a solution by taking advice or doing research.

Prioritise myself:
I will keep my life balanced by meeting friends, doing exercise or laughing.

Compartmentalise:
I will not let this event cloud my whole day; I will focus on something else now.

Utilise calming strategies:

When I:
- relax,
- breathe deeply,
- go for a run,
- shower,
- lie down,
- read,
- watch TV,
- climb into a mental helicopter
- practice mindfulness, meditation, my mind and body calm down.

Step Four: The Self Motivation Process

Endorse yourself for any growth no matter how small.

In the past I would have...

_____

_____

But this time I...

_____

_____

Tick off the traits that you strengthened when you worked down your anxiety:

☐ generosity	☐ peacefulness
☐ kindness	☐ self-discipline
☐ compassion	☐ forgiveness
☐ consideration	☐ courage
☐ helpfulness	☐ responsibility
☐ respectfulness	☐ reliability
☐ honesty	☐ loyalty
☐ fairness	☐ love
☐ patience	☐ humility

Rate your anxiety on a scale of 0 to 100%:

_____ %

O   W

Anxiety Management Worksheet

The purpose of this worksheet is to help you to see every stressful event as an opportunity for
1. greater understanding of yourself, your anxiety and the people around you, and
2. practicing tools to manage your anxiety.

Step One: An Event

Briefly describe an event when you became anxious. Give such details as time, place and people involved, and end with "That's when I began to work myself up..."

E

Rate your anxiety on a scale of 0 to 100%: [   ] %

Step Two: The Working-Up Process

Learn about your working up process by identifying your thoughts, feelings, behaviours and bodily reactions during the event. Tick the ones that most resonate with you.

Undermining Beliefs

I fear that I have lost...

- ☐ approval
- ☐ control
- ☐ co-operation
- ☐ face
- ☐ respect
- ☐ success
- ☐ trust
- ☐ validation
- ☐ love

This event proves that I am...

- ☐ stupid
- ☐ abnormal
- ☐ incompetent
- ☐ lazy
- ☐ irresponsible
- ☐ a total failure
- ☐ undisciplined
- ☐ untogether
- ☐ useless

B

I worry that I will suffer...

- ☐ mental collapse
- ☐ illness
- ☐ financial hardship

What I want is...

- ☐ total control
- ☐ respect
- ☐ success
- ☐ perfection
- ☐ comfort
- ☐ fairness
- ☐ tranquility
- ☐ all the answers
- ☐ for life to go smoothly
- ☐ to be all things to all people

Self-destructive Behaviour

Active

- ☐ get violent
- ☐ swear
- ☐ slam doors
- ☐ run away
- ☐ overeat
- ☐ harm myself
- ☐ criticise

Passive

- ☐ take it too seriously
- ☐ give up
- ☐ wallow in self pity
- ☐ sulk
- ☐ space out
- ☐ procrastinate
- ☐ give in
- ☐ be controlled

Intense Feelings

Angry feelings

- ☐ hateful
- ☐ aggravated
- ☐ annoyed
- ☐ hostile
- ☐ outraged
- ☐ punitive
- ☐ resentful
- ☐ vengeful

Fearful feelings

- ☐ helpless
- ☐ hopeless
- ☐ disappointed
- ☐ sad
- ☐ attacked
- ☐ worn out
- ☐ rejected
- ☐ jealous
- ☐ afraid
- ☐ exploited
- ☐ lonely
- ☐ abandoned
- ☐ guilty
- ☐ insulted
- ☐ confused
- ☐ disillusioned
- ☐ misunderstood
- ☐ trapped

Bodily Reactions (Limbic System)

I am uncomfortable because I am experiencing...

- ☐ tremors
- ☐ nausea
- ☐ sweaty palms
- ☐ stomach-ache
- ☐ pounding heart
- ☐ general tension
- ☐ fatigue
- ☐ imagination on fire
- ☐ headache
- ☐ dry mouth
- ☐ jaw clenching
- ☐ shortness of breath

Continued over

B   F   L

Step Three: The Working-Down Process

Begin with, "Suddenly I realised that I was anxious and that I had choices..." This is the step of self-leadership and trust in one's ability to handle the situation.

Choose helpful thoughts:

I choose to depersonalise
There is no intention to hurt me. He is doing the best he can with the tools he has at the moment.

I choose realism over romanticism
Life presents many obstacles. I lower or raise standards as needed.

There is no right or wrong
Unless it is a moral issue, I will see it simply as a difference of opinion and/or taste.

I choose the total view of positivity
Even though this event is negative, the total view of his behaviour is positive.

I surrender control
Since I cannot change this situation, I choose to let go of it

I choose to put this event in perspective
This event is not a catastrophe because it is not life threatening. It can be viewed as a trivial life event, a normal life problem that needs to be solved not dramatised.

I choose to view this event as average, falling within the normal range
This event is not exceptional; many people have gone through this.

It's temporary - "this too shall pass"
Life is constantly changing and moving through phases and this situation will also change.

Fears or facts?
Why fear? It may not happen!

I choose to focus on this as a learning experience
Every problem that comes my way is an opportunity for me to learn about my strengths and weaknesses, others and life.

Feel soothing emotions:

I choose to feel warm, loving emotions. I do this by focusing on my heart and letting love, trust forgiveness, compassion, hope or gratitude fill my heart space.

Behave constructively:

I choose to work in part acts:
I will break the overwhelming job into manageable parts.

Do the difficult:
I will face what I fear and act with self-discipline

I choose to solutionise:
I will find a solution by taking advice or doing research.

Prioritise myself:
I will keep my life balanced by meeting friends, doing exercise or laughing.

Compartmentalise:
I will not let this event cloud my whole day; I will focus on something else now.

Utilise calming strategies:

When I:
• relax,
• breathe deeply,
• go for a run,
• shower,
• lie down,
• read,
• watch TV,
• climb into a mental helicopter
• practice mindfulness, meditation, my mind and body calm down.

Step Four: The Self Motivation Process

Endorse yourself for any growth no matter how small.

In the past I would have...

_____

_____

But this time I...

_____

_____

Tick off the traits that you strengthened when you worked down your anxiety:

☐ generosity   ☐ peacefulness
☐ kindness   ☐ self-discipline
☐ compassion   ☐ forgiveness
☐ consideration   ☐ courage
☐ helpfulness   ☐ responsibility
☐ respectfulness ☐ reliability
☐ honesty   ☐ loyalty
☐ fairness   ☐ love
☐ patience   ☐ humility

Rate your anxiety on a scale of 0 to 100%:

[____]%

O   W

Session 8

Anxiety Management Worksheet

The purpose of this worksheet is to help you to see every stressful event as an opportunity for
1. greater understanding of yourself, your anxiety and the people around you, and
2. practicing tools to manage your anxiety.

Step One: An Event

Briefly describe an event when you became anxious. Give such details as time, place and people involved, and end with "That's when I began to work myself up..."

_____

_____ E

_____

Rate your anxiety on a scale of 0 to 100%: [   ] %

Step Two: The Working-Up Process

Learn about your working up process by identifying your thoughts, feelings, behaviours and bodily reactions during the event. Tick the ones that most resonate with you.

Undermining Beliefs

I fear that I have lost...
- ☐ approval
- ☐ control
- ☐ co-operation
- ☐ face
- ☐ respect
- ☐ success
- ☐ trust
- ☐ validation
- ☐ love

This event proves that I am...
- ☐ stupid
- ☐ abnormal
- ☐ incompetent
- ☐ lazy
- ☐ irresponsible
- ☐ a total failure
- ☐ undisciplined
- ☐ untogether
- ☐ useless

B

I worry that I will suffer...
- ☐ mental collapse
- ☐ illness
- ☐ financial hardship

What I want is...
- ☐ total control
- ☐ respect
- ☐ success
- ☐ perfection
- ☐ comfort
- ☐ fairness
- ☐ tranquility
- ☐ all the answers
- ☐ for life to go smoothly
- ☐ to be all things to all people

Self-destructive Behaviour

Active
- ☐ get violent
- ☐ swear
- ☐ slam doors
- ☐ run away
- ☐ overeat
- ☐ harm myself
- ☐ criticise

Passive
- ☐ take it too seriously
- ☐ give up
- ☐ wallow in self pity
- ☐ sulk
- ☐ space out
- ☐ procrastinate
- ☐ give in
- ☐ be controlled

Intense Feelings

Angry feelings
- ☐ hateful
- ☐ aggravated
- ☐ annoyed
- ☐ hostile
- ☐ outraged
- ☐ punitive
- ☐ resentful
- ☐ vengeful

Fearful feelings
- ☐ helpless
- ☐ hopeless
- ☐ disappointed
- ☐ sad
- ☐ attacked
- ☐ worn out
- ☐ rejected
- ☐ jealous
- ☐ afraid
- ☐ exploited
- ☐ lonely
- ☐ abandoned
- ☐ guilty
- ☐ insulted
- ☐ confused
- ☐ disillusioned
- ☐ misunderstood
- ☐ trapped

Bodily Reactions (Limbic System)

I am uncomfortable because I am experiencing...
- ☐ tremors
- ☐ nausea
- ☐ sweaty palms
- ☐ stomach-ache
- ☐ pounding heart
- ☐ general tension
- ☐ fatigue
- ☐ imagination on fire
- ☐ headache
- ☐ dry mouth
- ☐ jaw clenching
- ☐ shortness of breath

Continued over

B   F   L

Page 195

Step Three: The Working-Down Process

Begin with, "Suddenly I realised that I was anxious and that I had choices..." This is the step of self-leadership and trust in one's ability to handle the situation.

Choose helpful thoughts:

I choose to depersonalise
There is no intention to hurt me. He is doing the best he can with the tools he has at the moment.

I choose realism over romanticism
Life presents many obstacles. I lower or raise standards as needed.

There is no right or wrong
Unless it is a moral issue, I will see it simply as a difference of opinion and/or taste.

I choose the total view of positivity
Even though this event is negative, the total view of his behaviour is positive.

I surrender control
Since I cannot change this situation, I choose to let go of it

I choose to put this event in perspective
This event is not a catastrophe because it is not life threatening. It can be viewed as a trivial life event, a normal life problem that needs to be solved not dramatised.

I choose to view this event as average, falling within the normal range
This event is not exceptional; many people have gone through this.

It's temporary - "this too shall pass"
Life is constantly changing and moving through phases and this situation will also change.

Fears or facts?
Why fear? It may not happen!

I choose to focus on this as a learning experience
Every problem that comes my way is an opportunity for me to learn about my strengths and weaknesses, others and life.

Feel soothing emotions:

I choose to feel warm, loving emotions. I do this by focusing on my heart and letting love, trust forgiveness, compassion, hope or gratitude fill my heart space.

Behave constructively:

I choose to work in part acts:
I will break the overwhelming job into manageable parts.

Do the difficult:
I will face what I fear and act with self-discipline

I choose to solutionise:
I will find a solution by taking advice or doing research.

Prioritise myself:
I will keep my life balanced by meeting friends, doing exercise or laughing.

Compartmentalise:
I will not let this event cloud my whole day; I will focus on something else now.

Utilise calming strategies:

When I:
- relax,
- breathe deeply,
- go for a run,
- shower,
- lie down,
- read,
- watch TV,
- climb into a mental helicopter
- practice mindfulness, meditation, my mind and body calm down.

Step Four: The Self Motivation Process

Endorse yourself for any growth no matter how small.

In the past I would have...

_____

_____

But this time I...

_____

_____

Tick off the traits that you strengthened when you worked down your anxiety:

☐	generosity	☐	peacefulness
☐	kindness	☐	self-discipline
☐	compassion	☐	forgiveness
☐	consideration	☐	courage
☐	helpfulness	☐	responsibility
☐	respectfulness	☐	reliability
☐	honesty	☐	loyalty
☐	fairness	☐	love
☐	patience	☐	humility

Rate your anxiety on a scale of 0 to 100%:

_____ %

O

W

Session 8

Anxiety Management Worksheet

The purpose of this worksheet is to help you to see every stressful event as an opportunity for
1. greater understanding of yourself, your anxiety and the people around you, and
2. practicing tools to manage your anxiety.

Step One: An Event

Briefly describe an event when you became anxious. Give such details as time, place and people involved, and end with "That's when I began to work myself up..."

_____

_____ E

_____

_____ Rate your anxiety on a scale of 0 to 100%: [　　] %

Step Two: The Working-Up Process

Learn about your working up process by identifying your thoughts, feelings, behaviours and bodily reactions during the event. Tick the ones that most resonate with you.

Undermining Beliefs

I fear that I have lost...
- ☐ approval
- ☐ control
- ☐ co-operation
- ☐ face
- ☐ respect
- ☐ success
- ☐ trust
- ☐ validation
- ☐ love

This event proves that I am...
- ☐ stupid
- ☐ abnormal
- ☐ incompetent
- ☐ lazy
- ☐ irresponsible
- ☐ a total failure
- ☐ undisciplined
- ☐ untogether
- ☐ useless

B

I worry that I will suffer...
- ☐ mental collapse
- ☐ illness
- ☐ financial hardship

What I want is...
- ☐ total control
- ☐ respect
- ☐ success
- ☐ perfection
- ☐ comfort
- ☐ fairness
- ☐ tranquility
- ☐ all the answers
- ☐ for life to go smoothly
- ☐ to be all things to all people

Self-destructive Behaviour

Active
- ☐ get violent
- ☐ swear
- ☐ slam doors
- ☐ run away
- ☐ overeat
- ☐ harm myself
- ☐ criticise

Passive
- ☐ take it too seriously
- ☐ give up
- ☐ wallow in self pity
- ☐ sulk
- ☐ space out
- ☐ procrastinate
- ☐ give in
- ☐ be controlled

Intense Feelings

Angry feelings
- ☐ hateful
- ☐ aggravated
- ☐ annoyed
- ☐ hostile
- ☐ outraged
- ☐ punitive
- ☐ resentful
- ☐ vengeful

Fearful feelings
- ☐ helpless
- ☐ hopeless
- ☐ disappointed
- ☐ sad

- ☐ attacked
- ☐ worn out
- ☐ rejected
- ☐ jealous
- ☐ afraid
- ☐ exploited
- ☐ lonely
- ☐ abandoned
- ☐ guilty
- ☐ insulted
- ☐ confused
- ☐ disillusioned
- ☐ misunderstood
- ☐ trapped

Bodily Reactions (Limbic System)

I am uncomfortable because I am experiencing...
- ☐ tremors
- ☐ nausea
- ☐ sweaty palms
- ☐ stomach-ache
- ☐ pounding heart
- ☐ general tension
- ☐ fatigue
- ☐ imagination on fire
- ☐ headache
- ☐ dry mouth
- ☐ jaw clenching
- ☐ shortness of breath

Continued over

B   F   L

Step Three: The Working-Down Process

Begin with, "Suddenly I realised that I was anxious and that I had choices..." This is the step of self-leadership and trust in one's ability to handle the situation.

Choose helpful thoughts:

I choose to depersonalise
There is no intention to hurt me. He is doing the best he can with the tools he has at the moment.

I choose realism over romanticism
Life presents many obstacles. I lower or raise standards as needed.

There is no right or wrong
Unless it is a moral issue, I will see it simply as a difference of opinion and/or taste.

I choose the total view of positivity
Even though this event is negative, the total view of his behaviour is positive.

I surrender control
Since I cannot change this situation, I choose to let go of it

I choose to put this event in perspective
This event is not a catastrophe because it is not life threatening. It can be viewed as a trivial life event, a normal life problem that needs to be solved not dramatised.

I choose to view this event as average, falling within the normal range
This event is not exceptional; many people have gone through this.

It's temporary - "this too shall pass"
Life is constantly changing and moving through phases and this situation will also change.

Fears or facts?
Why fear? It may not happen!

I choose to focus on this as a learning experience
Every problem that comes my way is an opportunity for me to learn about my strengths and weaknesses, others and life.

Feel soothing emotions:

I choose to feel warm, loving emotions. I do this by focusing on my heart and letting love, trust forgiveness, compassion, hope or gratitude fill my heart space.

Behave constructively:

I choose to work in part acts:
I will break the overwhelming job into manageable parts.

Do the difficult:
I will face what I fear and act with self-discipline

I choose to solutionise:
I will find a solution by taking advice or doing research.

Prioritise myself:
I will keep my life balanced by meeting friends, doing exercise or laughing.

Compartmentalise:
I will not let this event cloud my whole day; I will focus on something else now.

Utilise calming strategies:

When I:
- relax,
- breathe deeply,
- go for a run,
- shower,
- lie down,
- read,
- watch TV,
- climb into a mental helicopter
- practice mindfulness, meditation, my mind and body calm down.

Step Four: The Self Motivation Process

Endorse yourself for any growth no matter how small.

In the past I would have...

_____

But this time I...

_____

Tick off the traits that you strengthened when you worked down your anxiety:

☐ generosity   ☐ peacefulness
☐ kindness   ☐ self-discipline
☐ compassion   ☐ forgiveness
☐ consideration   ☐ courage
☐ helpfulness   ☐ responsibility
☐ respectfulness ☐ reliability
☐ honesty   ☐ loyalty
☐ fairness   ☐ love
☐ patience   ☐ humility

Rate your anxiety on a scale of 0 to 100%:

_____ %

O   W

Session 8

Anxiety Management Worksheet

The purpose of this worksheet is to help you to see every stressful event as an opportunity for
1. greater understanding of yourself, your anxiety and the people around you, and
2. practicing tools to manage your anxiety.

Step One: An Event

Briefly describe an event when you became anxious. Give such details as time, place and people involved, and end with "That's when I began to work myself up..."

E

Rate your anxiety on a scale of 0 to 100%: [ ] %

Step Two: The Working-Up Process

Learn about your working up process by identifying your thoughts, feelings, behaviours and bodily reactions during the event. Tick the ones that most resonate with you.

Undermining Beliefs

I fear that I have lost...
- [ ] approval
- [ ] control
- [ ] co-operation
- [ ] face
- [ ] respect
- [ ] success
- [ ] trust
- [ ] validation
- [ ] love

This event proves that I am...
- [ ] stupid
- [ ] abnormal
- [ ] incompetent
- [ ] lazy
- [ ] irresponsible
- [ ] a total failure
- [ ] undisciplined
- [ ] untogether
- [ ] useless

B

I worry that I will suffer...
- [ ] mental collapse
- [ ] illness
- [ ] financial hardship

What I want is...
- [ ] total control
- [ ] respect
- [ ] success
- [ ] perfection
- [ ] comfort
- [ ] fairness
- [ ] tranquility
- [ ] all the answers
- [ ] for life to go smoothly
- [ ] to be all things to all people

Self-destructive Behaviour

Active
- [ ] get violent
- [ ] swear
- [ ] slam doors
- [ ] run away
- [ ] overeat
- [ ] harm myself
- [ ] criticise

Passive
- [ ] take it too seriously
- [ ] give up
- [ ] wallow in self pity
- [ ] sulk
- [ ] space out
- [ ] procrastinate
- [ ] give in
- [ ] be controlled

Intense Feelings

Angry feelings
- [ ] hateful
- [ ] aggravated
- [ ] annoyed
- [ ] hostile
- [ ] outraged
- [ ] punitive
- [ ] resentful
- [ ] vengeful

Fearful feelings
- [ ] helpless
- [ ] hopeless
- [ ] disappointed
- [ ] sad

- [ ] attacked
- [ ] worn out
- [ ] rejected
- [ ] jealous
- [ ] afraid
- [ ] exploited
- [ ] lonely
- [ ] abandoned
- [ ] guilty
- [ ] insulted
- [ ] confused
- [ ] disillusioned
- [ ] misunderstood
- [ ] trapped

Bodily Reactions (Limbic System)

I am uncomfortable because I am experiencing...
- [ ] tremors
- [ ] nausea
- [ ] sweaty palms
- [ ] stomach-ache
- [ ] pounding heart
- [ ] general tension
- [ ] fatigue
- [ ] imagination on fire
- [ ] headache
- [ ] dry mouth
- [ ] jaw clenching
- [ ] shortness of breath

Continued over

B   F   L

Step Three: The Working-Down Process

Begin with, "Suddenly I realised that I was anxious and that I had choices..." This is the step of self-leadership and trust in one's ability to handle the situation.

Choose helpful thoughts:

I choose to depersonalise
There is no intention to hurt me. He is doing the best he can with the tools he has at the moment.

I choose realism over romanticism
Life presents many obstacles. I lower or raise standards as needed.

There is no right or wrong
Unless it is a moral issue, I will see it simply as a difference of opinion and/or taste.

I choose the total view of positivity
Even though this event is negative, the total view of his behaviour is positive.

I surrender control
Since I cannot change this situation, I choose to let go of it

I choose to put this event in perspective
This event is not a catastrophe because it is not life threatening. It can be viewed as a trivial life event, a normal life problem that needs to be solved not dramatised.

I choose to view this event as average, falling within the normal range
This event is not exceptional; many people have gone through this.

It's temporary - "this too shall pass"
Life is constantly changing and moving through phases and this situation will also change.

Fears or facts?
Why fear? It may not happen!

I choose to focus on this as a learning experience
Every problem that comes my way is an opportunity for me to learn about my strengths and weaknesses, others and life.

Feel soothing emotions:

I choose to feel warm, loving emotions. I do this by focusing on my heart and letting love, trust forgiveness, compassion, hope or gratitude fill my heart space.

Behave constructively:

I choose to work in part acts:
I will break the overwhelming job into manageable parts.

Do the difficult:
I will face what I fear and act with self-discipline

I choose to solutionise:
I will find a solution by taking advice or doing research.

Prioritise myself:
I will keep my life balanced by meeting friends, doing exercise or laughing.

Compartmentalise:
I will not let this event cloud my whole day; I will focus on something else now.

Utilise calming strategies:

When I:
- relax,
- breathe deeply,
- go for a run,
- shower,
- lie down,
- read,
- watch TV,
- climb into a mental helicopter
- practice mindfulness, meditation, my mind and body calm down.

Step Four: The Self Motivation Process

Endorse yourself for any growth no matter how small.

In the past I would have...

_____

_____

But this time I...

_____

_____

Tick off the traits that you strengthened when you worked down your anxiety:

☐ generosity	☐ peacefulness
☐ kindness	☐ self-discipline
☐ compassion	☐ forgiveness
☐ consideration	☐ courage
☐ helpfulness	☐ responsibility
☐ respectfulness	☐ reliability
☐ honesty	☐ loyalty
☐ fairness	☐ love
☐ patience	☐ humility

Rate your anxiety on a scale of 0 to 100%:

[_____]%

O

W

Session 8

Anxiety Management Worksheet

The purpose of this worksheet is to help you to see every stressful event as an opportunity for
1. greater understanding of yourself, your anxiety and the people around you, and
2. practicing tools to manage your anxiety.

Step One: An Event

Briefly describe an event when you became anxious. Give such details as time, place and people involved, and end with "That's when I began to work myself up..."

_____

_____ E

_____

_____ Rate your anxiety on a scale of 0 to 100%: [   ] %

Step Two: The Working-Up Process

Learn about your working up process by identifying your thoughts, feelings, behaviours and bodily reactions during the event. Tick the ones that most resonate with you.

Undermining Beliefs

I fear that I have lost...
- ☐ approval
- ☐ control
- ☐ co-operation
- ☐ face
- ☐ respect
- ☐ success
- ☐ trust
- ☐ validation
- ☐ love

This event proves that I am...
- ☐ stupid
- ☐ abnormal
- ☐ incompetent
- ☐ lazy
- ☐ irresponsible
- ☐ a total failure
- ☐ undisciplined
- ☐ untogether
- ☐ useless

B

I worry that I will suffer...
- ☐ mental collapse
- ☐ illness
- ☐ financial hardship

What I want is...
- ☐ total control
- ☐ respect
- ☐ success
- ☐ perfection
- ☐ comfort
- ☐ fairness
- ☐ tranquility
- ☐ all the answers
- ☐ for life to go smoothly
- ☐ to be all things to all people

Self-destructive Behaviour

Active
- ☐ get violent
- ☐ swear
- ☐ slam doors
- ☐ run away
- ☐ overeat
- ☐ harm myself
- ☐ criticise

Passive
- ☐ take it too seriously
- ☐ give up
- ☐ wallow in self pity
- ☐ sulk
- ☐ space out
- ☐ procrastinate
- ☐ give in
- ☐ be controlled

Intense Feelings

Angry feelings
- ☐ hateful
- ☐ aggravated
- ☐ annoyed
- ☐ hostile
- ☐ outraged
- ☐ punitive
- ☐ resentful
- ☐ vengeful

Fearful feelings
- ☐ helpless
- ☐ hopeless
- ☐ disappointed
- ☐ sad
- ☐ attacked
- ☐ worn out
- ☐ rejected
- ☐ jealous
- ☐ afraid
- ☐ exploited
- ☐ lonely
- ☐ abandoned
- ☐ guilty
- ☐ insulted
- ☐ confused
- ☐ disillusioned
- ☐ misunderstood
- ☐ trapped

Bodily Reactions (Limbic System)

I am uncomfortable because I am experiencing...
- ☐ tremors
- ☐ nausea
- ☐ sweaty palms
- ☐ stomach-ache
- ☐ pounding heart
- ☐ general tension
- ☐ fatigue
- ☐ imagination on fire
- ☐ headache
- ☐ dry mouth
- ☐ jaw clenching
- ☐ shortness of breath

Continued over

B   F   L

Page 201

Step Three: The Working-Down Process

Begin with, "Suddenly I realised that I was anxious and that I had choices…" This is the step of self-leadership and trust in one's ability to handle the situation.

Choose helpful thoughts:

I choose to depersonalise
There is no intention to hurt me. He is doing the best he can with the tools he has at the moment.

I choose realism over romanticism
Life presents many obstacles. I lower or raise standards as needed.

There is no right or wrong
Unless it is a moral issue, I will see it simply as a difference of opinion and/or taste.

I choose the total view of positivity
Even though this event is negative, the total view of his behaviour is positive.

I surrender control
Since I cannot change this situation, I choose to let go of it

I choose to put this event in perspective
This event is not a catastrophe because it is not life threatening. It can be viewed as a trivial life event, a normal life problem that needs to be solved not dramatised.

I choose to view this event as average, falling within the normal range
This event is not exceptional; many people have gone through this.

It's temporary - "this too shall pass"
Life is constantly changing and moving through phases and this situation will also change.

Fears or facts?
Why fear? It may not happen!

I choose to focus on this as a learning experience
Every problem that comes my way is an opportunity for me to learn about my strengths and weaknesses, others and life.

Feel soothing emotions:

I choose to feel warm, loving emotions. I do this by focusing on my heart and letting love, trust forgiveness, compassion, hope or gratitude fill my heart space.

Behave constructively:

I choose to work in part acts:
I will break the overwhelming job into manageable parts.

Do the difficult:
I will face what I fear and act with self-discipline

I choose to solutionise:
I will find a solution by taking advice or doing research.

Prioritise myself:
I will keep my life balanced by meeting friends, doing exercise or laughing.

Compartmentalise:
I will not let this event cloud my whole day; I will focus on something else now.

Utilise calming strategies:

When I:
- relax,
- breathe deeply,
- go for a run,
- shower,
- lie down,
- read,
- watch TV,
- climb into a mental helicopter
- practice mindfulness, meditation, my mind and body calm down.

Step Four: The Self Motivation Process

Endorse yourself for any growth no matter how small.

In the past I would have...

_____

_____

But this time I...

_____

_____

Tick off the traits that you strengthened when you worked down your anxiety:

☐ generosity	☐ peacefulness
☐ kindness	☐ self-discipline
☐ compassion	☐ forgiveness
☐ consideration	☐ courage
☐ helpfulness	☐ responsibility
☐ respectfulness	☐ reliability
☐ honesty	☐ loyalty
☐ fairness	☐ love
☐ patience	☐ humility

Rate your anxiety on a scale of 0 to 100%:

_____ %

O

W

NOTES

NOTES

Session 9

BEHAVIOURAL TOOL: FIND A SOLUTION

'I choose to solutionise. I will find a solution by taking advice or doing research.'

Frequently, when we encounter a problem, we feel overwhelmed and anxious. This may lead us to give up because the problem seems insurmountable. However, when you begin to look for a solution, your anxiety will slowly reduce.

To solve a problem you may need (A) to take advice or (B) to do further research.

A. Taking Advice

One way of attempting to find a solution is to ask somebody who is experienced in the problem area for advice. Many people believe that asking for advice is shameful and that the ideal way of operating is to be self-sufficient. Believe me, there is nothing shameful about needing advice. All the greatest minds in the world had mentors that were key to their success.

EXERCISE THIRTY-ONE

Do you find it difficult to ask for advice?   YES/NO

If no, who do you generally call on for advice?

_____

_____

If yes, why do you think this is so?

- You are shy
- You are too proud
- You do not trust anybody
- You worry you will lose face
- You do not want to expose your ignorance
- You believe in self-sufficiency
- There are no intelligent people around
- Other:

_____

_____

Having circled one or more of the above options, think of ways you can rectify the situation. Write them down:

_____

_____

The Advantages of Taking Advice

Taking advice can save you a lot of time. Why re-invent the wheel when somebody can direct you to a method that works?

You would be amazed at how much people around you know. Even people who lack formal education have a wealth of experience and knowledge. By asking for advice, you are also going to get emotional support (even if only indirectly). Suddenly, you are no longer alone, and there is somebody to assist you.

Who to Ask?

There is a wide range of people you could ask. Here is a short list of some of them:

- Family member
- Psychologist
- Business consultant
- Expert in the relevant field
- Colleague
- Friend
- Partner
- Religious leader

Criteria of Whom to Ask

There are only two criteria to bear in mind before deciding whom you will ask. At times, it is beneficial to get several opinions.

- The person you ask must have your benefit at heart. It is no good asking a competitor or antagonist.
- You must respect the person you ask and be willing to give their words consideration.

B. Doing Further Research

When a process breaks down, it is often a result of insufficient groundwork. Thus, rather than giving up, spacing out or catastrophising, it is preferable to go back to the drawing board.

You may need to read books, go on a course, refer to old notes, or travel to obtain the answers you are seeking.

Doing further research can be done individually or in collaboration with others. Collaboration will frequently incorporate asking for advice.

Illustration

Tim is an architect who specialises in corporate designs. When he submits a proposal for a building, it is often knocked back. This is commonplace where design is involved because the first suggestion is the artist's idea and needs to be approved of by the customer.

In the early stages of his career, Tim would give up and withdraw from a job if his design was not accepted immediately. With years of experience behind him, Tim now knows that design is a collaborative process that occurs over time. Currently, if a proposal is not accepted, he will go back to the drawing board, do additional research and submit an improved design.

Illustration

Minnie is in year 11 at school. There is a lot of work to do at this level and her teachers drive her hard. When she first consulted with me, she described how she would cry if her essay earned a poor mark.

After a few sessions, Minnie grasped that her teachers were preparing her for her final exams. She changed her perception. Now when she receives a poor mark, she meets with the relevant teacher to learn how she can improve.

Illustration

Joe has a new job as a graduate lawyer. He is overwhelmed by the amount of work allocated to him plus the complexity. For a while, he wanted to give up and flunk out because it felt so overwhelming.

After learning that there is no shame in asking for advice, and assistance, he approached a few senior lawyers. To his happy surprise, he found that they understood his situation completely, having gone through it themselves. They were helpful, supportive and non-judgmental.

EXERCISE THIRTY-TWO

Imagine that you have submitted a work-related proposal and it is sent back to you asking you to amend and improve it. (If you are at school, imagine you have submitted a school project instead. If you are at home full time, imagine a family member criticises your cooking.)

Do you think you would:

- give up

- give in

- space out

- run away

- change your job

- scream at the manager/teacher/family member

- fear the worst

- other

_____

_____

Explain how doing any of these things would be helpful to you.

_____

_____

Would you ever think about re-working the proposal until it is acceptable? YES/NO

If yes, how would you go about doing it?

_____

_____

If no, what is the reason?

- You do not believe you'd get a second chance

- You cannot persevere

- You need immediate recognition

- You do not believe that your work could ever be deficient

- You wouldn't give the manager the satisfaction

- You're prepared to try everything only once

- Other

_____

_____

COGNITIVE TOOL: REALISM

'I choose realism over romanticism. Life presents many obstacles. I lower or raise standards as needed.'

Much of our stress is caused by wanting things a certain way but they pan out differently. We all have 'romantic' ideals of how life should be. I call it 'the house with the picket fence' vision. When we do not get the house/partner/riches/job of our dreams, we become upset, anxious and maybe even depressed.

Hollywood enchants us with fairy-tales, while our real life experiences are very different. We are often faced with not finding a life partner, no house, illness, divorce, job loss and so on.

By approaching life with a realistic view, a lot of the internal stress is alleviated. A realistic view, by the way, is not a pessimistic view ('Nothing ever works out'). It is a balanced view and could be stated philosophically as follows:

Life is an obstacle course.

Sometimes we soar over the

obstacle, other times we struggle over it,

and on rare occasions we do not get over it.

Life can never be constantly smooth.

No matter who we are,

where we come from

or what we do.

The positive outcome of thinking in this realistic way is that when an obstacle comes along, we do not get stressed or shocked. Nor do we start a negative commentary in our heads believing that what is happening is unfair, should not be happening, does not happen to others, is caused by our stupidity etc.

When negative self-talk is generated, you double the number of problems that you have. For example, let's imagine that you lost your purse. That is a problem. You have to deal with it and it certainly is inconvenient and a loss, especially if you lost cash. But when you start to blame yourself for losing your purse, calling yourself stupid, irresponsible and a loser, you now have two problems. Besides sorting out the purse, you now have to cope with your low self-esteem and other negative emotions.

It is preferable and very calming to think that what happened (a lost purse) is a normal life event, and merely an obstacle that needs to be overcome.

EXERCISE THIRTY-THREE

Some commonly held romantic beliefs are itemised below. Please tick those that pertain to you, and add others that are not mentioned. After that, compare your romantic views with the realistic views. Notice how you calm down when you see things realistically.

Romantic views

☐ Life can be smooth sailing at all times.

☐ Ultimately, there are always happy endings.

☐ As long as I please my boss, I will have a secure job.

☐ If I try hard enough, I will be a millionaire overnight.

☐ If I am kind all the time, everyone will like me.

☐ Life is fair and society just.

☐ If I work hard, I will get the reward I deserve.

Realistic views

☐ Life is an obstacle course with smooth times and difficult times.

☐ Often, things work out well but sometimes they do not.

☐ While pleasing a boss is important, other factors may result in my losing my job.

☐ While there are a few instant successes, most people become millionaires over a long period of time. I will work toward that goal in the long term.

☐ Some people respond to kindness with friendship. Others do not care either way.

☐ While these are values I aspire to, I have seen situations that do not seem fair or just.

☐ Sometimes hard work does not pay off.

Are there any romantic views that you have that may be causing you stress? Write down a realistic view that can help you feel less deprived and stressed.

_____

_____

_____

_____

DAILY MONITORING DIARY

WEEK ENDING _____

Day	M	T	W	T	F	S	S
Overall Anxiety Rating for the day (0-10)							

1. EXERCISE

How long?
Anxiety level before (0-10)
Anxiety level after (0-10)

2. BREATHING & RELAXATION

How long?
Anxiety level before (0-10)
Anxiety level after (0-10)

3. CATASTROPHIC THINKING

How often this type of thought occurred
Belief in thoughts before challenging (0-10)
Belief in thoughts after challenging (0-10)

4. FEARS NOT FACTS

How often this type of thought occurred
Belief in thoughts before challenging (0-10)
Belief in thoughts after challenging (0-10)

5. PERVASIVE PESSIMISTIC THINKING

How often this type of thought occurred
Belief in thoughts before challenging (0-10)
Belief in thoughts after challenging (0-10)

6. PERMANENT PESSIMISTIC THINKING

How often this type of thought occurred
Belief in thoughts before challenging (0-10)
Belief in thoughts after challenging (0-10)

7. MINDFULNESS (FORMAL, GROUNDING, INFORMAL MINDFULNESS)

How long?
Anxiety level before (0-10)
Anxiety level after (0-10)

8. EXCEPTIONAL THINKING

How often this type of thought occurred
Belief in thoughts before challenging (0-10)
Belief in thoughts after challenging (0-10)

9. TAKING IT PERSONALLY

How often this type of thought occurred
Belief in thoughts before challenging (0-10)
Belief in thoughts after challenging (0-10)

10. ROMANTIC THINKING

How often this type of thought occurred
Belief in thoughts before challenging (0-10)
Belief in thoughts after challenging (0-10)

Session 9

Anxiety Management Worksheet

The purpose of this worksheet is to help you to see every stressful event as an opportunity for
1. greater understanding of yourself, your anxiety and the people around you, and
2. practicing tools to manage your anxiety.

Step One: An Event

Briefly describe an event when you became anxious. Give such details as time, place and people involved, and end with "That's when I began to work myself up..."

_____

_____ E

_____

_____ Rate your anxiety on a scale of 0 to 100%: [____] %

Step Two: The Working-Up Process

Learn about your working up process by identifying your thoughts, feelings, behaviours and bodily reactions during the event. Tick the ones that most resonate with you.

Undermining Beliefs

I fear that I have lost...
- ☐ approval
- ☐ control
- ☐ co-operation
- ☐ face
- ☐ respect
- ☐ success
- ☐ trust
- ☐ validation
- ☐ love

This event proves that I am...
- ☐ stupid
- ☐ abnormal
- ☐ incompetent
- ☐ lazy
- ☐ irresponsible
- ☐ a total failure
- ☐ undisciplined
- ☐ untogether
- ☐ useless

B

I worry that I will suffer...
- ☐ mental collapse
- ☐ illness
- ☐ financial hardship

What I want is...
- ☐ total control
- ☐ respect
- ☐ success
- ☐ perfection
- ☐ comfort
- ☐ fairness
- ☐ tranquility
- ☐ all the answers
- ☐ for life to go smoothly
- ☐ to be all things to all people

Self-destructive Behaviour

Active
- ☐ get violent
- ☐ swear
- ☐ slam doors
- ☐ run away
- ☐ overeat
- ☐ harm myself
- ☐ criticise

Passive
- ☐ take it too seriously
- ☐ give up
- ☐ wallow in self pity
- ☐ sulk
- ☐ space out
- ☐ procrastinate
- ☐ give in
- ☐ be controlled

Intense Feelings

Angry feelings
- ☐ hateful
- ☐ aggravated
- ☐ annoyed
- ☐ hostile
- ☐ outraged
- ☐ punitive
- ☐ resentful
- ☐ vengeful

Fearful feelings
- ☐ helpless
- ☐ hopeless
- ☐ disappointed
- ☐ sad
- ☐ attacked
- ☐ worn out
- ☐ rejected
- ☐ jealous
- ☐ afraid
- ☐ exploited
- ☐ lonely
- ☐ abandoned
- ☐ guilty
- ☐ insulted
- ☐ confused
- ☐ disillusioned
- ☐ misunderstood
- ☐ trapped

Bodily Reactions (Limbic System)

I am uncomfortable because I am experiencing...
- ☐ tremors
- ☐ nausea
- ☐ sweaty palms
- ☐ stomach-ache
- ☐ pounding heart
- ☐ general tension
- ☐ fatigue
- ☐ imagination on fire
- ☐ headache
- ☐ dry mouth
- ☐ jaw clenching
- ☐ shortness of breath

Continued over

B   F   L

Step Three: The Working-Down Process

Begin with, "Suddenly I realised that I was anxious and that I had choices..." This is the step of self-leadership and trust in one's ability to handle the situation.

Choose helpful thoughts:

I choose to depersonalise
There is no intention to hurt me. He is doing the best he can with the tools he has at the moment.

I choose realism over romanticism
Life presents many obstacles. I lower or raise standards as needed.

There is no right or wrong
Unless it is a moral issue, I will see it simply as a difference of opinion and/or taste.

I choose the total view of positivity
Even though this event is negative, the total view of his behaviour is positive.

I surrender control
Since I cannot change this situation, I choose to let go of it

I choose to put this event in perspective
This event is not a catastrophe because it is not life threatening. It can be viewed as a trivial life event, a normal life problem that needs to be solved not dramatised.

I choose to view this event as average, falling within the normal range
This event is not exceptional; many people have gone through this.

It's temporary - "this too shall pass"
Life is constantly changing and moving through phases and this situation will also change.

Fears or facts?
Why fear? It may not happen!

I choose to focus on this as a learning experience
Every problem that comes my way is an opportunity for me to learn about my strengths and weaknesses, others and life.

Feel soothing emotions:

I choose to feel warm, loving emotions. I do this by focusing on my heart and letting love, trust forgiveness, compassion, hope or gratitude fill my heart space.

Behave constructively:

I choose to work in part acts:
I will break the overwhelming job into manageable parts.

Do the difficult:
I will face what I fear and act with self-discipline

I choose to solutionise:
I will find a solution by taking advice or doing research.

Prioritise myself:
I will keep my life balanced by meeting friends, doing exercise or laughing.

Compartmentalise:
I will not let this event cloud my whole day; I will focus on something else now.

Utilise calming strategies:

When I:
- relax,
- breathe deeply,
- go for a run,
- shower,
- lie down,
- read,
- watch TV,
- climb into a mental helicopter
- practice mindfulness, meditation, my mind and body calm down.

Step Four: The Self Motivation Process

Endorse yourself for any growth no matter how small.

In the past I would have...

_____

_____

But this time I...

_____

_____

Tick off the traits that you strengthened when you worked down your anxiety:

☐ generosity	☐ peacefulness	Rate your anxiety
☐ kindness	☐ self-discipline	on a scale of
☐ compassion	☐ forgiveness	0 to 100%:
☐ consideration	☐ courage	
☐ helpfulness	☐ responsibility	
☐ respectfulness	☐ reliability	
☐ honesty	☐ loyalty	
☐ fairness	☐ love	
☐ patience	☐ humility	☐ %

O

W

Anxiety Management Worksheet

The purpose of this worksheet is to help you to see every stressful event as an opportunity for
1. greater understanding of yourself, your anxiety and the people around you, and
2. practicing tools to manage your anxiety.

Step One: An Event

Briefly describe an event when you became anxious. Give such details as time, place and people involved, and end with "That's when I began to work myself up..."

E

Rate your anxiety on a scale of 0 to 100%: _____ %

Step Two: The Working-Up Process

Learn about your working up process by identifying your thoughts, feelings, behaviours and bodily reactions during the event. Tick the ones that most resonate with you.

Undermining Beliefs

I fear that I have lost...
- ☐ approval
- ☐ control
- ☐ co-operation
- ☐ face
- ☐ respect
- ☐ success
- ☐ trust
- ☐ validation
- ☐ love

This event proves that I am...
- ☐ stupid
- ☐ abnormal
- ☐ incompetent
- ☐ lazy
- ☐ irresponsible
- ☐ a total failure
- ☐ undisciplined
- ☐ untogether
- ☐ useless

B

I worry that I will suffer...
- ☐ mental collapse
- ☐ illness
- ☐ financial hardship

What I want is...
- ☐ total control
- ☐ respect
- ☐ success
- ☐ perfection
- ☐ comfort
- ☐ fairness
- ☐ tranquility
- ☐ all the answers
- ☐ for life to go smoothly
- ☐ to be all things to all people

Self-destructive Behaviour

Active
- ☐ get violent
- ☐ swear
- ☐ slam doors
- ☐ run away
- ☐ overeat
- ☐ harm myself
- ☐ criticise

Passive
- ☐ take it too seriously
- ☐ give up
- ☐ wallow in self pity
- ☐ sulk
- ☐ space out
- ☐ procrastinate
- ☐ give in
- ☐ be controlled

Intense Feelings

Angry feelings
- ☐ hateful
- ☐ aggravated
- ☐ annoyed
- ☐ hostile
- ☐ outraged
- ☐ punitive
- ☐ resentful
- ☐ vengeful

Fearful feelings
- ☐ helpless
- ☐ hopeless
- ☐ disappointed
- ☐ sad
- ☐ attacked
- ☐ worn out
- ☐ rejected
- ☐ jealous
- ☐ afraid
- ☐ exploited
- ☐ lonely
- ☐ abandoned
- ☐ guilty
- ☐ insulted
- ☐ confused
- ☐ disillusioned
- ☐ misunderstood
- ☐ trapped

Bodily Reactions (Limbic System)

I am uncomfortable because I am experiencing...
- ☐ tremors
- ☐ nausea
- ☐ sweaty palms
- ☐ stomach-ache
- ☐ pounding heart
- ☐ general tension
- ☐ fatigue
- ☐ imagination on fire
- ☐ headache
- ☐ dry mouth
- ☐ jaw clenching
- ☐ shortness of breath

Continued over

B   F   L

Step Three: The Working-Down Process

Begin with, "Suddenly I realised that I was anxious and that I had choices..." This is the step of self-leadership and trust in one's ability to handle the situation.

Choose helpful thoughts:

I choose to depersonalise
There is no intention to hurt me. He is doing the best he can with the tools he has at the moment.

I choose realism over romanticism
Life presents many obstacles. I lower or raise standards as needed.

There is no right or wrong
Unless it is a moral issue, I will see it simply as a difference of opinion and/or taste.

I choose the total view of positivity
Even though this event is negative, the total view of his behaviour is positive.

I surrender control
Since I cannot change this situation, I choose to let go of it

I choose to put this event in perspective
This event is not a catastrophe because it is not life threatening. It can be viewed as a trivial life event, a normal life problem that needs to be solved not dramatised.

I choose to view this event as average, falling within the normal range
This event is not exceptional; many people have gone through this.

It's temporary - "this too shall pass"
Life is constantly changing and moving through phases and this situation will also change.

Fears or facts?
Why fear? It may not happen!

I choose to focus on this as a learning experience
Every problem that comes my way is an opportunity for me to learn about my strengths and weaknesses, others and life.

Feel soothing emotions:

I choose to feel warm, loving emotions. I do this by focusing on my heart and letting love, trust forgiveness, compassion, hope or gratitude fill my heart space.

Behave constructively:

I choose to work in part acts:
I will break the overwhelming job into manageable parts.

Do the difficult:
I will face what I fear and act with self-discipline

I choose to solutionise:
I will find a solution by taking advice or doing research.

Prioritise myself:
I will keep my life balanced by meeting friends, doing exercise or laughing.

Compartmentalise:
I will not let this event cloud my whole day; I will focus on something else now.

Utilise calming strategies:

When I:
• relax,
• breathe deeply,
• go for a run,
• shower,
• lie down,
• read,
• watch TV,
• climb into a mental helicopter
• practice mindfulness, meditation, my mind and body calm down.

Step Four: The Self Motivation Process

Endorse yourself for any growth no matter how small.

In the past I would have...

_____

_____

But this time I...

_____

_____

Tick off the traits that you strengthened when you worked down your anxiety:

☐ generosity   ☐ peacefulness
☐ kindness   ☐ self-discipline
☐ compassion   ☐ forgiveness
☐ consideration   ☐ courage
☐ helpfulness   ☐ responsibility
☐ respectfulness ☐ reliability
☐ honesty   ☐ loyalty
☐ fairness   ☐ love
☐ patience   ☐ humility

Rate your anxiety on a scale of 0 to 100%:

[____]%

O   W

Anxiety Management Worksheet

The purpose of this worksheet is to help you to see every stressful event as an opportunity for
1. greater understanding of yourself, your anxiety and the people around you, and
2. practicing tools to manage your anxiety.

Step One: An Event

Briefly describe an event when you became anxious. Give such details as time, place and people involved, and end with "That's when I began to work myself up..."

_____

_____   E

_____

_____ Rate your anxiety on a scale of 0 to 100%: [   ] %

Step Two: The Working-Up Process

Learn about your working up process by identifying your thoughts, feelings, behaviours and bodily reactions during the event. Tick the ones that most resonate with you.

Undermining Beliefs

I fear that I have lost...
- ☐ approval
- ☐ control
- ☐ co-operation
- ☐ face
- ☐ respect
- ☐ success
- ☐ trust
- ☐ validation
- ☐ love

This event proves that I am...
- ☐ stupid
- ☐ abnormal
- ☐ incompetent
- ☐ lazy
- ☐ irresponsible
- ☐ a total failure
- ☐ undisciplined
- ☐ untogether
- ☐ useless

B

I worry that I will suffer...
- ☐ mental collapse
- ☐ illness
- ☐ financial hardship

What I want is...
- ☐ total control
- ☐ respect
- ☐ success
- ☐ perfection
- ☐ comfort
- ☐ fairness
- ☐ tranquility
- ☐ all the answers
- ☐ for life to go smoothly
- ☐ to be all things to all people

Self-destructive Behaviour

Active
- ☐ get violent
- ☐ swear
- ☐ slam doors
- ☐ run away
- ☐ overeat
- ☐ harm myself
- ☐ criticise

Passive
- ☐ take it too seriously
- ☐ give up
- ☐ wallow in self pity
- ☐ sulk
- ☐ space out
- ☐ procrastinate
- ☐ give in
- ☐ be controlled

Intense Feelings

Angry feelings
- ☐ hateful
- ☐ aggravated
- ☐ annoyed
- ☐ hostile
- ☐ outraged
- ☐ punitive
- ☐ resentful
- ☐ vengeful

Fearful feelings
- ☐ helpless
- ☐ hopeless
- ☐ disappointed
- ☐ sad
- ☐ attacked
- ☐ worn out
- ☐ rejected
- ☐ jealous
- ☐ afraid
- ☐ exploited
- ☐ lonely
- ☐ abandoned
- ☐ guilty
- ☐ insulted
- ☐ confused
- ☐ disillusioned
- ☐ misunderstood
- ☐ trapped

Bodily Reactions (Limbic System)

I am uncomfortable because I am experiencing...
- ☐ tremors
- ☐ nausea
- ☐ sweaty palms
- ☐ stomach-ache
- ☐ pounding heart
- ☐ general tension
- ☐ fatigue
- ☐ imagination on fire
- ☐ headache
- ☐ dry mouth
- ☐ jaw clenching
- ☐ shortness of breath

Continued over

B   F   L

Step Three: The Working-Down Process

Begin with, "Suddenly I realised that I was anxious and that I had choices..." This is the step of self-leadership and trust in one's ability to handle the situation.

Choose helpful thoughts:

I choose to depersonalise
There is no intention to hurt me. He is doing the best he can with the tools he has at the moment.

I choose realism over romanticism
Life presents many obstacles. I lower or raise standards as needed.

There is no right or wrong
Unless it is a moral issue, I will see it simply as a difference of opinion and/or taste.

I choose the total view of positivity
Even though this event is negative, the total view of his behaviour is positive.

I surrender control
Since I cannot change this situation, I choose to let go of it

I choose to put this event in perspective
This event is not a catastrophe because it is not life threatening. It can be viewed as a trivial life event, a normal life problem that needs to be solved not dramatised.

I choose to view this event as average, falling within the normal range
This event is not exceptional; many people have gone through this.

It's temporary - "this too shall pass"
Life is constantly changing and moving through phases and this situation will also change.

Fears or facts?
Why fear? It may not happen!

I choose to focus on this as a learning experience
Every problem that comes my way is an opportunity for me to learn about my strengths and weaknesses, others and life.

Feel soothing emotions:

I choose to feel warm, loving emotions. I do this by focusing on my heart and letting love, trust forgiveness, compassion, hope or gratitude fill my heart space.

Behave constructively:

I choose to work in part acts:
I will break the overwhelming job into manageable parts.

Do the difficult:
I will face what I fear and act with self-discipline

I choose to solutionise:
I will find a solution by taking advice or doing research.

Prioritise myself:
I will keep my life balanced by meeting friends, doing exercise or laughing.

Compartmentalise:
I will not let this event cloud my whole day; I will focus on something else now.

Utilise calming strategies:

When I:
• relax,
• breathe deeply,
• go for a run,
• shower,
• lie down,
• read,
• watch TV,
• climb into a mental helicopter
• practice mindfulness, meditation, my mind and body calm down.

Step Four: The Self Motivation Process

Endorse yourself for any growth no matter how small.

In the past I would have...

_____

But this time I...

_____

Tick off the traits that you strengthened when you worked down your anxiety:

☐ generosity   ☐ peacefulness
☐ kindness   ☐ self-discipline
☐ compassion   ☐ forgiveness
☐ consideration   ☐ courage
☐ helpfulness   ☐ responsibility
☐ respectfulness   ☐ reliability
☐ honesty   ☐ loyalty
☐ fairness   ☐ love
☐ patience   ☐ humility

Rate your anxiety on a scale of 0 to 100%:

_____%

O   W

Anxiety Management Worksheet

The purpose of this worksheet is to help you to see every stressful event as an opportunity for
1. greater understanding of yourself, your anxiety and the people around you, and
2. practicing tools to manage your anxiety.

Step One: An Event

Briefly describe an event when you became anxious. Give such details as time, place and people involved, and end with "That's when I began to work myself up…"

_____

_____   E

_____

_____ Rate your anxiety on a scale of 0 to 100%: [   ] %

Step Two: The Working-Up Process

Learn about your working up process by identifying your thoughts, feelings, behaviours and bodily reactions during the event. Tick the ones that most resonate with you.

Undermining Beliefs

I fear that I have lost…
- ☐ approval
- ☐ control
- ☐ co-operation
- ☐ face
- ☐ respect
- ☐ success
- ☐ trust
- ☐ validation
- ☐ love

This event proves that I am…
- ☐ stupid
- ☐ abnormal
- ☐ incompetent
- ☐ lazy
- ☐ irresponsible
- ☐ a total failure
- ☐ undisciplined
- ☐ untogether
- ☐ useless

B

I worry that I will suffer…
- ☐ mental collapse
- ☐ illness
- ☐ financial hardship

What I want is…
- ☐ total control
- ☐ respect
- ☐ success
- ☐ perfection
- ☐ comfort
- ☐ fairness
- ☐ tranquility
- ☐ all the answers
- ☐ for life to go smoothly
- ☐ to be all things to all people

Self-destructive Behaviour

Active
- ☐ get violent
- ☐ swear
- ☐ slam doors
- ☐ run away
- ☐ overeat
- ☐ harm myself
- ☐ criticise

Passive
- ☐ take it too seriously
- ☐ give up
- ☐ wallow in self pity
- ☐ sulk
- ☐ space out
- ☐ procrastinate
- ☐ give in
- ☐ be controlled

Intense Feelings

Angry feelings
- ☐ hateful
- ☐ aggravated
- ☐ annoyed
- ☐ hostile
- ☐ outraged
- ☐ punitive
- ☐ resentful
- ☐ vengeful

Fearful feelings
- ☐ helpless
- ☐ hopeless
- ☐ disappointed
- ☐ sad

- ☐ attacked
- ☐ worn out
- ☐ rejected
- ☐ jealous
- ☐ afraid
- ☐ exploited
- ☐ lonely
- ☐ abandoned
- ☐ guilty
- ☐ insulted
- ☐ confused
- ☐ disillusioned
- ☐ misunderstood
- ☐ trapped

Bodily Reactions (Limbic System)

I am uncomfortable because I am experiencing…
- ☐ tremors
- ☐ nausea
- ☐ sweaty palms
- ☐ stomach-ache
- ☐ pounding heart
- ☐ general tension
- ☐ fatigue
- ☐ imagination on fire
- ☐ headache
- ☐ dry mouth
- ☐ jaw clenching
- ☐ shortness of breath

Continued over

B   F   L

Step Three: The Working-Down Process

Begin with, "Suddenly I realised that I was anxious and that I had choices..." This is the step of self-leadership and trust in one's ability to handle the situation.

Choose helpful thoughts:

I choose to depersonalise
There is no intention to hurt me. He is doing the best he can with the tools he has at the moment.

I choose realism over romanticism
Life presents many obstacles. I lower or raise standards as needed.

There is no right or wrong
Unless it is a moral issue, I will see it simply as a difference of opinion and/or taste.

I choose the total view of positivity
Even though this event is negative, the total view of his behaviour is positive.

I surrender control
Since I cannot change this situation, I choose to let go of it

I choose to put this event in perspective
This event is not a catastrophe because it is not life threatening. It can be viewed as a trivial life event, a normal life problem that needs to be solved not dramatised.

I choose to view this event as average, falling within the normal range
This event is not exceptional; many people have gone through this.

It's temporary - "this too shall pass"
Life is constantly changing and moving through phases and this situation will also change.

Fears or facts?
Why fear? It may not happen!

I choose to focus on this as a learning experience
Every problem that comes my way is an opportunity for me to learn about my strengths and weaknesses, others and life.

Feel soothing emotions:

I choose to feel warm, loving emotions. I do this by focusing on my heart and letting love, trust forgiveness, compassion, hope or gratitude fill my heart space.

Behave constructively:

I choose to work in part acts:
I will break the overwhelming job into manageable parts.

Do the difficult:
I will face what I fear and act with self-discipline

I choose to solutionise:
I will find a solution by taking advice or doing research.

Prioritise myself:
I will keep my life balanced by meeting friends, doing exercise or laughing.

Compartmentalise:
I will not let this event cloud my whole day; I will focus on something else now.

Utilise calming strategies:

When I:
- relax,
- breathe deeply,
- go for a run,
- shower,
- lie down,
- read,
- watch TV,
- climb into a mental helicopter
- practice mindfulness, meditation, my mind and body calm down.

Step Four: The Self Motivation Process

Endorse yourself for any growth no matter how small.

In the past I would have...

_____

_____

But this time I...

_____

_____

Tick off the traits that you strengthened when you worked down your anxiety:

☐ generosity	☐ peacefulness	
☐ kindness	☐ self-discipline	
☐ compassion	☐ forgiveness	
☐ consideration	☐ courage	
☐ helpfulness	☐ responsibility	
☐ respectfulness	☐ reliability	
☐ honesty	☐ loyalty	
☐ fairness	☐ love	
☐ patience	☐ humility	

Rate your anxiety on a scale of 0 to 100%:

_____ %

O   W

Anxiety Management Worksheet

The purpose of this worksheet is to help you to see every stressful event as an opportunity for
1. greater understanding of yourself, your anxiety and the people around you, and
2. practicing tools to manage your anxiety.

Step One: An Event

Briefly describe an event when you became anxious. Give such details as time, place and people involved, and end with "That's when I began to work myself up..."

_____

_____   E

_____

_____ Rate your anxiety on a scale of 0 to 100%: [   ] %

Step Two: The Working-Up Process

Learn about your working up process by identifying your thoughts, feelings, behaviours and bodily reactions during the event. Tick the ones that most resonate with you.

Undermining Beliefs

I fear that I have lost...
- ☐ approval
- ☐ control
- ☐ co-operation
- ☐ face
- ☐ respect
- ☐ success
- ☐ trust
- ☐ validation
- ☐ love

This event proves that I am...
- ☐ stupid
- ☐ abnormal
- ☐ incompetent
- ☐ lazy
- ☐ irresponsible
- ☐ a total failure
- ☐ undisciplined
- ☐ untogether
- ☐ useless

B

I worry that I will suffer...
- ☐ mental collapse
- ☐ illness
- ☐ financial hardship

What I want is...
- ☐ total control
- ☐ respect
- ☐ success
- ☐ perfection
- ☐ comfort
- ☐ fairness
- ☐ tranquility
- ☐ all the answers
- ☐ for life to go smoothly
- ☐ to be all things to all people

Self-destructive Behaviour

Active
- ☐ get violent
- ☐ swear
- ☐ slam doors
- ☐ run away
- ☐ overeat
- ☐ harm myself
- ☐ criticise

Passive
- ☐ take it too seriously
- ☐ give up
- ☐ wallow in self pity
- ☐ sulk
- ☐ space out
- ☐ procrastinate
- ☐ give in
- ☐ be controlled

Intense Feelings

Angry feelings
- ☐ hateful
- ☐ aggravated
- ☐ annoyed
- ☐ hostile
- ☐ outraged
- ☐ punitive
- ☐ resentful
- ☐ vengeful

Fearful feelings
- ☐ helpless
- ☐ hopeless
- ☐ disappointed
- ☐ sad

- ☐ attacked
- ☐ worn out
- ☐ rejected
- ☐ jealous
- ☐ afraid
- ☐ exploited
- ☐ lonely
- ☐ abandoned
- ☐ guilty
- ☐ insulted
- ☐ confused
- ☐ disillusioned
- ☐ misunderstood
- ☐ trapped

Bodily Reactions (Limbic System)

I am uncomfortable because I am experiencing...
- ☐ tremors
- ☐ nausea
- ☐ sweaty palms
- ☐ stomach-ache
- ☐ pounding heart
- ☐ general tension
- ☐ fatigue
- ☐ imagination on fire
- ☐ headache
- ☐ dry mouth
- ☐ jaw clenching
- ☐ shortness of breath

Continued over

B   F   L

Step Three: The Working-Down Process

Begin with, "Suddenly I realised that I was anxious and that I had choices..." This is the step of self-leadership and trust in one's ability to handle the situation.

Choose helpful thoughts:

I choose to depersonalise
There is no intention to hurt me. He is doing the best he can with the tools he has at the moment.

I choose realism over romanticism
Life presents many obstacles. I lower or raise standards as needed.

There is no right or wrong
Unless it is a moral issue, I will see it simply as a difference of opinion and/or taste.

I choose the total view of positivity
Even though this event is negative, the total view of his behaviour is positive.

I surrender control
Since I cannot change this situation, I choose to let go of it

I choose to put this event in perspective
This event is not a catastrophe because it is not life threatening. It can be viewed as a trivial life event, a normal life problem that needs to be solved not dramatised.

I choose to view this event as average, falling within the normal range
This event is not exceptional; many people have gone through this.

It's temporary - "this too shall pass"
Life is constantly changing and moving through phases and this situation will also change.

Fears or facts?
Why fear? It may not happen!

I choose to focus on this as a learning experience
Every problem that comes my way is an opportunity for me to learn about my strengths and weaknesses, others and life.

Feel soothing emotions:

I choose to feel warm, loving emotions. I do this by focusing on my heart and letting love, trust forgiveness, compassion, hope or gratitude fill my heart space.

Behave constructively:

I choose to work in part acts:
I will break the overwhelming job into manageable parts.

Do the difficult:
I will face what I fear and act with self-discipline

I choose to solutionise:
I will find a solution by taking advice or doing research.

Prioritise myself:
I will keep my life balanced by meeting friends, doing exercise or laughing.

Compartmentalise:
I will not let this event cloud my whole day; I will focus on something else now.

Utilise calming strategies:

When I:
- relax,
- breathe deeply,
- go for a run,
- shower,
- lie down,
- read,
- watch TV,
- climb into a mental helicopter
- practice mindfulness, meditation, my mind and body calm down.

Step Four: The Self Motivation Process

Endorse yourself for any growth no matter how small.

In the past I would have...

_____

But this time I...

_____

Tick off the traits that you strengthened when you worked down your anxiety:

- ☐ generosity
- ☐ kindness
- ☐ compassion
- ☐ consideration
- ☐ helpfulness
- ☐ respectfulness
- ☐ honesty
- ☐ fairness
- ☐ patience
- ☐ peacefulness
- ☐ self-discipline
- ☐ forgiveness
- ☐ courage
- ☐ responsibility
- ☐ reliability
- ☐ loyalty
- ☐ love
- ☐ humility

Rate your anxiety on a scale of 0 to 100%:

_____ %

O   W

Anxiety Management Worksheet

The purpose of this worksheet is to help you to see every stressful event as an opportunity for
1. greater understanding of yourself, your anxiety and the people around you, and
2. practicing tools to manage your anxiety.

Step One: An Event

Briefly describe an event when you became anxious. Give such details as time, place and people involved, and end with "That's when I began to work myself up..."

_____

_____ E

_____

_____ Rate your anxiety on a scale of 0 to 100%: [   ] %

Step Two: The Working-Up Process

Learn about your working up process by identifying your thoughts, feelings, behaviours and bodily reactions during the event. Tick the ones that most resonate with you.

Undermining Beliefs

I fear that I have lost...
- ☐ approval
- ☐ control
- ☐ co-operation
- ☐ face
- ☐ respect
- ☐ success
- ☐ trust
- ☐ validation
- ☐ love

This event proves that I am...
- ☐ stupid
- ☐ abnormal
- ☐ incompetent
- ☐ lazy
- ☐ irresponsible
- ☐ a total failure
- ☐ undisciplined
- ☐ untogether
- ☐ useless

B

I worry that I will suffer...
- ☐ mental collapse
- ☐ illness
- ☐ financial hardship

What I want is...
- ☐ total control
- ☐ respect
- ☐ success
- ☐ perfection
- ☐ comfort
- ☐ fairness
- ☐ tranquility
- ☐ all the answers
- ☐ for life to go smoothly
- ☐ to be all things to all people

Self-destructive Behaviour

Active
- ☐ get violent
- ☐ swear
- ☐ slam doors
- ☐ run away
- ☐ overeat
- ☐ harm myself
- ☐ criticise

Passive
- ☐ take it too seriously
- ☐ give up
- ☐ wallow in self pity
- ☐ sulk
- ☐ space out
- ☐ procrastinate
- ☐ give in
- ☐ be controlled

Intense Feelings

Angry feelings
- ☐ hateful
- ☐ aggravated
- ☐ annoyed
- ☐ hostile
- ☐ outraged
- ☐ punitive
- ☐ resentful
- ☐ vengeful

Fearful feelings
- ☐ helpless
- ☐ hopeless
- ☐ disappointed
- ☐ sad

- ☐ attacked
- ☐ worn out
- ☐ rejected
- ☐ jealous
- ☐ afraid
- ☐ exploited
- ☐ lonely
- ☐ abandoned
- ☐ guilty
- ☐ insulted
- ☐ confused
- ☐ disillusioned
- ☐ misunderstood
- ☐ trapped

Bodily Reactions (Limbic System)

I am uncomfortable because I am experiencing...
- ☐ tremors
- ☐ nausea
- ☐ sweaty palms
- ☐ stomach-ache
- ☐ pounding heart
- ☐ general tension
- ☐ fatigue
- ☐ imagination on fire
- ☐ headache
- ☐ dry mouth
- ☐ jaw clenching
- ☐ shortness of breath

Continued over

B   F   L

Step Three: The Working-Down Process

Begin with, "Suddenly I realised that I was anxious and that I had choices..." This is the step of self-leadership and trust in one's ability to handle the situation.

Choose helpful thoughts:

I choose to depersonalise
There is no intention to hurt me. He is doing the best he can with the tools he has at the moment.

I choose realism over romanticism
Life presents many obstacles. I lower or raise standards as needed.

There is no right or wrong
Unless it is a moral issue, I will see it simply as a difference of opinion and/or taste.

I choose the total view of positivity
Even though this event is negative, the total view of his behaviour is positive.

I surrender control
Since I cannot change this situation, I choose to let go of it

I choose to put this event in perspective
This event is not a catastrophe because it is not life threatening. It can be viewed as a trivial life event, a normal life problem that needs to be solved not dramatised.

I choose to view this event as average, falling within the normal range
This event is not exceptional; many people have gone through this.

It's temporary - "this too shall pass"
Life is constantly changing and moving through phases and this situation will also change.

Fears or facts?
Why fear? It may not happen!

I choose to focus on this as a learning experience
Every problem that comes my way is an opportunity for me to learn about my strengths and weaknesses, others and life.

Feel soothing emotions:

I choose to feel warm, loving emotions. I do this by focusing on my heart and letting love, trust forgiveness, compassion, hope or gratitude fill my heart space.

Behave constructively:

I choose to work in part acts:
I will break the overwhelming job into manageable parts.

Do the difficult:
I will face what I fear and act with self-discipline

I choose to solutionise:
I will find a solution by taking advice or doing research.

Prioritise myself:
I will keep my life balanced by meeting friends, doing exercise or laughing.

Compartmentalise:
I will not let this event cloud my whole day; I will focus on something else now.

Utilise calming strategies:

When I:
- relax,
- breathe deeply,
- go for a run,
- shower,
- lie down,
- read,
- watch TV,
- climb into a mental helicopter
- practice mindfulness, meditation, my mind and body calm down.

Step Four: The Self Motivation Process

Endorse yourself for any growth no matter how small.

In the past I would have...

_____

_____

But this time I...

_____

_____

Tick off the traits that you strengthened when you worked down your anxiety:

☐ generosity ☐ peacefulness
☐ kindness ☐ self-discipline
☐ compassion ☐ forgiveness
☐ consideration ☐ courage
☐ helpfulness ☐ responsibility
☐ respectfulness ☐ reliability
☐ honesty ☐ loyalty
☐ fairness ☐ love
☐ patience ☐ humility

Rate your anxiety on a scale of 0 to 100%:

☐ %

O   W

Anxiety Management Worksheet

The purpose of this worksheet is to help you to see every stressful event as an opportunity for
1. greater understanding of yourself, your anxiety and the people around you, and
2. practicing tools to manage your anxiety.

Step One: An Event

Briefly describe an event when you became anxious. Give such details as time, place and people involved, and end with "That's when I began to work myself up..."

_____

_____ E

_____ Rate your anxiety on a scale of 0 to 100%: [　　] %

Step Two: The Working-Up Process

Learn about your working up process by identifying your thoughts, feelings, behaviours and bodily reactions during the event. Tick the ones that most resonate with you.

Undermining Beliefs

I fear that I have lost...
- ☐ approval
- ☐ control
- ☐ co-operation
- ☐ face
- ☐ respect
- ☐ success
- ☐ trust
- ☐ validation
- ☐ love

This event proves that I am...
- ☐ stupid
- ☐ abnormal
- ☐ incompetent
- ☐ lazy
- ☐ irresponsible
- ☐ a total failure
- ☐ undisciplined
- ☐ untogether
- ☐ useless

B

I worry that I will suffer...
- ☐ mental collapse
- ☐ illness
- ☐ financial hardship

What I want is...
- ☐ total control
- ☐ respect
- ☐ success
- ☐ perfection
- ☐ comfort
- ☐ fairness
- ☐ tranquility
- ☐ all the answers
- ☐ for life to go smoothly
- ☐ to be all things to all people

Self-destructive Behaviour

Active
- ☐ get violent
- ☐ swear
- ☐ slam doors
- ☐ run away
- ☐ overeat
- ☐ harm myself
- ☐ criticise

Passive
- ☐ take it too seriously
- ☐ give up
- ☐ wallow in self pity
- ☐ sulk
- ☐ space out
- ☐ procrastinate
- ☐ give in
- ☐ be controlled

Intense Feelings

Angry feelings
- ☐ hateful
- ☐ aggravated
- ☐ annoyed
- ☐ hostile
- ☐ outraged
- ☐ punitive
- ☐ resentful
- ☐ vengeful

Fearful feelings
- ☐ helpless
- ☐ hopeless
- ☐ disappointed
- ☐ sad

- ☐ attacked
- ☐ worn out
- ☐ rejected
- ☐ jealous
- ☐ afraid
- ☐ exploited
- ☐ lonely
- ☐ abandoned
- ☐ guilty
- ☐ insulted
- ☐ confused
- ☐ disillusioned
- ☐ misunderstood
- ☐ trapped

Bodily Reactions (Limbic System)

I am uncomfortable because I am experiencing...
- ☐ tremors
- ☐ nausea
- ☐ sweaty palms
- ☐ stomach-ache
- ☐ pounding heart
- ☐ general tension
- ☐ fatigue
- ☐ imagination on fire
- ☐ headache
- ☐ dry mouth
- ☐ jaw clenching
- ☐ shortness of breath

Continued over

B　　　　　　　　F　　　　　　　　L

Step Three: The Working-Down Process

Begin with, "Suddenly I realised that I was anxious and that I had choices..." This is the step of self-leadership and trust in one's ability to handle the situation.

Choose helpful thoughts:

I choose to depersonalise
There is no intention to hurt me. He is doing the best he can with the tools he has at the moment.

I choose realism over romanticism
Life presents many obstacles. I lower or raise standards as needed.

There is no right or wrong
Unless it is a moral issue, I will see it simply as a difference of opinion and/or taste.

I choose the total view of positivity
Even though this event is negative, the total view of his behaviour is positive.

I surrender control
Since I cannot change this situation, I choose to let go of it

I choose to put this event in perspective
This event is not a catastrophe because it is not life threatening. It can be viewed as a trivial life event, a normal life problem that needs to be solved not dramatised.

I choose to view this event as average, falling within the normal range
This event is not exceptional; many people have gone through this.

It's temporary - "this too shall pass"
Life is constantly changing and moving through phases and this situation will also change.

Fears or facts?
Why fear? It may not happen!

I choose to focus on this as a learning experience
Every problem that comes my way is an opportunity for me to learn about my strengths and weaknesses, others and life.

Feel soothing emotions:

I choose to feel warm, loving emotions. I do this by focusing on my heart and letting love, trust forgiveness, compassion, hope or gratitude fill my heart space.

Behave constructively:

I choose to work in part acts:
I will break the overwhelming job into manageable parts.

Do the difficult:
I will face what I fear and act with self-discipline

I choose to solutionise:
I will find a solution by taking advice or doing research.

Prioritise myself:
I will keep my life balanced by meeting friends, doing exercise or laughing.

Compartmentalise:
I will not let this event cloud my whole day; I will focus on something else now.

Utilise calming strategies:

When I:
- relax,
- breathe deeply,
- go for a run,
- shower,
- lie down,
- read,
- watch TV,
- climb into a mental helicopter
- practice mindfulness, meditation, my mind and body calm down.

Step Four: The Self Motivation Process

Endorse yourself for any growth no matter how small.

In the past I would have...
_____
_____

But this time I...
_____
_____

Tick off the traits that you strengthened when you worked down your anxiety:

- ☐ generosity
- ☐ kindness
- ☐ compassion
- ☐ consideration
- ☐ helpfulness
- ☐ respectfulness
- ☐ honesty
- ☐ fairness
- ☐ patience
- ☐ peacefulness
- ☐ self-discipline
- ☐ forgiveness
- ☐ courage
- ☐ responsibility
- ☐ reliability
- ☐ loyalty
- ☐ love
- ☐ humility

Rate your anxiety on a scale of 0 to 100%:

☐ %

O

W

NOTES

NOTES

Session 10

COGNITIVE TOOL: RIGHT OR WRONG

'There is no right or wrong. Unless it is a moral issue, I will see it simply as a difference of opinion and/or taste.'

Every person has an inner voice that tells you when something is right or wrong, good or bad. That inner voice is the awful feeling you have when you tell a lie or have yelled at another person excessively.

Stephen Covey describes the inner voice as a moral compass that tells us when we have done something wrong. Covey explains that just like a compass will always point North, so too our moral compass is there to guide us to do what is right.

Simply put, we all instinctively know the difference between right and wrong.

So much of our daily stress and anger comes from believing a person has done something **wrong** to us. However, when we dig deep into our moral compass, we frequently find that the behaviour was not wrong but based on a difference of taste or opinion.

Using the Right or Wrong tool will help you to discern if somebody actually committed an 'offence' or merely acted in a way that differs from the way you would act. Utilising this tool will set you free — free from the unnecessary stress which arises from incorrectly judging others.

Illustration

Fred likes to wear formal clothing, in particular, expensive suits. Once he invited friends over for a drink for his birthday, and was horrified that one friend (Jack) arrived in a tracksuit. He felt it was unacceptable and therefore yelled at Jack about it. Jack was confused. For the life of him he could not work out what he had done that merited such an attack.

Over time, Fred realised that few people actually wear suits anymore and that fashion had changed. Once he accepted that fashion varies and that different people follow fashion in different ways, he felt calm.

Illustration

Trish spends a good deal of her time observing others, judging them and stewing about their behaviour. For example:

- Trish believes that Sonya is a bad mother because she feeds on schedule and Trish believes in demand feeding.

- Trish criticises Peter for taking his son to footy matches because her opinion is that footy is violent.

- Trish views Margaret as the worst hostess ever because she uses plastic, disposable cutlery. According to Trish, any decent hostess knows that only silverware will do.

The truth is that there is ongoing debate about how to nurse babies. There is no consensus about footy or style of cutlery; these things are personal choices made by individuals and families based on their own views, tastes and personal moral compass. Trish would be so much more relaxed and content if she learnt to use the Right or Wrong tool.

By working through parts A, B and C of exercise 34, you will illuminate your inner moral compass. You will establish a range of behaviours for reference in the future. Your reference list will assist you to clarify if a behaviour that is bothering you is 'wrong' and merits judgement, or not.

EXERCISE THIRTY-FOUR

PART A

Here is a list of behaviours that are seen as immoral or bad by most cultures and societies. Feel free to add any others in the space provided.

- Murder

- Pedophilia

- Stealing

- Kidnapping

- Adultery

- Perjury

- Rape

- _____
  _____

Do you disagree with any of these? If so, why?

_____

_____

PART B

Here is a list of behaviours often seen as unethical in the Western world. Feel free to add any others in the space provided.

- Opening someone else's mail

- Invading a person's privacy

- Breaking a promise/commitment

- Gossiping

- Breaking a confidence

- Telling lies

- _____
  _____

- _____
  _____

Do you disagree with any of these? If so, why?

_____

_____

PART C

The list of unacceptable behaviours below was compiled by a team I worked with in a large corporation. If you work in a team, add your own additional unacceptable behaviours at the bottom of the list.

- Taking time out to smoke when a job needs to be done

- Coming late to work

- Dressing inappropriately

- Leaving without checking if it is OK with others

- Not being punctual

- Answering somebody else's calls without permission

- Swearing

- Not helping others

- _____
  _____

Here is a list of expectations commonly held by families:

- Taking ones plate to the sink

- Making ones bed

- Taking laundry to the laundry bin

- Contributing to the telephone bill

- Discussing family conflicts with others

Please make your own list of expectations you hold for your family below.

_____

_____

_____

_____

_____

What expectations do your family hold for you?

_____

_____

_____

_____

In sum, the list in Part A would be agreed upon by nearly everybody. The list in Part B would be agreed upon by most people in Western society.

The list in Part C is specific to each unique company, team or family.

It is important that you have clarified your expectations with your family or team before you can judge them. Only once you have all articulated and agreed to abide by your shared expectations, would it be appropriate for you to judge them negatively if the expectations are broken.

You may be wondering why we should judge at all. After all, is it not an ideal to accept everyone and everything? I think not. I believe that there are behaviours that are unacceptable. Our moral compass warns us that something is amiss so that we can protect ourselves.

Illustration

Freda's second husband did not have children of his own and embraced her daughter Emily (10) as his own. However, when he began to spend large chunks of time with Emily, Freda did not feel comfortable. Freda became vigilant and, sure enough, she caught him walking into the bathroom when Emily was in the shower. She had to protect Emily no matter the cost. She could not use this tool. On the contrary, she judged the behaviour as inappropriate and took strong action. She ended her second marriage.

In other words, if a moral code has been infringed upon, this tool would not be appropriate. Nor would it be useful if unethical behaviour or broken expectations were noted.

The comprehensive list of behaviours that you completed above is now your reference point. Tell yourself that all other behaviours that annoy, frustrate or infuriate you are merely a difference of opinion and taste and let them go. You will find that you are more relaxed overall when you 'live and let live'.

EXERCISE THIRTY-FIVE

Think of a person around whom you feel stressed. Name him/her.

_____

_____

_____

List the behaviours he/she is doing that may be causing you stress.

_____

_____

_____

Can any of the behaviours on this list be found on lists you compiled in parts A, B or C? YES/NO

If yes, then you cannot utilise this tool. Think of another person and try again. If no, tell yourself 'Unless it is a moral issue, I will see it simply as a difference of opinion and/or taste.'

CALMING TOOL: CLIMBING INTO A MENTAL HELICOPTER

This is a great tool to use when you begin to work yourself up and are not in a position to physically exit a situation. The helicopter is the vehicle of choice because it can hover above a situation. In other words, it is present but not right in the middle of the situation.

Illustration

You are sitting in a board meeting. There is a lot of tension between team members. You do not want to be dragged into the tension. You will be presenting your proposal shortly and want to stay calm.

You have few options. You cannot leave the room as that would be unprofessional. You cannot do deep breathing or relaxation as that would be inappropriate. What you can do is visualise yourself climbing into a mental helicopter. Imagine your tense feelings hovering above, not being caught up in the tension.

This is an effective tool because your body and conscious rational mind are fully present in the moment and able to perform with excellence, while your potentially damaging emotions are at a distance.

Illustration

You are at a family dinner. Your mother-in-law is picking on your husband. You want to interfere, to stick up for him or to leave. However, you know it will upset the rest of the family, including your husband, who is used to his mother's ways.

While sitting at the table, climb into your mental helicopter. Let all your judgements and animosity hover above while you display warmth and enthusiasm to the rest of the family.

Please note: Climbing into a mental helicopter is not spacing out or disassociating. It is making an active choice to put your emotions out of centre. They are there, you are aware of them, you can tap into them at any time. However, for peace and calm, you choose to keep them in the helicopter until it is an appropriate time to deal with them.

DAILY MONITORING DIARY

WEEK ENDING _____

Day	M	T	W	T	F	S	S
Overall Anxiety Rating for the day (0-10)							

1. EXERCISE

How long?
Anxiety level before (0-10)
Anxiety level after (0-10)

2. BREATHING & RELAXATION

How long?
Anxiety level before (0-10)
Anxiety level after (0-10)

3. CATASTROPHIC THINKING

How often this type of thought occurred
Belief in thoughts before challenging (0-10)
Belief in thoughts after challenging (0-10)

4. FEARS NOT FACTS

How often this type of thought occurred
Belief in thoughts before challenging (0-10)
Belief in thoughts after challenging (0-10)

5. PERVASIVE PESSIMISTIC THINKING

How often this type of thought occurred
Belief in thoughts before challenging (0-10)
Belief in thoughts after challenging (0-10)

6. PERMANENT PESSIMISTIC THINKING

How often this type of thought occurred
Belief in thoughts before challenging (0-10)
Belief in thoughts after challenging (0-10)

7. MINDFULNESS (FORMAL, GROUNDING, INFORMAL MINDFULNESS)

How long?
Anxiety level before (0-10)
Anxiety level after (0-10)

8. EXCEPTIONAL THINKING

How often this type of thought occurred
Belief in thoughts before challenging (0-10)
Belief in thoughts after challenging (0-10)

9. TAKING IT PERSONALLY

How often this type of thought occurred
Belief in thoughts before challenging (0-10)
Belief in thoughts after challenging (0-10)

10. ROMANTIC THINKING

How often this type of thought occurred
Belief in thoughts before challenging (0-10)
Belief in thoughts after challenging (0-10)

11. NEGATIVE JUDGEMENTAL THINKING

How often this type of thought occurred
Belief in thoughts before challenging (0-10)
Belief in thoughts after challenging (0-10)

Anxiety Management Worksheet

The purpose of this worksheet is to help you to see every stressful event as an opportunity for
1. greater understanding of yourself, your anxiety and the people around you, and
2. practicing tools to manage your anxiety.

Step One: An Event

Briefly describe an event when you became anxious. Give such details as time, place and people involved, and end with "That's when I began to work myself up..."

E

_____ Rate your anxiety on a scale of 0 to 100%: [   ] %

Step Two: The Working-Up Process

Learn about your working up process by identifying your thoughts, feelings, behaviours and bodily reactions during the event. Tick the ones that most resonate with you.

Undermining Beliefs

I fear that I have lost...
- ☐ approval
- ☐ control
- ☐ co-operation
- ☐ face
- ☐ respect
- ☐ success
- ☐ trust
- ☐ validation
- ☐ love

This event proves that I am...
- ☐ stupid
- ☐ abnormal
- ☐ incompetent
- ☐ lazy
- ☐ irresponsible
- ☐ a total failure
- ☐ undisciplined
- ☐ untogether
- ☐ useless

B

I worry that I will suffer...
- ☐ mental collapse
- ☐ illness
- ☐ financial hardship

What I want is...
- ☐ total control
- ☐ respect
- ☐ success
- ☐ perfection
- ☐ comfort
- ☐ fairness
- ☐ tranquility
- ☐ all the answers
- ☐ for life to go smoothly
- ☐ to be all things to all people

Self-destructive Behaviour

Active
- ☐ get violent
- ☐ swear
- ☐ slam doors
- ☐ run away
- ☐ overeat
- ☐ harm myself
- ☐ criticise

Passive
- ☐ take it too seriously
- ☐ give up
- ☐ wallow in self pity
- ☐ sulk
- ☐ space out
- ☐ procrastinate
- ☐ give in
- ☐ be controlled

Intense Feelings

Angry feelings
- ☐ hateful
- ☐ aggravated
- ☐ annoyed
- ☐ hostile
- ☐ outraged
- ☐ punitive
- ☐ resentful
- ☐ vengeful

Fearful feelings
- ☐ helpless
- ☐ hopeless
- ☐ disappointed
- ☐ sad

- ☐ attacked
- ☐ worn out
- ☐ rejected
- ☐ jealous
- ☐ afraid
- ☐ exploited
- ☐ lonely
- ☐ abandoned
- ☐ guilty
- ☐ insulted
- ☐ confused
- ☐ disillusioned
- ☐ misunderstood
- ☐ trapped

Bodily Reactions (Limbic System)

I am uncomfortable because I am experiencing...
- ☐ tremors
- ☐ nausea
- ☐ sweaty palms
- ☐ stomach-ache
- ☐ pounding heart
- ☐ general tension
- ☐ fatigue
- ☐ imagination on fire
- ☐ headache
- ☐ dry mouth
- ☐ jaw clenching
- ☐ shortness of breath

Continued over

B   F   L

Step Three: The Working-Down Process

Begin with, "Suddenly I realised that I was anxious and that I had choices..." This is the step of self-leadership and trust in one's ability to handle the situation.

Choose helpful thoughts:

I choose to depersonalise
There is no intention to hurt me. He is doing the best he can with the tools he has at the moment.

I choose realism over romanticism
Life presents many obstacles. I lower or raise standards as needed.

There is no right or wrong
Unless it is a moral issue, I will see it simply as a difference of opinion and/or taste.

I choose the total view of positivity
Even though this event is negative, the total view of his behaviour is positive.

I surrender control
Since I cannot change this situation, I choose to let go of it

I choose to put this event in perspective
This event is not a catastrophe because it is not life threatening. It can be viewed as a trivial life event, a normal life problem that needs to be solved not dramatised.

I choose to view this event as average, falling within the normal range
This event is not exceptional; many people have gone through this.

It's temporary - "this too shall pass"
Life is constantly changing and moving through phases and this situation will also change.

Fears or facts?
Why fear? It may not happen!

I choose to focus on this as a learning experience
Every problem that comes my way is an opportunity for me to learn about my strengths and weaknesses, others and life.

Feel soothing emotions:

I choose to feel warm, loving emotions. I do this by focusing on my heart and letting love, trust forgiveness, compassion, hope or gratitude fill my heart space.

Behave constructively:

I choose to work in part acts:
I will break the overwhelming job into manageable parts.

Do the difficult:
I will face what I fear and act with self-discipline

I choose to solutionise:
I will find a solution by taking advice or doing research.

Prioritise myself:
I will keep my life balanced by meeting friends, doing exercise or laughing.

Compartmentalise:
I will not let this event cloud my whole day; I will focus on something else now.

Utilise calming strategies:

When I:
- relax,
- breathe deeply,
- go for a run,
- shower,
- lie down,
- read,
- watch TV,
- climb into a mental helicopter
- practice mindfulness, meditation, my mind and body calm down.

Step Four: The Self Motivation Process

Endorse yourself for any growth no matter how small.

In the past I would have...

_____

_____

But this time I...

_____

_____

Tick off the traits that you strengthened when you worked down your anxiety:

☐ generosity	☐ peacefulness	Rate your anxiety
☐ kindness	☐ self-discipline	on a scale of
☐ compassion	☐ forgiveness	0 to 100%:
☐ consideration	☐ courage	
☐ helpfulness	☐ responsibility	
☐ respectfulness	☐ reliability	
☐ honesty	☐ loyalty	
☐ fairness	☐ love	
☐ patience	☐ humility	☐ %

O   W

Session 10

Anxiety Management Worksheet

The purpose of this worksheet is to help you to see every stressful event as an opportunity for
1. greater understanding of yourself, your anxiety and the people around you, and
2. practicing tools to manage your anxiety.

Step One: An Event

Briefly describe an event when you became anxious. Give such details as time, place and people involved, and end with "That's when I began to work myself up..."

_____

_____ E

_____

_____ Rate your anxiety on a scale of 0 to 100%: [   ] %

Step Two: The Working-Up Process

Learn about your working up process by identifying your thoughts, feelings, behaviours and bodily reactions during the event. Tick the ones that most resonate with you.

Undermining Beliefs

I fear that I have lost...
- ☐ approval
- ☐ control
- ☐ co-operation
- ☐ face
- ☐ respect
- ☐ success
- ☐ trust
- ☐ validation
- ☐ love

This event proves that I am...
- ☐ stupid
- ☐ abnormal
- ☐ incompetent
- ☐ lazy
- ☐ irresponsible
- ☐ a total failure
- ☐ undisciplined
- ☐ untogether
- ☐ useless

B

I worry that I will suffer...
- ☐ mental collapse
- ☐ illness
- ☐ financial hardship

What I want is...
- ☐ total control
- ☐ respect
- ☐ success
- ☐ perfection
- ☐ comfort
- ☐ fairness
- ☐ tranquility
- ☐ all the answers
- ☐ for life to go smoothly
- ☐ to be all things to all people

Self-destructive Behaviour

Active
- ☐ get violent
- ☐ swear
- ☐ slam doors
- ☐ run away
- ☐ overeat
- ☐ harm myself
- ☐ criticise

Passive
- ☐ take it too seriously
- ☐ give up
- ☐ wallow in self pity
- ☐ sulk
- ☐ space out
- ☐ procrastinate
- ☐ give in
- ☐ be controlled

Intense Feelings

Angry feelings
- ☐ hateful
- ☐ aggravated
- ☐ annoyed
- ☐ hostile
- ☐ outraged
- ☐ punitive
- ☐ resentful
- ☐ vengeful

Fearful feelings
- ☐ helpless
- ☐ hopeless
- ☐ disappointed
- ☐ sad

- ☐ attacked
- ☐ worn out
- ☐ rejected
- ☐ jealous
- ☐ afraid
- ☐ exploited
- ☐ lonely
- ☐ abandoned
- ☐ guilty
- ☐ insulted
- ☐ confused
- ☐ disillusioned
- ☐ misunderstood
- ☐ trapped

Bodily Reactions (Limbic System)

I am uncomfortable because I am experiencing...
- ☐ tremors
- ☐ nausea
- ☐ sweaty palms
- ☐ stomach-ache
- ☐ pounding heart
- ☐ general tension
- ☐ fatigue
- ☐ imagination on fire
- ☐ headache
- ☐ dry mouth
- ☐ jaw clenching
- ☐ shortness of breath

Continued over

B   F   L

Step Three: The Working-Down Process

Begin with, "Suddenly I realised that I was anxious and that I had choices…" This is the step of self-leadership and trust in one's ability to handle the situation.

Choose helpful thoughts:

I choose to depersonalise
There is no intention to hurt me. He is doing the best he can with the tools he has at the moment.

I choose realism over romanticism
Life presents many obstacles. I lower or raise standards as needed.

There is no right or wrong
Unless it is a moral issue, I will see it simply as a difference of opinion and/or taste.

I choose the total view of positivity
Even though this event is negative, the total view of his behaviour is positive.

I surrender control
Since I cannot change this situation, I choose to let go of it

I choose to put this event in perspective
This event is not a catastrophe because it is not life threatening. It can be viewed as a trivial life event, a normal life problem that needs to be solved not dramatised.

I choose to view this event as average, falling within the normal range
This event is not exceptional; many people have gone through this.

It's temporary - "this too shall pass"
Life is constantly changing and moving through phases and this situation will also change.

Fears or facts?
Why fear? It may not happen!

I choose to focus on this as a learning experience
Every problem that comes my way is an opportunity for me to learn about my strengths and weaknesses, others and life.

Feel soothing emotions:

I choose to feel warm, loving emotions. I do this by focusing on my heart and letting love, trust forgiveness, compassion, hope or gratitude fill my heart space.

Behave constructively:

I choose to work in part acts:
I will break the overwhelming job into manageable parts.

Do the difficult:
I will face what I fear and act with self-discipline

I choose to solutionise:
I will find a solution by taking advice or doing research.

Prioritise myself:
I will keep my life balanced by meeting friends, doing exercise or laughing.

Compartmentalise:
I will not let this event cloud my whole day; I will focus on something else now.

Utilise calming strategies:

When I:
- relax,
- breathe deeply,
- go for a run,
- shower,
- lie down,
- read,
- watch TV,
- climb into a mental helicopter
- practice mindfulness, meditation, my mind and body calm down.

Step Four: The Self Motivation Process

Endorse yourself for any growth no matter how small.

In the past I would have...

_____

_____

But this time I...

_____

_____

Tick off the traits that you strengthened when you worked down your anxiety:

☐ generosity ☐ peacefulness
☐ kindness ☐ self-discipline
☐ compassion ☐ forgiveness
☐ consideration ☐ courage
☐ helpfulness ☐ responsibility
☐ respectfulness ☐ reliability
☐ honesty ☐ loyalty
☐ fairness ☐ love
☐ patience ☐ humility

Rate your anxiety on a scale of 0 to 100%:

_____%

O   W

Anxiety Management Worksheet

The purpose of this worksheet is to help you to see every stressful event as an opportunity for
1. greater understanding of yourself, your anxiety and the people around you, and
2. practicing tools to manage your anxiety.

Step One: An Event

Briefly describe an event when you became anxious. Give such details as time, place and people involved, and end with "That's when I began to work myself up..."

E

Rate your anxiety on a scale of 0 to 100%: ____ %

Step Two: The Working-Up Process

Learn about your working up process by identifying your thoughts, feelings, behaviours and bodily reactions during the event. Tick the ones that most resonate with you.

Undermining Beliefs

I fear that I have lost...
- ☐ approval
- ☐ control
- ☐ co-operation
- ☐ face
- ☐ respect
- ☐ success
- ☐ trust
- ☐ validation
- ☐ love

This event proves that I am...
- ☐ stupid
- ☐ abnormal
- ☐ incompetent
- ☐ lazy
- ☐ irresponsible
- ☐ a total failure
- ☐ undisciplined
- ☐ untogether
- ☐ useless

B

I worry that I will suffer...
- ☐ mental collapse
- ☐ illness
- ☐ financial hardship

What I want is...
- ☐ total control
- ☐ respect
- ☐ success
- ☐ perfection
- ☐ comfort
- ☐ fairness
- ☐ tranquility
- ☐ all the answers
- ☐ for life to go smoothly
- ☐ to be all things to all people

Self-destructive Behaviour

Active
- ☐ get violent
- ☐ swear
- ☐ slam doors
- ☐ run away
- ☐ overeat
- ☐ harm myself
- ☐ criticise

Passive
- ☐ take it too seriously
- ☐ give up
- ☐ wallow in self pity
- ☐ sulk
- ☐ space out
- ☐ procrastinate
- ☐ give in
- ☐ be controlled

Intense Feelings

Angry feelings
- ☐ hateful
- ☐ aggravated
- ☐ annoyed
- ☐ hostile
- ☐ outraged
- ☐ punitive
- ☐ resentful
- ☐ vengeful

Fearful feelings
- ☐ helpless
- ☐ hopeless
- ☐ disappointed
- ☐ sad
- ☐ attacked
- ☐ worn out
- ☐ rejected
- ☐ jealous
- ☐ afraid
- ☐ exploited
- ☐ lonely
- ☐ abandoned
- ☐ guilty
- ☐ insulted
- ☐ confused
- ☐ disillusioned
- ☐ misunderstood
- ☐ trapped

Bodily Reactions (Limbic System)

I am uncomfortable because I am experiencing...
- ☐ tremors
- ☐ nausea
- ☐ sweaty palms
- ☐ stomach-ache
- ☐ pounding heart
- ☐ general tension
- ☐ fatigue
- ☐ imagination on fire
- ☐ headache
- ☐ dry mouth
- ☐ jaw clenching
- ☐ shortness of breath

Continued over

B   F   L

Step Three: The Working-Down Process

Begin with, "Suddenly I realised that I was anxious and that I had choices..." This is the step of self-leadership and trust in one's ability to handle the situation.

Choose helpful thoughts:

I choose to depersonalise
There is no intention to hurt me. He is doing the best he can with the tools he has at the moment.

I choose realism over romanticism
Life presents many obstacles. I lower or raise standards as needed.

There is no right or wrong
Unless it is a moral issue, I will see it simply as a difference of opinion and/or taste.

I choose the total view of positivity
Even though this event is negative, the total view of his behaviour is positive.

I surrender control
Since I cannot change this situation, I choose to let go of it

I choose to put this event in perspective
This event is not a catastrophe because it is not life threatening. It can be viewed as a trivial life event, a normal life problem that needs to be solved not dramatised.

I choose to view this event as average, falling within the normal range
This event is not exceptional; many people have gone through this.

It's temporary - "this too shall pass"
Life is constantly changing and moving through phases and this situation will also change.

Fears or facts?
Why fear? It may not happen!

I choose to focus on this as a learning experience
Every problem that comes my way is an opportunity for me to learn about my strengths and weaknesses, others and life.

Feel soothing emotions:

I choose to feel warm, loving emotions. I do this by focusing on my heart and letting love, trust forgiveness, compassion, hope or gratitude fill my heart space.

Behave constructively:

I choose to work in part acts:
I will break the overwhelming job into manageable parts.

Do the difficult:
I will face what I fear and act with self-discipline

I choose to solutionise:
I will find a solution by taking advice or doing research.

Prioritise myself:
I will keep my life balanced by meeting friends, doing exercise or laughing.

Compartmentalise:
I will not let this event cloud my whole day; I will focus on something else now.

Utilise calming strategies:

When I:
- relax,
- breathe deeply,
- go for a run,
- shower,
- lie down,
- read,
- watch TV,
- climb into a mental helicopter
- practice mindfulness, meditation, my mind and body calm down.

Step Four: The Self Motivation Process

Endorse yourself for any growth no matter how small.

In the past I would have...

_____

_____

But this time I...

_____

_____

Tick off the traits that you strengthened when you worked down your anxiety:

☐ generosity	☐ peacefulness	
☐ kindness	☐ self-discipline	
☐ compassion	☐ forgiveness	
☐ consideration	☐ courage	
☐ helpfulness	☐ responsibility	
☐ respectfulness	☐ reliability	
☐ honesty	☐ loyalty	
☐ fairness	☐ love	
☐ patience	☐ humility	

Rate your anxiety on a scale of 0 to 100%:

_____ %

O

W

Anxiety Management Worksheet

The purpose of this worksheet is to help you to see every stressful event as an opportunity for
1. greater understanding of yourself, your anxiety and the people around you, and
2. practicing tools to manage your anxiety.

Step One: An Event

Briefly describe an event when you became anxious. Give such details as time, place and people involved, and end with "That's when I began to work myself up..."

E

Rate your anxiety on a scale of 0 to 100%: ____ %

Step Two: The Working-Up Process

Learn about your working up process by identifying your thoughts, feelings, behaviours and bodily reactions during the event. Tick the ones that most resonate with you.

Undermining Beliefs

I fear that I have lost...

- ☐ approval
- ☐ success
- ☐ control
- ☐ trust
- ☐ co-operation
- ☐ validation
- ☐ face
- ☐ love
- ☐ respect

This event proves that I am...

- ☐ stupid
- ☐ a total failure
- ☐ abnormal
- ☐ undisciplined
- ☐ incompetent
- ☐ untogether
- ☐ lazy
- ☐ useless
- ☐ irresponsible

B

I worry that I will suffer...

- ☐ mental collapse
- ☐ illness
- ☐ financial hardship

What I want is...

- ☐ total control
- ☐ tranquility
- ☐ respect
- ☐ all the answers
- ☐ success
- ☐ for life to go smoothly
- ☐ perfection
- ☐ comfort
- ☐ to be all things to all people
- ☐ fairness

Self-destructive Behaviour

Active

- ☐ get violent
- ☐ swear
- ☐ slam doors
- ☐ run away
- ☐ overeat
- ☐ harm myself
- ☐ criticise

Passive

- ☐ take it too seriously
- ☐ give up
- ☐ wallow in self pity
- ☐ sulk
- ☐ space out
- ☐ procrastinate
- ☐ give in
- ☐ be controlled

Intense Feelings

Angry feelings

- ☐ hateful
- ☐ attacked
- ☐ aggravated
- ☐ worn out
- ☐ annoyed
- ☐ rejected
- ☐ hostile
- ☐ jealous
- ☐ outraged
- ☐ afraid
- ☐ punitive
- ☐ exploited
- ☐ resentful
- ☐ lonely
- ☐ vengeful
- ☐ abandoned
- ☐ guilty

Fearful feelings

- ☐ insulted
- ☐ helpless
- ☐ confused
- ☐ hopeless
- ☐ disillusioned
- ☐ disappointed
- ☐ misunderstood
- ☐ sad
- ☐ trapped

Bodily Reactions (Limbic System)

I am uncomfortable because I am experiencing...

- ☐ tremors
- ☐ nausea
- ☐ sweaty palms
- ☐ stomach-ache
- ☐ pounding heart
- ☐ general tension
- ☐ fatigue
- ☐ imagination on fire
- ☐ headache
- ☐ dry mouth
- ☐ jaw clenching
- ☐ shortness of breath

Continued over

B   F   L

Step Three: The Working-Down Process

Begin with, "Suddenly I realised that I was anxious and that I had choices..." This is the step of self-leadership and trust in one's ability to handle the situation.

Choose helpful thoughts:

I choose to depersonalise
There is no intention to hurt me. He is doing the best he can with the tools he has at the moment.

I choose realism over romanticism
Life presents many obstacles. I lower or raise standards as needed.

There is no right or wrong
Unless it is a moral issue, I will see it simply as a difference of opinion and/or taste.

I choose the total view of positivity
Even though this event is negative, the total view of his behaviour is positive.

I surrender control
Since I cannot change this situation, I choose to let go of it

I choose to put this event in perspective
This event is not a catastrophe because it is not life threatening. It can be viewed as a trivial life event, a normal life problem that needs to be solved not dramatised.

I choose to view this event as average, falling within the normal range
This event is not exceptional; many people have gone through this.

It's temporary - "this too shall pass"
Life is constantly changing and moving through phases and this situation will also change.

Fears or facts?
Why fear? It may not happen!

I choose to focus on this as a learning experience
Every problem that comes my way is an opportunity for me to learn about my strengths and weaknesses, others and life.

Feel soothing emotions:

I choose to feel warm, loving emotions. I do this by focusing on my heart and letting love, trust forgiveness, compassion, hope or gratitude fill my heart space.

Behave constructively:

I choose to work in part acts:
I will break the overwhelming job into manageable parts.

Do the difficult:
I will face what I fear and act with self-discipline

I choose to solutionise:
I will find a solution by taking advice or doing research.

Prioritise myself:
I will keep my life balanced by meeting friends, doing exercise or laughing.

Compartmentalise:
I will not let this event cloud my whole day; I will focus on something else now.

Utilise calming strategies:

When I:
- relax,
- breathe deeply,
- go for a run,
- shower,
- lie down,
- read,
- watch TV,
- climb into a mental helicopter
- practice mindfulness, meditation, my mind and body calm down.

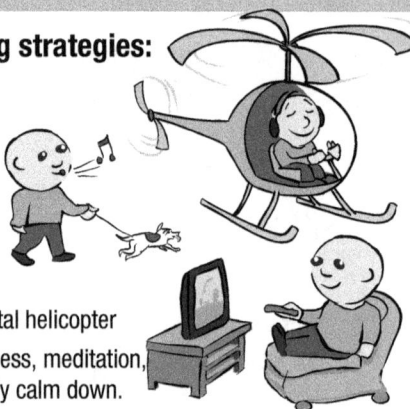

Step Four: The Self Motivation Process

Endorse yourself for any growth no matter how small.

In the past I would have...

_____

_____

But this time I...

_____

_____

Tick off the traits that you strengthened when you worked down your anxiety:

☐ generosity	☐ peacefulness	
☐ kindness	☐ self-discipline	
☐ compassion	☐ forgiveness	
☐ consideration	☐ courage	
☐ helpfulness	☐ responsibility	
☐ respectfulness	☐ reliability	
☐ honesty	☐ loyalty	
☐ fairness	☐ love	
☐ patience	☐ humility	

Rate your anxiety on a scale of 0 to 100%:

_____ %

O   W

Anxiety Management Worksheet

The purpose of this worksheet is to help you to see every stressful event as an opportunity for
1. greater understanding of yourself, your anxiety and the people around you, and
2. practicing tools to manage your anxiety.

Step One: An Event

Briefly describe an event when you became anxious. Give such details as time, place and people involved, and end with "That's when I began to work myself up..."

_____

_____ E

_____ Rate your anxiety on a scale of 0 to 100%: [   ] %

Step Two: The Working-Up Process

Learn about your working up process by identifying your thoughts, feelings, behaviours and bodily reactions during the event. Tick the ones that most resonate with you.

Undermining Beliefs

I fear that I have lost...
- ☐ approval
- ☐ control
- ☐ co-operation
- ☐ face
- ☐ respect
- ☐ success
- ☐ trust
- ☐ validation
- ☐ love

This event proves that I am...
- ☐ stupid
- ☐ abnormal
- ☐ incompetent
- ☐ lazy
- ☐ irresponsible
- ☐ a total failure
- ☐ undisciplined
- ☐ untogether
- ☐ useless

B

I worry that I will suffer...
- ☐ mental collapse
- ☐ illness
- ☐ financial hardship

What I want is...
- ☐ total control
- ☐ respect
- ☐ success
- ☐ perfection
- ☐ comfort
- ☐ fairness
- ☐ tranquility
- ☐ all the answers
- ☐ for life to go smoothly
- ☐ to be all things to all people

Self-destructive Behaviour

Active
- ☐ get violent
- ☐ swear
- ☐ slam doors
- ☐ run away
- ☐ overeat
- ☐ harm myself
- ☐ criticise

Passive
- ☐ take it too seriously
- ☐ give up
- ☐ wallow in self pity
- ☐ sulk
- ☐ space out
- ☐ procrastinate
- ☐ give in
- ☐ be controlled

Intense Feelings

Angry feelings
- ☐ hateful
- ☐ aggravated
- ☐ annoyed
- ☐ hostile
- ☐ outraged
- ☐ punitive
- ☐ resentful
- ☐ vengeful

Fearful feelings
- ☐ helpless
- ☐ hopeless
- ☐ disappointed
- ☐ sad

- ☐ attacked
- ☐ worn out
- ☐ rejected
- ☐ jealous
- ☐ afraid
- ☐ exploited
- ☐ lonely
- ☐ abandoned
- ☐ guilty
- ☐ insulted
- ☐ confused
- ☐ disillusioned
- ☐ misunderstood
- ☐ trapped

Bodily Reactions (Limbic System)

I am uncomfortable because I am experiencing...
- ☐ tremors
- ☐ nausea
- ☐ sweaty palms
- ☐ stomach-ache
- ☐ pounding heart
- ☐ general tension
- ☐ fatigue
- ☐ imagination on fire
- ☐ headache
- ☐ dry mouth
- ☐ jaw clenching
- ☐ shortness of breath

Continued over

B   F   L

Step Three: The Working-Down Process

Begin with, "Suddenly I realised that I was anxious and that I had choices..." This is the step of self-leadership and trust in one's ability to handle the situation.

Choose helpful thoughts:

I choose to depersonalise
There is no intention to hurt me. He is doing the best he can with the tools he has at the moment.

I choose realism over romanticism
Life presents many obstacles. I lower or raise standards as needed.

There is no right or wrong
Unless it is a moral issue, I will see it simply as a difference of opinion and/or taste.

I choose the total view of positivity
Even though this event is negative, the total view of his behaviour is positive.

I surrender control
Since I cannot change this situation, I choose to let go of it

I choose to put this event in perspective
This event is not a catastrophe because it is not life threatening. It can be viewed as a trivial life event, a normal life problem that needs to be solved not dramatised.

I choose to view this event as average, falling within the normal range
This event is not exceptional; many people have gone through this.

It's temporary - "this too shall pass"
Life is constantly changing and moving through phases and this situation will also change.

Fears or facts?
Why fear? It may not happen!

I choose to focus on this as a learning experience
Every problem that comes my way is an opportunity for me to learn about my strengths and weaknesses, others and life.

Feel soothing emotions:

I choose to feel warm, loving emotions. I do this by focusing on my heart and letting love, trust forgiveness, compassion, hope or gratitude fill my heart space.

Behave constructively:

I choose to work in part acts:
I will break the overwhelming job into manageable parts.

Do the difficult:
I will face what I fear and act with self-discipline

I choose to solutionise:
I will find a solution by taking advice or doing research.

Prioritise myself:
I will keep my life balanced by meeting friends, doing exercise or laughing.

Compartmentalise:
I will not let this event cloud my whole day; I will focus on something else now.

Utilise calming strategies:

When I:
- relax,
- breathe deeply,
- go for a run,
- shower,
- lie down,
- read,
- watch TV,
- climb into a mental helicopter
- practice mindfulness, meditation, my mind and body calm down.

Step Four: The Self Motivation Process

Endorse yourself for any growth no matter how small.

In the past I would have...

But this time I...

Tick off the traits that you strengthened when you worked down your anxiety:

- generosity
- kindness
- compassion
- consideration
- helpfulness
- respectfulness
- honesty
- fairness
- patience
- peacefulness
- self-discipline
- forgiveness
- courage
- responsibility
- reliability
- loyalty
- love
- humility

Rate your anxiety on a scale of 0 to 100%:

_____%

O W

Anxiety Management Worksheet

The purpose of this worksheet is to help you to see every stressful event as an opportunity for
1. greater understanding of yourself, your anxiety and the people around you, and
2. practicing tools to manage your anxiety.

Step One: An Event

Briefly describe an event when you became anxious. Give such details as time, place and people involved, and end with "That's when I began to work myself up..."

E

Rate your anxiety on a scale of 0 to 100%: ____ %

Step Two: The Working-Up Process

Learn about your working up process by identifying your thoughts, feelings, behaviours and bodily reactions during the event. Tick the ones that most resonate with you.

Undermining Beliefs

I fear that I have lost...
- approval
- control
- co-operation
- face
- respect
- success
- trust
- validation
- love

This event proves that I am...
- stupid
- abnormal
- incompetent
- lazy
- irresponsible
- a total failure
- undisciplined
- untogether
- useless

B

I worry that I will suffer...
- mental collapse
- illness
- financial hardship

What I want is...
- total control
- respect
- success
- perfection
- comfort
- fairness
- tranquility
- all the answers
- for life to go smoothly
- to be all things to all people

Self-destructive Behaviour

Active
- get violent
- swear
- slam doors
- run away
- overeat
- harm myself
- criticise

Passive
- take it too seriously
- give up
- wallow in self pity
- sulk
- space out
- procrastinate
- give in
- be controlled

Intense Feelings

Angry feelings
- hateful
- aggravated
- annoyed
- hostile
- outraged
- punitive
- resentful
- vengeful

Fearful feelings
- helpless
- hopeless
- disappointed
- sad
- attacked
- worn out
- rejected
- jealous
- afraid
- exploited
- lonely
- abandoned
- guilty
- insulted
- confused
- disillusioned
- misunderstood
- trapped

Bodily Reactions (Limbic System)

I am uncomfortable because I am experiencing...
- tremors
- nausea
- sweaty palms
- stomach-ache
- pounding heart
- general tension
- fatigue
- imagination on fire
- headache
- dry mouth
- jaw clenching
- shortness of breath

Continued over

B   F   L

Step Three: The Working-Down Process

Begin with, "Suddenly I realised that I was anxious and that I had choices..." This is the step of self-leadership and trust in one's ability to handle the situation.

Choose helpful thoughts:

I choose to depersonalise
There is no intention to hurt me. He is doing the best he can with the tools he has at the moment.

I choose realism over romanticism
Life presents many obstacles. I lower or raise standards as needed.

There is no right or wrong
Unless it is a moral issue, I will see it simply as a difference of opinion and/or taste.

I choose the total view of positivity
Even though this event is negative, the total view of his behaviour is positive.

I surrender control
Since I cannot change this situation, I choose to let go of it

I choose to put this event in perspective
This event is not a catastrophe because it is not life threatening. It can be viewed as a trivial life event, a normal life problem that needs to be solved not dramatised.

I choose to view this event as average, falling within the normal range
This event is not exceptional; many people have gone through this.

It's temporary - "this too shall pass"
Life is constantly changing and moving through phases and this situation will also change.

Fears or facts?
Why fear? It may not happen!

I choose to focus on this as a learning experience
Every problem that comes my way is an opportunity for me to learn about my strengths and weaknesses, others and life.

Feel soothing emotions:

I choose to feel warm, loving emotions. I do this by focusing on my heart and letting love, trust forgiveness, compassion, hope or gratitude fill my heart space.

Behave constructively:

I choose to work in part acts:
I will break the overwhelming job into manageable parts.

Do the difficult:
I will face what I fear and act with self-discipline

I choose to solutionise:
I will find a solution by taking advice or doing research.

Prioritise myself:
I will keep my life balanced by meeting friends, doing exercise or laughing.

Compartmentalise:
I will not let this event cloud my whole day; I will focus on something else now.

Utilise calming strategies:

When I:
• relax,
• breathe deeply,
• go for a run,
• shower,
• lie down,
• read,
• watch TV,
• climb into a mental helicopter
• practice mindfulness, meditation, my mind and body calm down.

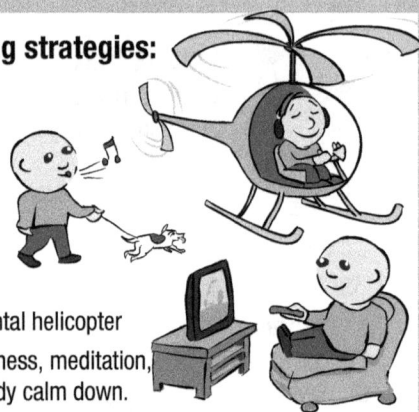

Step Four: The Self Motivation Process

Endorse yourself for any growth no matter how small.

In the past I would have...

_____

_____

But this time I...

_____

_____

Tick off the traits that you strengthened when you worked down your anxiety:

☐ generosity ☐ peacefulness
☐ kindness ☐ self-discipline
☐ compassion ☐ forgiveness
☐ consideration ☐ courage
☐ helpfulness ☐ responsibility
☐ respectfulness ☐ reliability
☐ honesty ☐ loyalty
☐ fairness ☐ love
☐ patience ☐ humility

Rate your anxiety on a scale of 0 to 100%:

☐ %

O   W

Anxiety Management Worksheet

The purpose of this worksheet is to help you to see every stressful event as an opportunity for
1. greater understanding of yourself, your anxiety and the people around you, and
2. practicing tools to manage your anxiety.

Step One: An Event

Briefly describe an event when you became anxious. Give such details as time, place and people involved, and end with "That's when I began to work myself up..."

_____

_____ E

_____

_____ Rate your anxiety on a scale of 0 to 100%: [   ] %

Step Two: The Working-Up Process

Learn about your working up process by identifying your thoughts, feelings, behaviours and bodily reactions during the event. Tick the ones that most resonate with you.

Undermining Beliefs

I fear that I have lost...
- approval
- control
- co-operation
- face
- respect
- success
- trust
- validation
- love

This event proves that I am...
- stupid
- abnormal
- incompetent
- lazy
- irresponsible
- a total failure
- undisciplined
- untogether
- useless

B

I worry that I will suffer...
- mental collapse
- illness
- financial hardship

What I want is...
- total control
- respect
- success
- perfection
- comfort
- fairness
- tranquility
- all the answers
- for life to go smoothly
- to be all things to all people

Self-destructive Behaviour

Active
- get violent
- swear
- slam doors
- run away
- overeat
- harm myself
- criticise

Passive
- take it too seriously
- give up
- wallow in self pity
- sulk
- space out
- procrastinate
- give in
- be controlled

Intense Feelings

Angry feelings
- hateful
- aggravated
- annoyed
- hostile
- outraged
- punitive
- resentful
- vengeful

Fearful feelings
- helpless
- hopeless
- disappointed
- sad
- attacked
- worn out
- rejected
- jealous
- afraid
- exploited
- lonely
- abandoned
- guilty
- insulted
- confused
- disillusioned
- misunderstood
- trapped

Bodily Reactions (Limbic System)

I am uncomfortable because I am experiencing...
- tremors
- nausea
- sweaty palms
- stomach-ache
- pounding heart
- general tension
- fatigue
- imagination on fire
- headache
- dry mouth
- jaw clenching
- shortness of breath

Continued over

B   F   L

Step Three: The Working-Down Process

Begin with, "Suddenly I realised that I was anxious and that I had choices..." This is the step of self-leadership and trust in one's ability to handle the situation.

Choose helpful thoughts:

I choose to depersonalise
There is no intention to hurt me. He is doing the best he can with the tools he has at the moment.

I choose realism over romanticism
Life presents many obstacles. I lower or raise standards as needed.

There is no right or wrong
Unless it is a moral issue, I will see it simply as a difference of opinion and/or taste.

I choose the total view of positivity
Even though this event is negative, the total view of his behaviour is positive.

I surrender control
Since I cannot change this situation, I choose to let go of it

I choose to put this event in perspective
This event is not a catastrophe because it is not life threatening. It can be viewed as a trivial life event, a normal life problem that needs to be solved not dramatised.

I choose to view this event as average, falling within the normal range
This event is not exceptional; many people have gone through this.

It's temporary - "this too shall pass"
Life is constantly changing and moving through phases and this situation will also change.

Fears or facts?
Why fear? It may not happen!

I choose to focus on this as a learning experience
Every problem that comes my way is an opportunity for me to learn about my strengths and weaknesses, others and life.

Feel soothing emotions:

I choose to feel warm, loving emotions. I do this by focusing on my heart and letting love, trust forgiveness, compassion, hope or gratitude fill my heart space.

Behave constructively:

I choose to work in part acts:
I will break the overwhelming job into manageable parts.

Do the difficult:
I will face what I fear and act with self-discipline

I choose to solutionise:
I will find a solution by taking advice or doing research.

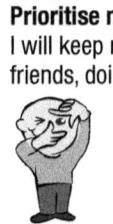

Prioritise myself:
I will keep my life balanced by meeting friends, doing exercise or laughing.

Compartmentalise:
I will not let this event cloud my whole day; I will focus on something else now.

Utilise calming strategies:

When I:
- relax,
- breathe deeply,
- go for a run,
- shower,
- lie down,
- read,
- watch TV,
- climb into a mental helicopter
- practice mindfulness, meditation, my mind and body calm down.

Step Four: The Self Motivation Process

Endorse yourself for any growth no matter how small.

In the past I would have...

_____

_____

But this time I...

_____

_____

Tick off the traits that you strengthened when you worked down your anxiety:

☐ generosity	☐ peacefulness	
☐ kindness	☐ self-discipline	
☐ compassion	☐ forgiveness	
☐ consideration	☐ courage	
☐ helpfulness	☐ responsibility	
☐ respectfulness	☐ reliability	
☐ honesty	☐ loyalty	
☐ fairness	☐ love	
☐ patience	☐ humility	

Rate your anxiety on a scale of 0 to 100%:

[____]%

O

W

NOTES

NOTES

Summing up the ten sessions

In what ways do you think you have grown over the past weeks?

_____

_____

_____

_____

_____

_____

What changes have you noticed within yourself?

_____

_____

_____

_____

_____

_____

What have you learned about yourself?

_____

_____

_____

_____

_____

What have you gained from the techniques you've practiced?

_____

_____

_____

_____

_____

_____

What skills have you been using the most and finding helpful in reducing anxiety?

_____
_____
_____
_____
_____
_____

What has been difficult for you during this course?

_____
_____
_____
_____
_____
_____

How do you plan on keeping up with practicing the tools you've acquired over this time?

_____
_____
_____
_____
_____
_____

What are your plans to keep up the practice of relaxation/mindfulness/ meditation/ exercise?

_____
_____
_____
_____
_____
_____

CONCLUSION

You have now learned a process. You will need to keep practicing it, in order to continue to manage your anxiety. Practice and repetition is the key. Remember to keep using your Anxiety Management Worksheets.

Thank you for working with us. Please feel free to contact the team at Anxiety Solutions for further help on. Our website is at www.anxietysolutionscbt.com where you can receive all the latest information on anxiety and its management.

FEEDBACK FORM

Please take a minute to fill out the feedback form provided on page 255 and hand in to your psychologist. Your feedback will help us continue to improve and provide excellent treatment.

FEEDBACK FORM

Date: _____

Name: (optional) _____

Occupation/Position/Professional Classification:_____

Age: _____

Gender: Male / Female   (please circle)

Thank you for taking a few minutes to complete this evaluation form. The information you provide will be used in planning future sessions.

1. Where did you hear about this treatment course?

_____

_____

_____

2. What did you expect to gain from this treatment course?

_____

_____

_____

_____

3. How interesting did you find the treatment sessions? (please tick)

Very interesting	❏
Fairly interesting	❏
Not really interesting	❏

4. Did you think the treatment sessions were… (please tick)

Too unsophisticated	❏
Just right	❏
Too complicated	❏
Not easy to follow	❏

5. Did you think the treatment sessions had… (please tick)

Too much information, not enough group discussion	❏
Not enough information, too much group discussion	❏
The right balance of information and group discussion	❏

6. **Did you find the topics covered...** (please tick)

Relevant and applicable ❏

Not relevant ❏

Not applicable to real-life situations ❏

7. **How effective was the Psychologist?** (please tick)

Very effective ❏

Fairly effective ❏

Not very effective ❏

8. **Did you find the presentation of material...**(please tick)

Excellent ❏

Good ❏

Average ❏

Poor ❏

9. **What did you think of the quality of the manual?** (please tick)

Excellent ❏

Good ❏

Average ❏

Poor ❏

10. **Overall, did you feel the treatment course was...**(please tick)

Worthwhile ❏

Okay ❏

Disappointing ❏

11. **Any final comments/suggestions?**

_____

_____

_____

_____

_____

_____

_____

_____